Venus: Don't Go There

Venus: Don't Go There

Unveiling a Biblical Hell

MICHAEL T. SANTINI

iUniverse®

VENUS: DON'T GO THERE
UNVEILING A BIBLICAL HELL

iUniverse books may be ordered through booksellers or by contacting:

iUniverse
1663 Liberty Drive
Bloomington, IN 47403
www.iuniverse.com
844-349-9409

ISBN: 978-1-6632-3348-6 (sc)
ISBN: 978-1-6632-3349-3 (e)

Library of Congress Control Number: 2022902328

Print information available on the last page.

iUniverse rev. date: 02/10/2022

Cover: Transit of Venus on the Face of the Sun
*   NASA Solar Dynamic Observatory*
*   June 6, 2012*
*   Goddard Space Flight Center*

To my daughter,
Veronica Santini,
who created many happy memories during her
childhood upbringing (birthday, April 12).

In memory of
Maria Santini (1936–2012),
my beloved mother, who tirelessly raised her children
and remained dedicated to their well-being.

CONTENTS

Chapter 3

Chapter 4

Chapter 5

Chapter 6

Chapter 7

Chapter 8

FIGURES

TABLES

PREFACE

No one is ever forgotten in this world. Every person is special to God and loved in a personal way. An eternal expression of his love is the ability to continue living after physical death. All individuals have an immortal aspect to their being—a soul that keeps on going after one's passing. Yet, as living and breathing mortal beings, time on the planet is finite. Our bodily presence is a fragile and fleeting commodity. Here today and gone tomorrow, the self will move on to a permanent destiny. Is not the certainty of death a cause to prepare for the next life? And if so, what purpose is there for living in the world now, and what ultimate intention does our mortality serve?

When visiting the cemetery to pay my respects to friends and family, I sometimes roam around to see the burial sites of other people. As I read the names, lifespans, and inscriptions on the headstones, my mind begins to drift toward spiritual matters. I realize the dead body remains in the ground, but the soul departs, alive and well, with memories and feelings fully intact. A particularly engaging epitaph will cause me to stop and contemplate the person. One question coming to mind is their eternal fate. I ask myself, "Where did the soul of this individual go, heaven or Hades?"

To speak about heaven as our home is not a figure of speech. Jesus tells us in John 14:2 that he has gone "to prepare a place" for you. It is a forever residence. Heaven is where we belong. Death has no power over the believer. The loss of a loved one may bring grief, but the transition from life to death is only a door. It is a pathway to a new life free from pain and sorrow. The majesty of the destination supplants the challenging process of getting old and then dying. The faithful person will encounter God face-to-face and experience unsurpassed joy, peace, and splendor. But what can be said about the unfaithful? What can be said about those who fail to properly prepare?

The alternate fate is certainly one of gloom and despair. All our time, all our effort, and all our determination to make the best of life on Earth can end in disaster because of spiritual neglect, unbelief, and hard-heartedness. Hell is a destiny to be avoided at all costs. You simply do not want to go there. Many people find hell a hard concept to accept, and to some, it's even irritating. Why is this so? Perhaps it is due to an indifference toward sin. Human transgression is a grave matter that goes way over our heads. Our sin is infinitely bad because it is rebellion against an eternally splendid and holy God. Consequently, the exacting penalty for being found guilty is a never-ending sentence.

Working several years ago on a classified space program, I was on travel in Los Angeles for the business week to engage in a series of engineering meetings with another defense contractor.[1] During one gathering, some dapper young engineers were discussing a design topic. And then it started. Every fifteen to twenty minutes someone would say, "Where the hell is the data?" or "Who the hell is responsible

---

1   Twenty-five years of aerospace engineering at Lockheed Martin and The Boeing Company brought opportunity for travel in order to integrate major defense systems. The plethora of funding for large defense contracts is normally spread to suppliers, subcontractors, associates, and teammates around the country. Meeting technical requirements and coordinating schedules for delivery of various components and support services is essential to the success of a program.

for that?" or "When the hell will they finish?" or "What the hell was he thinking?" It quickly became apparent that this brash, cliquish group of professionals was joking about hell. Hell may be many things, but it is certainly not funny.

The last six years of my work in aerospace included going to school at night to earn a graduate degree from Fuller Theological Seminary. From start to finish, including summer months, my free hours and weekends were filled with reading theology books and writing papers. Supplementing my knowledge of the Bible with a formal education was a valuable experience. The effort built a solid foundation for full-time doctoral study following retirement from The Boeing Company. In retrospect, the time and energy spent slowly absorbing rational and systematic views of God aided immensely in understanding how to properly interpret the scriptures.

Background in the sciences and scriptures allows access to both worlds. God ordains the sciences to work together with faith in the Bible, allowing for a clearer view of some passages. The coming of Jesus in bodily form unveils a close intertwining of the physical universe and the eternal realm. God has taken a permanent stake in the material universe because the resurrected Christ remains a God-man forever. The God-and-man linkage allows for an inseparable joining between the physical and spiritual domain. A future linking will be demonstrated at the second coming of Christ. God's spiritual and eternal kingdom of heaven will physically unfold on planet Earth.

After the final judgment of humankind, the question of where perdition is located will come into view. Places of loss and banishment will be away from paradisical Earth. If heaven is on the third planet from the sun, then where is hell or the lake of fire? After all, there are plenty of places outside the confines of Mother Earth. In order for hell to be a physically real place—just as heaven will be on a renewed

Earth—it could be situated on another planet. Examples would be Venus or even an exoplanet. For those who express indifference by denying God or choose to be amused by hell, being sequestered to one of these worlds in the solar system, galaxy, or beyond will be no laughing matter.

As mortals, we only have a limited view of the immortal aspects of being. People are not independently qualified to make judgments on eternal matters. We are reliant on God to give proper insight on the subject. Fortunately, the word of God is not silent concerning the afterlife. In the Gospels, Jesus speaks about heaven. He also happens to author the original doctrine of hell. This text examines his warnings and description of perdition, making details come alive within the solar system. I am prayerful that those uncertain about their eternal destiny will consider the message. Heaven is a beautiful place, and no one—not a single soul—should miss it.

ACKNOWLEDGMENTS

Research for the first edition of this book began in late 2011. At the time, I was a graduate student at San Francisco Theological Seminary. Having submitted my dissertation for review to the faculty, I was waiting for feedback. After the response, I would perform revisions and get final approval of the thesis. In the meantime, the process would provide plenty of free time to read, as it would be months before spring graduation in 2012. In preparing to write my first book, I felt confident in my ability to research, document, and organize a large body of information.

Publication of the first release came in late 2014 under the title *Venus: Don't Go There—What Science and Religion Reveal about Life after Death*. In 2016, minor changes were made for an update to the release. The additions included a formal introduction and glossary to help the reader. Thanks to the NASA Solar Dynamic Observatory, a fresh cover photo of Venus crossing the sun gave the book a compelling new look. After the modest update, I thought about the next step. The reader would need greater clarity about everlasting places being *in the cosmos*. The best support would come by identifying three locations: the physical universe, an eternity connecting to that universe, and an "ethereal realm" of nothing, which connects to neither one.

Researching the second edition began in late 2016. New information is brought to the table on the close relationship between the physical universe and eternity, which compares to the ethereal realm. The ethereal is the "nothing" that remains outside the expanding universe. The addition of three new sections will (1) compare science with the creation sciences, (2) give exoplanets as viable options for perdition, and (3) provide geological data for Hades—the current place of banishment—being located near the center of the earth. The changes for the second edition were so extensive that a rerelease was in order. It is now *Venus: Don't Go There— Unveiling a Biblical Hell.*

Many thanks go to Barry Applewhite, Paul Meyer, and Rebekah McKamie, who provided editorial coverage for the book. Their careful review aided immensely in the final release. Appreciation goes to artist Paul Martin, who willingly took on the challenge of creating imagery for the locust invasion in the book of Revelation. Sincere gratitude goes to Joel Hamme for his review of Greek and Hebrew language usage. Many thanks go to Andrew Smith for his production of graphic art for the text. Finally, I would like to give thanks to the insight and leading of the Holy Spirit. The researching, organizing, and composing of this volume are in cooperation with the Lord Jesus Christ.

INTRODUCTION

The Rosetta stone from early Egypt was a dark, granite rock that bore inscriptions of the Egyptian and Greek languages. The discovery of the engraving in 1799, and eventual decipherment by the 1820s, brought a reliable way of understanding hieroglyphics—the Egyptian picture script. It was an essential archaeological find, allowing for the appreciation of ancient Nile civilizations. The translation faithfully decodes the language of symbols found at pyramids and numerous excavation sites around the Egyptian world. Information from the stone is useful for interpreting the inscriptions on many artifacts. The animals, birds, and other figures became meaningful to archaeologists and historians.

The terms and jargon from two fields of study require similar correspondence in the English language. It is especially true when the two are brought together in one writing. In this text, there are biblical and theological discussions as well as scientific details. Describing the association of faith and science requires a bridging, as two diverse fields undergo comparison and contrast. The reader must understand the terminology. Knowing the basics in meaning is important for better comprehension. With this in mind, an expansive glossary appears in the back matter. The lexicon includes a critical mass of biblical and scientific terms that the reader encounters in the body of the text.

The Bible contains a long history of human beings living

on the earth, which includes records of natural events, such as those found in the Genesis creation account. When people who appreciate science attempt to evaluate these scriptures for accuracy, the creation text is usually compared to accepted facts. The cosmological, geological, and biological findings of science (including the claims of natural evolution) are critically measured against the biblical content. In doing the inquiry, four approaches or models find use. The list is as follows:

- **Sovereign model**
  The Sovereign model sees biblical faith and science as independent, respectable domains with no overlap. If two different "truths" about the creation of humanity exist, people are expected to live with the schism. It is a model accepting that ultimate truth cannot be known in this life.

- **Conflict model**
  The Conflict model puts the scriptures and science at odds with one another. Proponents of Young Earth creationism, who insist the earth is 10,000 years old, lock in battle with people such as evolutionary biologist and atheist Richard Dawkins, who sees religious faith as dangerous and lacking in any evidence.

- **Complementary model**
  The Complementary model works to find overlap and agreement. It limits encroachment by conforming the biblical creation account to scientific findings. Those accepting theistic evolution are adherents to the model. Their ideas include agreeing with the universe's age of 13.8 billion years, while accepting the natural evolution of humanity.

- **Fruitful Integration model**
  The Fruitful Integration model shows that biblical faith and science are consistent. It steps out by challenging questionable theology advertised as being "true" while reexamining science's presentation of the "facts." Old Earth creationism is part of this model. Included are separate metaphysical propositions about space, time, and being, which attempt to create a complete vision.

This text pursues the Fruitful Integration model and will address the rift between faith and science. We will cover agnostic thinking by relevant scientists, as well as skepticism toward science by Christian torchbearers of the faith. With narrow thinking coming from leadership, it is no surprise faith and science lack assimilation. One scientist, Max Planck, came to realize that most disputes, even within the scientific community, were rooted in pride. He said, "A new scientific truth does not triumph by convincing its opponents and making them see the light, but rather, because its opponents eventually die, and a new generation grows up being familiar with it."

An important update to the rerelease provides insight into the connection between eternity and the material universe. The fundamental properties of space, time, mass, and gravity are active in both eternity and the physical realm. A new section appraises science and its relationship to creation science. A properly understood creation science helps to grasp the universe's origin and the origin of life itself. The segment on Hades expands to include a geological review of possible locations under Earth's surface. A new section on the recent findings of exoplanets reveals how harsh conditions on these worlds can correlate to hell or the lake of fire. Finally, the addition of an appendix explains both the English use and biblical meaning of "morning star."

The truth from the Bible, the sciences, and theology, as

well as input from the metaphysical realm, blend together to form a fruitful integration. The resulting work produces compelling evidence for eternal places, such as heaven and hell, being in the physical universe. While going through the list of terms below, the author recommends referring to the glossary. In reading through these definitions, you will be aided in the ability to understand the science and biblical theology of the book.

The author accepts...   as well as...

Revelation (special)   **Revelation (general)**

The Bible warns against...   And does *not* imply...

Eternal Separation   **Annihilationism**
                             Universalism

The Bible faithfully teaches... Science arguably teaches...

Creationism   **Evolution (natural)**

The author embraces...   And questions...

Old Earth Creationism   **Young Earth Creationism**

A biblical view of the creation sciences will include Adam and Eve being the biological parents of all humanity.

This means accepting...   And denying ...

Progressive Creation   **Theistic Evolution**

This study supports the...	While refuting the...
End of the age	**End of the world**
Before creation, there was...	God made the universe...
God's Eternal Realm	***Ex nihilo***
God's kingdom is now in...	God's kingdom is not in the...
Eternity (see Figure 7)	**Ethereal**

This writing holds to traditional Christian views while bringing biblical teaching, theology, space science, and geology together. It maintains the truth of Genesis while showing how its verses make room for a universe that is billions of years old. As such, the writing does not accept Young Earth creationism as it causes a chasm between faith and science. Theistic evolution is shown to be problematic for its unbridled support of natural evolution. Natural evolution is a forensic science that fails to incorporate the scientific method. Finally, the text provides support for the eternal banishment of the unrighteous person, which is in keeping with what the scriptures teach.

Additional terms setting the stage for the reader include:

Co-presence
Heaven (celestial)
Exoplanet
Extra dimensions (space and time)
Hades
Hell
Intermediate State
Lake of Fire

Metaphysics
Physical Universe
Resurrected Spiritual Body
Soul

The understanding of biblical passages and planetary science will blend together in a meaningful way. By proposing the intertwining of eternity with our world, this book gives evidence for heaven, Hades, and hell (or the lake of fire) having material substance in the physical universe. In the present, heaven is located in the cosmic realm, while Hades is within the earth. In the future, heaven will relocate to the earth, and after final judgment, hell (the lake of fire) will be on a planetary body. Although Venus is a highly probable location for banishment, it remains tentative because of the myriad of exoplanet discoveries in the galaxy.

Following the evangelical pattern, the author accepts the divine inspiration, trustworthiness, and authority of the Bible in matters of faith and conduct. In creating and preserving the cosmos, God has endowed our world with unwavering order and clarity, which is the basis for scientific investigation. In Genesis 1:26, the Creator bestows dominion on humanity. Dominion includes maintaining the animal kingdom, plant life, and natural resources while helping to keep the planet's environment safe and clean. As such, scientific discovery and technological innovation are for sustaining life and for the continual progress of human civilization.

We move confidently into the body of the text, fully appreciating that we live on an exclusive planet. The establishing hand of the Creator now guides and cares for the world. In rare fashion, the earth is capable of supporting a vast taxonomy of organisms. One view, the mediocrity principle, believes there is nothing unusual or special about planet Earth. Contradicting this inaccuracy, we see a world with multifaceted plant and animal life. God's providence has manifested itself in biological complexity and intelligent life, which has set our globe apart as a special place in the solar system, the Milky Way, and the innumerable galaxies of the universe.

ABBREVIATIONS

AVO   Akatsuki Venus Orbiter
CO_2 carbon dioxide
CMBR   cosmic microwave background radiation
ESA   European Space Agency
Gk.   Greek
GPS   global positioning system
GUT   Grand Unified Theory
Heb.   Hebrew
H_2SO_4 sulfuric acid
IASP   International Association of Seismology and Physics
IAU   International Astronomical Union
ID   Intelligent Design
IRIS   Incorporated Research Institutes for Seismology
ISRO   Indian Space Research Organization
IUS   inertial upper stage
JAXA   Japan Aerospace Exploration Agency
KJV   King James Version
LHC   Large Hadron Collider
LUCA   Last Universal Common Ancestor
N_2 (diatomic) nitrogen
NASA   National Aeronautics and Space Administration
NKJV   New King James Version

NRL	Naval Research Laboratory
NRSV	New Revised Standard Version
NT	New Testament
NTP	normal temperature and pressure
OEC	Old Earth creationism
OT	Old Testament
SAR	synthetic aperture radar
SO_2	sulfur dioxide
TE	Theistic evolution
ToE	Theory of Everything
USGS	United States Geological Survey
USSR	Union of Soviet Socialist Republics
YEC	Young Earth creationism

BIBLICAL REFERENCES

Unless otherwise noted, the text references the New Revised Standard Version (NRSV) Bible translation. The NRSV sets a standard for the twenty-first century by drawing on newly available sources. These sources include the Dead Sea Scrolls, other newfound manuscripts, archaeological finds from the ancient Near East, and new insights of Greek and Hebrew grammar. The NRSV is available in a standard edition, with or without the Apocrypha. The approved Roman Catholic edition uses the same text as the Protestant publication. A Common Bible version is available, which includes all books belonging to the Protestant, Roman Catholic, and Orthodox canons.

Chapter 1

Revelation through the Sciences

*The heavens are telling
the glory of God;
and the firmament
proclaims his handiwork.*

Psalm 19:1

By the will of God all things were created and have their
being. By his command the heavenly bodies came into
existence; the vast expanse of interstellar space, galaxies,
stars, the planets in their courses, and this fragile Earth,
our island home. From the original elements God brought
forth the human race in his image, bestowing upon them
memory, reason, and skill. He made us rulers of creation,
with providence, self-sufficiency, and the ability to imagine.
As intelligent beings, we often think beyond the physical into
the transcendent, asking the question, "What is the purpose
of it all?"

The setting of the sun is picturesque to couples walking
hand-in-hand, to singles, to young and old alike. As physically
confined yet incurably curious beings, we look in wonder at
moonlit skies and dark, starry nights. Across the firmament

1

extends a seemingly infinite number of celestial bodies of varying brightness, forming constellations such as the Big and Little Dipper, Hercules, Orion, Cassiopeia, and Pisces. The night sky stirs our imagination. The star cluster of the Pleiades generates folklore tales of seven sisters. Some even dream about *Star Trek* voyages into outer space, asking theatrically, "Scotty, are you there? Beam me up!"

Looking at images from the Hubble Space Telescope (HST), one is amazed by the beauty and diversity of celestial objects. From colorful nebulas to swirling, bleached galaxies, the HST manages to uncover a kaleidoscope of stunning panoramas in the firmament. On the ground, amateur astronomers peer into the night sky with small telescopes to examine the surface of Jupiter, to search for a double star, or to study the craters of the moon. In the midst of exploration, you can take the time to appreciate the goodness of God for creating the glorious heavens.

The paradox of the beautiful night sky is the adverse conditions of deep space. Without a capsule or space suit for environmental control, a person cannot survive beyond Earth's envelope. Our friendly planet provides a safe haven; but beyond the atmosphere, adversity looms. Nearby celestial bodies are less than appealing for humans in this life. Perhaps the same can be said for spiritual beings in the afterlife. If the conditions of a planet align closely with biblical depictions of hell, we might take notice. From there, we can organize a faith- and science-based presentation arguing for worlds such as Venus, or possibly an exoplanet, to be a prototypical place for eternal separation.

In the Gospels, Jesus tells his followers that hell is a location set apart for the unrighteous. Yet, the idea of a permanent place of loss and separation endures skepticism from some churchgoers. One reason is that the Bible provides a less-than-complete description of eternal places. Nebulous concepts persist about places such as perdition, making it difficult to grasp, unthinkable, or even fictional. One way to provide a sense of certainty is to give convincing evidence for the afterlife existing in the material universe. From there, biblical passages pertaining to hell and the lake of fire can connect to the environments of nearby worlds.

The Nature of Revelation

How does an infinite and all-powerful deity show himself to finite humans? It comes through the process of divine revelation, which is self-disclosure and communication from God. Through divine revelation, God gives knowledge to humans. The word "revelation" denotes a "revealing." It is the unfolding or making plain of that which is hidden. God's revelation comes about through two avenues: special revelation and general revelation. As the source of power and truth, God makes his existence and character traits known using these two avenues.

Special revelation refers to the record of God's words and actions in the Holy Scriptures. In freeing the Hebrews from Egyptian slavery and bringing them to the Promised Land, the Lord God conveys knowledge about himself to a particular people at specific times and places. The recording of many Old Testament events in Israel's history serves as special revelation, as do dreams and visions received by his people. Many of these dreams provide critical pieces of knowledge to direct people to do the right thing at the right time. In the New Testament, the disclosure of Jesus Christ as Lord and Savior falls under the category of special revelation.

Several examples of revelatory dreams and visions are in the scriptures. In the Old Testament, Abimelech receives a warning in a dream to return Abraham's wife to him, which he obeys. The prophet Daniel receives an accurate understanding of Nebuchadnezzar's dream in a night vision, which he then relates to the king. In the New Testament,

3

Joseph receives direction in a dream to take Mary as his wife. Dreams guide him to flee with his family to Egypt and later return. Ananias assists the apostle Paul in receiving his sight because of a divine vision. Finally, Paul himself receives direction to preach the gospel in Macedonia as the result of a vision.

The most common avenue for special revelation comes to readers through studying the Bible, which is the written record of the prophets and apostles. The biblical text provides a trustworthy way to reveal information from God. The Christian life relies primarily on the study of sacred Scripture, which can lead and guide a person. In 2 Timothy 3:16–17, Paul states, "All scripture is inspired by God and is useful for teaching, for reproof, for correction, and for training in righteousness, so that everyone who belongs to God may be proficient, equipped for every good work." God's principles jump off the page to encourage, to enlighten, and to give daily instruction.

The ultimate form of special revelation is the bringing forth of the person of Jesus Christ. God became a human being in the person of Jesus. He identifies with us, teaches us, guides us, reveals God the Father to us, and ultimately provides salvation for us. The Bible is the place where the Son of God is revealed to humankind. The scarlet thread of redemption is evident from Genesis to Revelation. The Old Testament looks toward his coming and the New Testament brings his fulfillment. He is the One to be born, to suffer, and to die for the atonement of sin. Jesus delivers a person from darkness into light and gives the Holy Spirit as a guide for a new life.

A special revelation originating with Jesus warns about perdition. In the Gospels, he describes "hell" as the eternal fire and where the fire is never quenched. Later, in the book of Revelation, the Bible uses the phrase "lake of fire" as another term for perdition. The lake of fire is the place where unsaved people go after Judgment Day. Similar to the fires of hell, the torment of those in the lake of fire is forever and ever. The idea of everlasting fire brings "hell" and the "lake of fire" together. Since Revelation is filled with metaphors, it is not unusual to use lake of fire as a substitute for hell.[2] So, special revelation can reveal that hell and the lake of fire are one and the same.

General revelation, on the other hand, is the self-disclosure of God through observation, experience, innate conscience, and reason. The revealing of God in this manner finds backing in the scriptures. In Romans 1:19–20, the apostle Paul affirms, "For what can be known about God is plain to them, because God has shown it to them. Ever since the creation of the world his eternal power and divine nature, invisible though they are, have been understood and seen through the things he has made." In other words, truths about God are actually present in the observable universe.

Knowledge of God is arrived at through reasoning about the creation. Humans have the capacity to uncover, to interpret, to comprehend, and to evaluate certain truths. For example, when staring into the vastness of the night sky, one might say, "There must be a God and he must be infinite." God exists and is definitely an infinite being, but in what way? General revelation is incomplete. The Bible will illustrate God's character—showing, for example, that his forgiveness toward repentant people is infinite. Still, observation brings some truth about God when looking into deep space. The idea of a real and infinite God does not depart from the intent of the scriptures.

Saint Thomas Aquinas, the great theologian of the thirteenth century, gave strong support to general revelation

---

2   In the gospels, the unquenchable flames of hell correlate to the lake of fire, which is forever and ever in the book of Revelation. Walter A. Elwell, ed., *Baker Encyclopedia of the Bible* (Grand Rapids, MI: Baker Book House, 1988), 1,299.

in his formulation of natural theology. Natural theology is the term for seeing the existence of God by observing the natural world and using human reason. Aquinas maintains there is a valid, objective understanding of a higher being that is attainable in nature, history, and human personality. For example, the perfect order and harmony of our solar system, planet, and natural surroundings is a witness to his being. God remains unseen, yet his wisdom shines through the underpinning of our tranquil environment.

In 1885, an annual series of lectures was commissioned by Lord Adam Gifford. Known as the Gifford Lectures, the talks are given annually at Scottish universities and deal with the topic of natural theology.[3] The lectures began in 1888 and have been delivered continuously since that time, excluding the World War II period. In dealing with various topics, expert lecturers discuss natural theology as a science. Discussing natural theology as a science requires a shift in epistemology. Natural theology is no longer general revelation, but rather, is thought of as a scientific worldview. It becomes a way to philosophize ideas and beliefs through observation.

In being a worldview, natural theology does not seek to offer revelatory evidence for the existence of God. Rather, the thinking attempts to provide a coherent summary of the world around us.[4] It is an integrated vision of humankind's place in the universe. It draws from religious and biblical views to bring together the finest knowledge from areas such as science, history, and the arts. The vision is sacred because it centers on the reality of an all-powerful and transcendent deity. Being a philosophical view, natural theology becomes

---

3   Gifford Lectures, The University of Edinburgh, College of Arts, Humanities and Social Sciences, https://www.ed.ac.uk/arts-humanities-soc-sci/news-events/lectures/gifford-lectures (accessed July 25, 2020).

4   John Polkinghorne, *Belief in God in an Age of Science* (London: Yale University Press, 2003), 10–11.

an area of study where faith can hold an intelligent position. The Christian use of natural theology will be a topic in Chapter 3.

To summarize, God's revelation consists of special revelation and general revelation. For all practical purposes, special revelation comes through reading and understanding the Bible. The biblical text provides you with revelation about God so that you can know who he is. On the other hand, general revelation communicates to all of humanity. It conveys God's existence, power, and glory, so that no one is left without evidence. Finally, natural theology began as a belief in support of general revelation but has evolved into a worldview. This important way of thinking helps to reveal how God works in the physical realm.

Seeing Venus as a Hell–Lake of Fire

The sun and orbiting bodies originate from diffuse nebula material in the galaxy. The molecular cloud of interstellar gas and dust gradually congeals and forms celestial structures. The center eventually became the sun. The forming of the planets arose from the material that remained in the outer sections, which partitioned out and flattened into a rotating, circumstellar disc. The continuing gravity collapse was responsible for the planets, moons, asteroids, comets, and other small bodies that solidified in the solar system. Although Earth and neighboring Venus grew to about the same size, evolutionary processes molded two decisively different planets.

Scientific data from the Mariner, Pioneer, and Venera programs were the first to detail the planet's uninviting and extremely unpleasant environment. Soviet spacecraft in the 1970s and 1980s were able to release descent modules, which landed safely on the ground. Operating on the surface for only a few short minutes, camera systems took clear images of a dreary Venusian landscape. A topographical sweep made by the Magellan mission would show innumerable volcanoes and extensive volcanism on the surface. Many scientists consider the planet alive with ongoing volcanic activity. The conditions create a hot, barren place of exile for the lost.

Revelation is the last book of the Bible. Called the Apocalypse, it means "disclosure" or "unveiling." The prophetic and metaphorical writing by John the apostle reveals God's end-time plan for humanity, as well as for the earth. The text continues to mystify readers with its figurative language. As a result, some Christians assign a broad-brush or "warm and fuzzy" feeling to the complex series of events. Revelation, however, is not an indiscernible text written solely to provide hazy comfort to the believer. Activities occur in a coherent, sensible progression throughout the chapters, leading to a final crescendo before the return of Christ.

The final three chapters of Revelation are an important part of individual eschatology, Eschatology is the "study of last things" and concerns itself with what God has revealed about the final events of history. When the events relate to your death, resurrection, and eternal destiny, it becomes *individual* eschatology. The eschatology of Revelation includes the final judgment of humanity and the creation of a new heaven and earth. One way to understand the meaning of passages is through exegesis. Exegesis relies on an objective and critical interpretation of the text. It draws out and explains the meaning of words and passages in the Bible.

As part of the final judgment, the reader encounters the term "lake of fire" in Revelation 19:20, 20:10, 20:13–14, 20:15, and 21:8. The passages read as follows:

> **Rev. 19:20**—"And the beast was captured, and with it the false prophet who had performed in its presence the signs by which he deceived

8

those who had received the mark of the beast and those who worshiped its image. These two were thrown alive into *the lake of fire that burns with sulfur.*"

Rev. 20:10—"And the devil who had deceived them was thrown into *the lake of fire and sulfur,* where the beast and the false prophet were, and they will be tormented day and night forever and ever."

Rev. 20:13–14—"And the sea gave up the dead that were in it, Death and Hades gave up the dead that were in them, and all were judged according to what they had done. Then Death and Hades were thrown into *the lake of fire.* This is the second death, *the lake of fire.*"

Rev. 20:15— "and anyone whose name was not found written in the book of life was thrown into *the lake of fire.*"

Rev. 21:8—"But as for the cowardly, the faithless, the polluted, the murderers, the fornicators, the sorcerers, the idolaters, and all liars, their place will be in *the lake that burns with fire and sulfur,* which is the second death."

The last two passages (Rev. 20:15 and 21:8) pertain to lost souls, who are brought up out of Hades for a review of their lives. At the time of the final judgment, people arriving from the netherworld are equipped with an immortal spiritual body. A physical resurrection, as understood in the resurrection of Jesus Christ, comes to every person, regardless of whether one has done good or evil. In John 5:29, Jesus refers to both a resurrection unto life (to those doing good) and a resurrection unto condemnation (to those doing evil). After the review is complete, sentencing to the lake of fire occurs unless one's name is inscribed in the book of life.

The first word in the *lake of fire* is "lake," which derives from the Greek *limne*. The field of limnology is the study of lakes. Looking at a body of water can suggest an unchanging or homogeneous surface condition. You can grasp the smooth expanse of a body of water when standing on the edge of a large, calm lake. The shores of the Great Lakes bring this experience. When you look out on the tranquil water toward the horizon, the scene is vast, uniform, and unbroken. You experience a similar sensation staring at the parched landscape of planets such as Venus. Volcanism is global, creating an enormous and seemingly unchanging field of view.

The word fire (Gk. *pûr*) can represent the inner planet's hot surface temperature, which is estimated to be about 865°F. Clearly, Venus' milieu is one of fiery heat, compared to Earth's temperate climate. Overhead, a dense cloud cover blankets the planet. The atmospheric clouds retain the sun's heat in a greenhouse effect, facilitating isothermal conditions. An isothermal state means Venus maintains the same temperature around the globe, regardless of whether it is day or night. *Pûr*, from which the word "pyrotechnic" derives, can also refer to flashes of light or lightning. Lightning events are thought to occur regularly on the planet.

A significant factor relating Venus to the lake of fire is the presence of hot sulfur. The element of sulfur, or compounds chemically containing sulfur, are very predominant in the scorching environment. In the NRSV Bible, Revelation 19:20 and 21:8 tell the reader that the lake of fire "burns with sulfur" and "burns with fire and sulfur." In the KJV Bible, it reads "burning with brimstone" and "burneth with fire and brimstone." Brimstone is an old, nonscientific name for sulfur. In the periodic table, sulfur (S) is a nonmetallic, multivalent element. Valence tells about sulfur's ability to bond quickly and easily with other elements, often producing unpleasant and even deadly substances.

On Earth's surface, sulfur is able to ignite and then burn with a hot blue flame. Sulfur is difficult to approach when on fire because the suffocating fumes of sulfur dioxide make it hard to breathe. Molten sulfur is a hot, amber-colored liquid that is used in manufacturing. It is often transported in bulk quantity using double-walled railway tank cars. It has a variety of industrial applications and is key in making fertilizers and sulfuric acid. On Venus, sulfur is a far more abundant element than on Earth. It appears both in basic form and in chemical combination with hydrogen and oxygen.

Sulfur is so abundant on Venus that scientists delineate a sulfur cycle. The sulfur cycle divides the atmosphere into four thermal zones, with sulfur activity being traced in each zone. On Earth, the hydrologic or water cycle describes water motion on and above the planet's surface. The same is true for the sulfur cycle of Venus. The atmosphere is primarily carbon dioxide (CO_2) and nitrogen (N_2), but it houses significant levels of sulfur dioxide (SO_2) from volcanic outgassing. At higher altitudes, the copious cloud cover is composed primarily of sulfur dioxide and sulfuric acid (H_2SO_4) droplets. Additionally, the volcanic rocks on the surface contain elemental sulfur.[5]

Considering the scriptures and scientific findings of intense heat and sulfur on Venus, the planet can be thought of in a metaphysical sense to be the lake of fire. In viewing the cover of this book, our interest continues to grow. The photograph shows the transit of the planet across the sun

---

5   Using X-ray florescence spectrometers, Soviet spacecraft found the chemical makeup of surface rocks to contain high levels of sulfur. V. L. Barsukov ed., *Venus Geology, Geochemistry and Geophysics: Research Results from the USSR* (Tucson, AZ: The University of Arizona Press, 1992), 166.

on June 6, 2012, by the Solar Dynamic Observatory.[6] A planetary transit happens when either Mercury or Venus traverses directly between the sun and the earth. Venus transits are uncommon astronomical events, with the 2012 occurrence being the last of the twenty-first century. As the planet makes its way across the fiery surface of the sun, you can imagine a world immersed in a lake of fire.

Revelation 20:13–14 states, "the sea gave up the dead." People who die at sea have no remains. The preservation of even the skeletal structure is not possible. Ocean tides and currents scatter bodily remains, which settle at varying locations and depths. Fish and crustaceans consume the flesh and bone. To the apostle John, the sea transcends a mere body of water. In first-century Europe, maritime travel was a dangerous affair. Loss of the entire ship, including passengers and cargo, was an accepted risk for seafarers. The oceans were an unconquerable and fearful nemesis. John's allusion to the sea is of a place of untimely passage; an erratic, all-consuming place of turbulence and uncertainty.[7]

The scripture goes on to refer to both Death and Hades as giving up the dead. The use of "Death" (Gk. *thanatos*) is as a personified noun. Death is an eternal state of existence that has dominion over the soul. To every human being, death will manifest in the physical termination of life. To the lost soul, Death has a worse outcome. It ultimately results in spiritual separation from God. When a person departs to the lake of fire, Death will accompany him or her and become the second death. To the saved soul that ends up in

---

6   The NASA mission was launched in 2010 to study the synergy of the Sun–Earth system. NASA Science Visualization Studio, "Venus Transit 2012 from Solar Dynamics Observatory," https://svs.gsfc.nasa.gov/3940 (accessed Oct. 28, 2020).

7   In Rev. 13:1, the beast rising from the sea links large bodies of water with turbulence and instability. Michael D. Coogan, ed., *The New Oxford Annotated Bible: New Revised Standard Version* (New York: Oxford University Press, 2001), 437, 446 [NT].

the paradise of heaven, the presence of God replaces Death, which Revelation 21:4 renders as being no more.

Hades is the place of departed souls under the earth, where the unrighteous go after leaving the body. Revelation 20:13–14 shows the term "Hades" (Gk. *Hádes*) can have both a physical and a nonphysical meaning. The first use of Hades (giving up the dead) is as a physical place of confinement under the earth. The second use of Hades (thrown into the lake of fire) is in being a spiritual domain of wickedness. Spiritual Hades is the global initiative of Satan and his demonic army. It extends throughout all the nations, creating evil and mayhem. The global spiritual incursion will remain in place until the final judgment.

Hades and hell are two different places with hell not being formally introduced until the NT. Unfortunately, the King James Version Bible incorrectly use the word "hell" in several OT passages. Thankfully, the New King James Version Bible revises the passages to use Sheol, an OT equivalent to Hades. In the Gospels, Jesus introduces "hell" as a final destination for the unrighteous. Early in his ministry, he provides important teaching in the Sermon on the Mount. The sermon contains the basic tenets of Christian discipleship. In this teaching, Jesus speaks for the first time about being "thrown into hell," which has both a familiar and unpleasant connotation with Jewish listeners.

The word "hell" comes from the Greek noun *gehenna* and refers to the valley of "Hinnom." To a resident of Jerusalem, Hinnom was the primary disposal site for garbage from the city. It was situated in a deep, narrow gorge southeast of the city. Identified as "Tophet" in the book of Jeremiah, it was originally an area where idolatrous Israelites sacrificed their young children to the gods Moloch and Baal. Conducting these wicked acts was part of worshipping the deities of Semitic culture. By the first century, the valley of Hinnom had become the infamous dumping site for the city's garbage.

In Nehemiah 3:14, we read about the rebuilding of the Dung Gate at the southern end of Jerusalem. People moved trash and dung through the gate for burning in the valley of Hinnom. Unlike modern disposal sites that differentiate between garbage and toxic waste, *gehenna* accepted every form of refuse. Israelites regarded the valley of Hinnom as a place of devastation and loss due to the deposit of dead bodies, including animals, criminals, and enemies slain in battle. Never-ending burning kept the accumulation of corpses and rubbish in check, though the activities led to offensive sights and foul smells in the valley. Over time, the negative images of the dumpsite became associated with unending fire and destruction.

Similar to the "unquenchable fire of hell" in the Gospels is the "lake of fire" in the book of Revelation. But what is an unquenchable lake of fire? Is it a sea of lighter fluid that cannot be put out? Are the resurrected spiritual bodies of unsaved people tossed off a precipice into a voracious inferno? Since we lack a full explanation, the human mind can make up terrible images. Beyond the absence of biblical details, the problem magnifies because hell and the lake of fire are eternal destinations. One purpose for writing this book is to address that difficulty. God provides rational, coherent, and morally principled answers, even for places such as hell.

Bible believers lacking a clear sense about hell or the lake of fire try to equate the destination to the unknown. I've heard some Christians refer to it as a "black hole." Black holes do exist in the cosmos, but are they even a valid metaphysical concept for spiritual beings? Supermassive black holes situate in the center of galaxies. Studies of orbiting stars near the center of the Milky Way have brought the black hole, Sagittarius A, to scientists' attention. A black hole has powerful gravity. It seems to act as a central hub for the rotation of stars about our galaxy. Close in, the gravitational pull of the black hole creates a force from which nothing can escape.

In April 2019, astronomers held an international press conference to release the first-ever image of a supermassive black hole.[8] It is 53 million light-years from the earth and located in the center of the elliptical galaxy Messier 87. In the image, light at the outer edge of the black hole is visible. Crossing the boundary or event horizon marks the "point of no return." Photons of light, which have no rest mass, are irreversibly drawn by gravity across the event horizon. Scientists speculate an object of any shape or size entering a black hole will be stretched as thin as a piece of spaghetti. The process is known as spaghettification or the "noodle effect."

Staring at one area of outer space for long periods has uncovered the activities of black holes. Together, three X-ray telescopes found a supermassive black hole known as XJ1500+154. It had been consuming a local star for over a decade.[9] The star and starlight itself are unable to resist the sucking action of the black hole. Cataclysmic forces are in play that are even able to consume massless photons. As such, the scientific findings of black holes do not correlate to biblical descriptions of perdition. Even in a metaphysical sense, it is difficult to fathom resurrected spiritual bodies as being coherent or able to survive the environment inside a black hole.

Some Bible teachers rationalize that hell and the lake

---

8   Using interferometry, the Event Horizon Telescope took a picture of a black hole. ScienceNews, "The First Picture of a Black Hole Opens a New Era of Astrophysics," https://www.sciencenews.org/article/blackholefirst-picture-event-horizon-telescope (accessed April 10, 2021).

9   In 2005, the Chandra X-ray Observatory, the Neil Gehrels Swift Observatory, and the High Throughput X-ray Spectroscopy Mission began watching the event. Astronomy, "A Supermassive Black Hole Spent More Than a Decade Consuming a Star," http://www.astronomy.com/news/2017/02/black-hole-record (accessed Feb. 9, 2020).

of fire are not in the realm of space and time, and as such, are beyond a logical grasp of the mind. This line of thinking is not only unbiblical but will draw the conversation to a close quickly. Upcoming chapters will address these ideas as ethereal destinations. The ethereal domain requires a place where nothing exists, including space, time, matter, and energy. The chances are small that unsaved spirits will go into nothing. In God's eternal realm, he creates the cosmos, which came from nothing (Lat. *ex nihilo*). The nothing has now moved beyond the edge of the universe. The ethereal realm of nothing draws a sharp contrast with eternity, which is shown to be part of the universe.

Hades in the Material Universe

Hades can also be thought to exist in the realm of space and time. This study deduces the physical location of Hades to be the same as the Old Testament location of Sheol. It is within the earth. The systematic theology of Charles Hodge, principal of Princeton Theological Seminary from 1851 to 1878, supports the notion. In all points, Hodge believes the Greek idea of Hades corresponds with the Hebrew notion of Sheol—the underworld destination of departed souls.[10] He uses the parable of the rich man and Lazarus in Luke 16 as a key reference for his belief. Sheol–Hades is a distinct underground setting designed for separation from God's immediate presence.

In Matthew 16:18, Jesus uses the word "Hades" in commending Peter, "And I tell you, you are Peter, and on this rock, I will build my church, and the gates of Hades will not prevail against it." In this application, Hades takes on the sense of a vast, evil empire. The spiritual domain of Hades is amorphous in shape, global in scope, and has a focus on

---

10   Charles Hodge, *Systematic Theology – Volume III*, http://www.ccel.org/ccel/hodge/theology3 (accessed Oct. 19, 2020).

lawlessness and malevolence. The empire will always work against the good intentions of God's church on the earth. The Lord views the domain of Hades as formidable. It is a coordinated, international operation of rebellion, hostility, and wickedness geared against the body of believers.

Satan and his demonic army operate within the spiritual domain of Hades, which covers the entire planet. It works in partnership with the physical location of Hades, which is under the earth's surface. The material location of Hades basically functions as a holding tank, where unrighteous souls and confined demons are kept. The spiritual domain of Hades serves Satan's purposes in being able to reach and plague humankind. The devil and his minions engage in spiritual warfare with Almighty God and the holy angels for the souls of the earth's inhabitants.

Hearing that Hades has "gates" brought concern to first-century listeners. Gates were robust and thoughtfully planned fortifications of ancient Near East cities. As such, the spiritual domain of Hades is a fortified, resilient operation with an established hierarchy. The spiritual terrain is powerful in sway and worldwide in scope. Satan leads the dark forces of the spiritual domain of Hades into continual conflict with the light of the kingdom of God. The goals of the spiritual domain of Hades are to accuse, to criticize, and to condemn God's people in the current church age.

After the second coming of Christ and final judgment, perdition awaits evil spirits and lost people. Planets or exoplanets similar to Venus can be eligible as a destination for Satan and his demonic army, the beast, the false prophet, and all unsaved humanity. The demons operating in the spiritual empire of Hades and the lost souls from physical Hades are cast into outer darkness, heading for the lake of fire. The discarding of physical Hades is like emptying a box or canister. You can dispose of the material inside and still keep the container. The contents within the boundaries of

Hades will empty out, but the enclosure remains under the planet's surface.

Omission of Perdition by the Church

The church has traditionally taught about Satan, sin, and the tragic fate of the unsaved, but present-day churchgoers hear less and less on the topic. When was the last time you listened to a preacher give a "fire and brimstone" sermon on the fate of the lost? With a great sigh of relief, many will say, "Not in a long time." Over the course of the last few decades, the topic of perdition has nearly vanished from the pulpit. When finally hearing a sermon on the subject, silence grips the audience. Hell is an unspeakably bad and fearful place. Many people in the church have close relationships with family, friends, and neighbors who have rejected the gospel.

Discussion about the afterlife receives neglect in the modern church era, which tends to focus on the here and now. Finding fulfillment in the present day is of great concern to the contemporary worshiper. Living the Christian life with an eye on eternity does not draw interest in an American culture geared toward instant gratification, financial success, and material wealth. Topics having a futuristic twist are not popular with adherents to the faith. Over time, heaven becomes fuzzy, and hell relegates to an artifact of times past. Yet, the Lord teaches us to gain an eternal perspective by laying up treasures in heaven while avoiding hell.

One problem with the hereafter is the lack of biblical imagery. Scripture does not enlighten the reader on the milieu of heaven and hell. As such, these places become mysterious, abstract, ever-so-distant from life, and seemingly lacking in concreteness. Considering nearby planets and far away exoplanets as places for perdition may bring validity to the subject. The research classifies as interdisciplinary, allowing for the crossing of boundaries between two or more academic disciplines, creating innovative findings and solutions. Through fruitful integration of the sciences and the Bible, something new and thought-provoking will be brought to the table.

The remaining three sections give an introductory overview of the scientific aspects of this book. The first segment, astronomy, discusses planetary bodies inside and outside the solar system. The second section is a short review of the history of space exploration. In studying planetary voyages, it turns out that Venus is one of the most visited bodies in the solar system. The third part covers artificial satellites. It briefly addresses the design, build, test, launch, and operation of spacecraft. Whether orbiting the earth or traveling to distant planets, these advanced systems are capable of returning valuable data about atmospheres and environments.

Astronomy

The Remick Observatory is on the grounds of Lockport High School in Lockport, New York. As a member of the Astronomy Club, I would make occasional visits to the observatory in order to look through the optical telescope. The facility contains an adjoining planetarium with star maps, planetary photographs, and sky-watching information. Memorizing facts about the planets and solar system was part of the fun. During evening viewing times, I could see the rings of Saturn and identify double star formations. Teachers and students alike sought a grander view of the heavens and a better appreciation of the night sky.

Back in the late '60s and early '70s, little was known about outer space. Scientists could not grasp how far the solar system was from the center of the Milky Way galaxy. Sorely missing was an understanding of the birth and death of stars, the Kuiper Belt, the Oort Cloud, black holes, exoplanets, and dark matter/energy. In terms of planets, nine were orbiting the sun; Mercury, Venus, Earth, Mars, Jupiter, Saturn, Uranus, Neptune, and Pluto, with an asteroid belt sitting between Mars and Jupiter. The 1990 launch of the Hubble Space Telescope would help to dramatically improve information about the solar system, galaxy, and observable universe.

One example of increasing knowledge was in the number of moons revolving around the planets. At the time of my 1973 high school graduation, Jupiter had 12 moons in its orbit, Saturn had 10, Uranus had 5, Neptune had 2, and Pluto had none. Today, the number of natural satellites circling Jupiter exceeds 70, Saturn exceeds 80, with Uranus, Neptune, and Pluto numbering 27, 14, and 5, respectively. The number of Saturn's moons excludes the dense ring structure, which has moonlets and innumerable small particles embedded in the halo. The dramatic revisions represent the technical advancements in observational astronomy.

The 1992 discovery of the Kuiper Belt opened new categories for planetary objects. The Kuiper Belt, which extends radially past Neptune, is a region of minor planets and small icy-rock bodies orbiting the sun. The discovery led to the 2006 downgrade of Pluto to a minor planet by the International Astronomical Union (IAU). The demotion was due to a portion of Pluto's orbit being closer to the sun than neighboring Neptune. The IAU definition of a planet requires it to have "cleared the neighborhood around its orbit."[11] The elliptical track of Pluto crosses sunward of Neptune's path

---

11 International Astronomical Union, "Resolution B5: Definition of a Planet in the Solar System," XXVIth IAU 26th General Assembly (Prague, Czech Republic: IAU, Aug. 24, 2006), 1.

during part of Pluto's orbit, resulting in its demotion from planet to minor planet.[12]

Under the current classification of planets by the IAU, there are eight planets and five minor or dwarf planets. Besides Pluto, the minor planets are Ceres, Haumea, Makemake, and Eris. Technically, there are thousands of minor planets in the solar system, but the bigger ones receive interest. Ceres is sometimes considered a large asteroid because it sits in the asteroid belt. Haumea, Makemake, and Eris are trans-Neptunian bodies in the Kuiper Belt with Pluto.

Our solar system contains two types of worlds: terrestrial planets and gas giants. Terrestrial planets have crusts that are composed of silicate rocks and metals. The word "terrestrial" derives from the Latin word, *terra*, which means "land" or "earth." The planets Mercury, Venus, Earth, and Mars are terrestrial planets. Terrestrial landscapes have features such as craters, volcanoes, canyons, mountains, and plains. The four planets have similar structures, consisting of a metallic core, a silicate mantle, and compact, rock-strewn surfaces. The lunar surface presents a volcanic landscape that reflects the appearance of a terrestrial planet.

Orbiting just beyond the asteroid belt is Jupiter, which is the largest planet in the solar system. Outside of Jupiter is the planet Saturn. Both worlds are gas giants composed of thick atmospheres of hydrogen and helium. Further out sit the ice giants Uranus and Neptune. Ice giants contain hydrogen and helium as well, but have more "ices" made up of water, ammonia, and methane. The vast majority of "gas and ice" in the giants is in liquid form. Moving toward the center of these planets, the gases compress, becoming a fluid. Due

---

12 The scientific community now recognizes Pluto as an important prototype of a new class of trans-Neptunian objects. International Astronomical Union, "IAU 2006 General Assembly: Result of the IAU Resolution Votes," http://www.iau.org/public_press/news/detail/iau0603/ (accessed Jan. 21, 2021).

to the lack of a hard surface, space exploration of gas giants consists mainly of orbital and flyby vehicles.

An exciting frontier is the exploration and discovery of exoplanets or extrasolar planets; that is, planets outside our solar system. People have supposed the existence of extrasolar planets for centuries, but scientists were unable to confirm them until the mid-1990s. The Kepler Space Telescope is the spacecraft responsible for finding over twenty-five hundred exoplanets. The NASA launch of the more recent Transiting Exoplanet Survey Satellite (TESS) in 2018 is expected to uncover an additional fifteen thousand exoplanets during its mission. The coverage area is much greater than previous telescopes, allowing for the observation of a wider star field.

Bolstering deep space search was the 2017 discovery of seven terrestrial planets around a single star called TRAPPIST-1.[13] The red dwarf star is thirty-nine light-years from our Sun and situates in the constellation of Aquarius. At least three planets classify as exo-Earths and are located in the habitable zone. An exo-Earth is an Earth-size planet. The habitable zone of a star allows a planet to have moderate temperatures and to retain liquid water on its surface. The star system garners special interest from astronomers because it may be capable of biological habitation.

Space Exploration

Formal space exploration began during the geopolitical tensions of the Cold War between the United States and the former Soviet Union. The launch of Sputnik 1 in October 1957 placed the first artificial satellite into orbit. The USSR

---

13 All seven planets (b-h) could contain liquid water, a key factor in finding life. NASA, "Spitzer Space Telescope Reveals New Exoplanet Discovery," https://exoplanets.nasa.gov/news/1419/nasatelescopereveals-largest-batch-of-earth-size-habitable-zone-planets-around-single-star/ (accessed Feb. 21, 2021).

spacecraft looked like a silver sphere with four long, whip-like antennas protruding from its body. A month later, a female dog named "Laika" boarded Sputnik 2 and became the first animal to orbit the planet. The United States responded in February and March 1958 by launching Explorer 1 and Vanguard 1. The mission successes began a technology race between the two countries, ushering in the Space Age.

The first person to venture into outer space was cosmonaut Yuri Gagarin of the Soviet Union. On the historic date of April 12, 1961, his Vostok 1 spacecraft performed a single orbit of the earth, completing a successful landing in 108 minutes. Following closely behind was American astronaut John Glenn, who orbited three times on February 20, 1962, in Friendship 7, a Mercury spacecraft launched from Cape Canaveral, Florida. Propelled by an Atlas LV-3B vehicle, the mission lasted around five hours.

After Yuri Gagarin's historic flight, the Soviet cosmonaut became an international celebrity, parading through the Soviet Union and its client states, visiting countries around the world, and receiving numerous honors and awards. April 12th became known as Cosmonautics Day, in honor of his achievement. His winning smile was a crowd pleaser and became part of his legacy. He suffered an untimely death while piloting a MiG-15 training jet in 1968.

Interestingly, the NASA launch of the first Space Shuttle mission was on April 12, 1981, which was twenty years to the date of Vostok 1. The highly successful Space Shuttle program completed a total of 135 missions. With these two feats in mind, space fans celebrated Yuri's Night exactly twenty years later, on April 12, 2001. It was a "world space party" honoring human spaceflight. In 2011, the United Nations General Assembly adopted resolution A/RES/65/271, declaring April 12 as the International Day of Human Space Flight. The day serves to commemorate the beginning of space flight for humankind all over the world.

With the evolution of dependable boosters came an ever-increasing payload weight. The design of the Saturn 5 super-heavy-lift launch vehicle for the Apollo program resulted in successful voyages to the moon. The chief architect, Wernher von Braun, became known as the "father of rocket science." Saturn 5 remains the tallest, heaviest, and most powerful rocket ever brought to operational status. The initiative, which began in the early 1960s, led to twelve men landing on the moon and returning safely.[14] The moon remains the only non-Earth place visited by humans.

The twenty-first century finds private companies like SpaceX reliably sending up and retrieving space rockets. A launch vehicle's first-stage motor and casing are expensive, so reuse is a priority. With great success, the Falcon 9 first-stage assembly can lift off, separate, and then steer back to a pad for relaunch following refurbishment. The family of Falcon rockets brings safety and financial prudence to the launch business from a commercial supplier. The purpose of reuse is to defray costs for future missions, especially manned missions to Mars. Certified in 2019 by the US Air Force, the Falcon 9 Heavy is a variant that will serve to carry humans into space.

Under the sponsorship of various nations, space vehicles continue to orbit the planet and explore the solar system. Similar to Earth's satellite systems, spacecraft travel to distant places is an unmanned venture, requiring both autonomous and robotic functioning. The primary purpose for visiting neighboring bodies is to investigate physical features and chemical composition. The study helps us grasp the evolutionary processes of our own world. Two favorite

---

14 The initial commitment to putting a man on the moon was made by President John F. Kennedy. New York Daily News, "President John F. Kennedy Announces He Wants to Put a Man on the Moon," https://www.nydailynews.com/news/national/jfk-announces-1961-put-man-moon-article-1.2648222 (accessed May 15, 2020).

targets of multiple spaceflights have been Venus and Mars. Historically, the former Soviet Union put strong effort toward Venus, while the United States has directed more effort toward Mars.

The start of spacecraft travel to Venus and Mars dates back to 1961, when launch events and spacecraft operations were less than reliable. Those years witnessed lift off malfunctions and many onboard equipment failures. Yet, in six successive decades of effort, multiple missions have successfully managed to fly by, orbit, land on, probe, and rove these neighboring worlds. In logging over three dozen missions to the inner planet, Venus has become one the most visited places in the solar system. The research provides a plethora of insight about the shrouded world.

Satellite Design and Operation

The word aerospace comes from the joining of "aero" and "space." "Aero" is from aeronautics, which is the science of flight. "Space" is the realm of both the inner and outer reaches of the planet, which generate two types of design challenges. Airplanes, missiles, and launch vehicles encounter the inner domain and must consider gravity and atmospheric drag. The outer atmosphere and deeper space contain orbiting satellites such as the International Space Station, as well as interplanetary vehicles. Design for the operation of these systems must consider radiant heating and cooling effects, as well as functioning in zero gravity and vacuum environments.

Knowing about the capability of spacecraft is helpful when reading about missions to other planets. In the literature on interplanetary exploration, discussion centers on the ability to achieve certain objectives. Some articles are for general audiences, while other publications aim toward more technically-minded people. In examining technical writing, it is beneficial to have background as to what goes into the design, build, and testing of space vehicles. Amazing as it may seem, the evolutionary cycle of spacecraft is so complex that it takes years—even more than a decade—to go from the concept phase to a satellite constellation being fully operational in space.

Satellite systems orbit the earth, collecting and relaying information to users around the globe. The five steps necessary to draw up, produce, and operate a space vehicle include (1) the concept and design phase, (2) the part procurement and manufacturing phase, (3) the development and test phase, (4) the launch event, and (5) the final operational phase, where communication and tasking of the satellite occurs. Strict quality control standards are critical throughout the process. With few exceptions, once vehicles blast off into space, they are not physically accessible. There are no plans made for maintenance and repair, so rigorous testing is necessary.

Spacecraft must withstand the titanic forces from vertical liftoff. The space vehicle sits on top of a launch system that is powered by rocket motors, using either solid or liquid propellant. In order to protect the space vehicle from the dynamic pressure of atmospheric ascent, it is encased by a payload fairing (a.k.a. the nose cone). The fairing is made of three vertical sections that are mechanically stitched together. Once the booster reaches the upper atmosphere, the fairing pyrotechnically unzips along the seams, with the pieces being jettisoned by the aerodynamic forces.

The power of the liftoff must work against the force of gravity. In order to overcome the gravity effect, the vehicle thrust, or g-force level, must exceed the pull of the planet. As an example, when traveling to the International Space Station, astronauts experience a downward pressure of 3 g during ascent. The g-force is strong enough to overcome the grip of the earth. Once in space, satellites must survive extreme conditions, including a high-vacuum environment and radiant heating and cooling effects. Thermal effects in a vacuum will cause "touch temperatures" on the sun side of vehicles to approach 250°F and on the dark side to be as cool as minus 200°F.

Satellites operate both autonomously and with commands from mission control. The commands will relay information such as turning electronic units on/off, downlinking health and status data, and establishing computer control modes. In addition to satisfying mission requirements, satellite programming includes housekeeping tasks and recovery functions. Recovery functions ensure satellite protection from catastrophic loss until personnel at the ground station can analyze telemetry data and resolve the anomalous condition. The criticality of autonomous, interwoven, and nuanced control features is one reason for stringent spacecraft testing.

Today, hundreds of large satellites circle the earth, with orbits varying in altitude, inclination, and eccentricity. The goal of artificial satellites is to improve, protect, and modernize civilization. The technology assists people in almost every part of the world. The genesis for designing and building spacecraft originates from government agencies and commercial enterprises. Satellites provide services such as (1) relaying location and providing navigation, as in the GPS or Global Positioning System; (2) surveillance and reconnaissance for national defense; (3) telecommunication for television, radio, and cell phones; and (4) climate monitoring for predicting weather changes, which can warn of impending dangers such as hurricanes and tornadoes.

The future of spacecraft points to a smaller size. Grouped by weight, varieties include the smallsat or mini (200 to 1000 lb.), the micro (20 to 200 lb.), and the nano (2 to 20 lb.). Starlink is a smallsat constellation that will provide the earth with global broadband internet access by using thousands of 570-pound satellites. It will provide fast, reliable, low-cost internet to rural communities and remote areas with no connectivity. One type of nano spacecraft is called the

CubeSat. It is about four inches long on each side. These miniaturized satellites reduce investment capital, allowing developing countries, universities, and small companies entry into space.[15]

---

15 Estonia's first-ever satellite was a CubeSat. The device investigates solar sail technology. It resulted in 29 bachelor's dissertations, 19 master's dissertations, and 5 doctoral theses. Estonia News, "ESTCube-1's 651-day Career: 53 Dissertations and a Marriage Proposal," http://news.err.ee/115186/ estcube-1-s-651daycareer-53-dissertations-and-a-marriage-proposal (accessed Aug. 7, 2020).

Chapter 2

Biblical Views of Perdition

*All scripture is inspired by God,
and is useful for teaching,
for reproof, for correction, and for
training in righteousness.*

2 Timothy 3:16

The great assurance from the Bible is the gift of eternal life. Jesus began his earthly ministry by proclaiming the good news about the kingdom of God. His primary mission was to tell people about a heavenly Father who loves them and has prepared a place for them. The paradise of heaven is the pinnacle of supreme happiness and peace, where God and the angels dwell. It is a glorious place of bliss—the ultimate fulfillment of the deepest human longing. All good that is found on the earth and in heaven comes from God himself. For a person to be cut off from such goodness can only result in serious deficiencies.

As a secondary feature of his teaching, Jesus speaks about the fate of those who choose to ignore the call to salvation. His sermons are full of gentleness, care, and compassion toward the multitude. Yet, he alerts the religious hypocrites and the wrongdoers about impending judgment. Instead of going to heaven, people can choose hell by failing to give ear to the message. In John 17:12, Jesus describes the scheming apostle, Judas Iscariot, as being "lost" (NRSV). The KJV translates this phrase more literally from the (Latin) Vulgate as "son of perdition." This became a common character reference to Judas Iscariot. Perdition serves as a place of separation from God and results in suffering due to being absent from everything good.

While researching this book, I occasionally found myself downhearted about the subject of hell. It is not a pleasant topic to think about. As a result, I would pick up a diametrically opposed text about heaven to cheer myself up. Contemplating heaven and hell can affect your state of mind, but they are not resident within the mind. A person cannot be in heaven or hell by using brainpower. The idea of a mental hell as the only hell is misleading. Heaven and hell are tangible locations in the physical universe, with heaven being desirable and hell being unwelcome.

The Bible provides testimony about the seriousness of human sin and the consequence of death resulting from sin. In understanding sin, death, and eternal loss, you must remember that the Bible teaches in a consistent manner. Personal and communal sin are pervasive problems to God. It reveals the incurable condition of fallen humanity. The hopeless tendency is for humans to sin, which is in sharp contrast to God's holy and perfect being. The idea is basic. People have to come to terms with the dilemma of wrongdoing in order to find a right relationship with God. This is where the simple message of the gospel comes into effect.

For the unprepared person, a huge risk presents itself. Depictions of hell are of an inescapable place of misery and loss. As such, giving attention to your eternal destiny should be the highest priority. Human life is fragile, and our time on the earth is short. In passing through the fleeting moments of the present age, the average person spends little time thinking about the afterlife. Yet, our bodies are stuck in an irreversible aging process. The mortal state dictates a birth that will eventually conclude in death. In the hereafter, one will have to account for the choices made in this life.

According to statistical data, approximately fifty-five million individuals die every year.[16] The data translates into 108 deaths per minute, or almost two people every second. The fate of these departed souls is either ascent to a paradise filled with eternal joy or descent to a sequestered place of sadness and regret. The news media gives plenty of attention to catastrophes taking scores of lives. Casualty rates from pandemics such as the coronavirus (COVID-19) can dominate the news for months at a time. Given less consideration is the moment by moment march into death by humanity.

God reveals his character progressively in the Bible, with Jesus bringing the full and complete unveiling of Yahweh. Yahweh is the one true God who has love for every individual and desires for us to call him "Father." Knowing this should shed some light on the Old Testament. Reprimand and punishment do not come from an intolerant supernatural being, but rather from a corrective Father who detests sin and desires the best for his children.

One historical event affecting all humankind was the flooding of the earth after only ten generations of human existence. The deluge was an unusual, sweeping sentence of the creation brought on by drastic circumstances. The number of people committing wicked and immoral acts had continued unabated, growing to such enormous proportion as to touch the entire population. Because of the condition, the Lord God had no choice but to drive the people to extinction. Only Noah, his family, and representative pairs of animals

---

16 The 2020 crude death rate estimate is 7.7 per 1,000. CIA World Factbook, "Field Listing – Death Rate," https://www.cia.gov/the-world-factbook/field/death-rate/ (accessed July 15, 2021).

were spared from the catastrophe because of Noah's godly character.[17]

One can view the mass extinction of human beings as divine retribution for unchecked bad behavior. The extent and severity of such judgment by a holy deity reveals the attitude of the Lord God toward deliberate, nonstop disobedience. The offenders gave neither thought to the Creator nor consideration to their acts of sin. People were eating and drinking, marrying and being given in marriage, right up until the flood came and destroyed them all. The event shows God's attitude toward unapologetic sin and is a foreshadowing of final, eternal judgment.[18]

In the New Testament age, the timeframe of God's final judgment toward sin and global wickedness stretches out because of the work of Jesus Christ. God's patience is a result of the divine mercy and grace purchased at the cross by Christ. God maintains compassion, favor, and blessing toward mortal creatures in the midst of defiance. One intention of this goodness and longsuffering is for people to understand the depth of his love. God's desire is for everyone to come to faith. In order to draw people in, his plan includes constant doses of kindness and benevolence throughout people's lives.

Ultimately, God allows people to control their own lives and destinies. In his book, *The Great Divorce*, C. S. Lewis states, "There are only two kinds of people in the end: those who say to God, 'Thy will be done,' and those to whom God says, 'Thy will be done.'"[19] Lewis believes every lost person

---

17 Whether the event was global or regional remains a matter of debate because humans occupied only a fraction of the planet when Noah constructed the ark. Reasons to Believe, "The Waters of the Flood," http://www.reasons.org/articles/the-waters-of-the-flood (accessed Nov. 5, 2020).

18 Robert A. Peterson, *Hell on Trial: The Case for Eternal Punishment* (Phillipsburg, NJ: Presbyterian and Reformed Publishing, 1995), 25.

19 C.S. Lewis, *The Great Divorce* (New York: MacMillan, 1946), 69.

has chosen his or her destiny, and that without self-choice, there could not be a hell.[20]

The netherworld of Sheol–Hades serves as a place of temporary separation from God until the Day of Judgment. In the Septuagint, which is the Greek translation of the Hebrew Bible, the word "Hades" substitutes for the Hebrew word "Sheol." The writers of the Septuagint consider the two words interchangeable. The idea of Sheol residing inside the planet carries forward from the Old into the New Testament. In Matthew 11:23, Jesus addresses the city dwellers of Capernaum as having to be "brought down" to Hades for their unbelief. The following sections focus on Sheol and other statements about Hades as being in an underground location.

Sheol in the Old Testament

The Old Testament does not give much insight into the hell of the New Testament, but it does imply afterlife in a place beneath the earth. Many books tell of departing souls going to the underworld of Sheol, a place of temporary confinement. The Hebrew word *Sh'ol* or *Sh'olaah* properly appears as "Sheol" in most Bible versions. It is the "place of departed souls" or the "state of the dead." As noted earlier, the exception is the King James Version, which translates Sheol as either "hell" or "grave," or even "pit." The use of grave or pit is adequate, but using the word "hell" is incorrect. Hell is a place of final separation and loss, which the Bible doesn't address until the Gospels.

Following death, the Hebrew Scriptures regard someone as "going down into the pit" or "descending into Sheol." The underworld is where the righteous and the unrighteous go.

---

20 Lewis asserts individual responsibility for choices made in life. One's eternal destiny is the result of a personal decision. He considers the doors of hell to be locked on the inside. Lewis, *Divorce*, 69.

Sheol is a place of darkness below the earth and is in the furthest recess from light. In the book of Job, Job cries out to conceal himself in Sheol until the wrath of the Lord passes. For disobedient Israelites, Isaiah reckons Sheol to have a vast appetite and large opening (Isaiah 5:14). The prayer of Hannah in 1 Samuel 2:6 states, "The Lord kills and brings to life; he brings down to Sheol and raises up." Many scriptures lead the reader to believe Sheol is an "all-consuming place" under the earth.

Going down into Sheol ranges from burial, to drowning, to falling into a large fissure caused by an earthquake. In Numbers 16:33, the rebellious Korah and his men come against Moses. As a result, the earth opens and consumes the dissenters alive, as they fall into Sheol. All openings on the earth go in a descending direction, placing Sheol on a nadir course. Nadir points in a direction that is directly under a specific location. On the celestial sphere, it is below an observer, following the line of gravitational pull downward. The path of nadir followed by burial, drowning, or plummeting will directly lead to the center of the earth.

In some Hebrew Scriptures, we can interpret Sheol as a welcoming place of rest for the faithful servant of Yahweh. In other passages, going to Sheol has a disciplinary flavor, where confinement is an early act of judgment. You can envision Sheol as a fully encompassing world of good and evil souls. The apocryphal book of Enoch introduces a division of souls in Sheol when discussing discrete "apartments" for the righteous and the unrighteous.[21] In expanding the Judaic understanding of the underworld, Jesus will also suggest a separation in Hades between good and evil spirits in the parable of Lazarus and the rich man (Luke 16).

---

21 The passage is from Enoch 22:1–14. The Ethiopian Orthodox Church regards the book of Enoch as canonical. Warren F. Draper trans., *The Book of Enoch* (Andover, MA: U.S. Act of Congress, 1882), 47.

Foretelling by the Prophets

The Old Testament has two books that contain passages addressing the never-ending problems of the unrighteous. The verse below closes the book of Isaiah, who ranks as one of Israel's most significant prophets. Isaiah 66:22–24 reads:

> For as the new heavens and the new earth, which I will make, shall remain before me, says the Lord; so shall your descendants and your name remain. From new moon to new moon, and from Sabbath to Sabbath, all flesh shall come to worship before me, says the Lord. And they shall go out and look at the dead bodies of the people who have rebelled against me; for their worm shall not die, their fire shall not be quenched, and they shall be an abhorrence to all flesh.

In the passage, Isaiah provides an end-time prediction for when God's people will come to worship on the holy mountain of Zion. The paragraph begins on a positive note, with the promise of faithful people being part of the new heavens and the new earth. Midway, the scene shifts to contrast the destiny of the faithless. The unsaved are understood to be alive and having to cope with an unceasing hardship and unquenchable fire. The hardship, or worm, is an unspecified type of weakness or suffering. The mention of fire is symbolic of perdition in the Bible.

A second scripture in Daniel describes an everlasting state of disgrace for a group of people. Daniel was a person of deep faith and piety. His book contains many end-time prophetic passages. Daniel 12:1–2 reads:

At that time Michael, the great prince, the
protector of your people, shall arise. There
shall be a time of anguish, such as has never
occurred since nations first came into existence.
But at that time your people shall be delivered,
everyone who is found written in the book.
Many of those who sleep in the dust of the earth
shall awake, some to everlasting life, and some
to shame and everlasting contempt.

Similar to the Isaiah passage, Daniel looks out to the
distant future of nations, including Israel. The "time of
anguish" spoken about is a period of unrivaled tribulation
in human history, where Michael the archangel stands
guard over God's people. The promise of deliverance is
having one's name "written in the book," a phrase found in
Revelation 20:15. Daniel's portrayal of a resurrection for both
the righteous and unrighteous is the only Old Testament
reference to such an event. Both groups will rise from the
dust, one to eternal life and the other to shame and endless
contempt.

The awakening of "those who sleep in the dust of the
earth" is not a literal reviving of souls. After physical death,
souls leave the human body fully conscious and require
no sleep. The Bible supports the idea of a person having a
perpetually living and active soul.[22] Daniel's reference to
"those who sleep" brings to mind the incorrect notion of "soul
sleep." Soul sleep advocates believe a person's soul enters
a state of deep sleep following death. The sleep requires a

---

22 Three accounts negate the idea of soul sleep. Saul's encounter with the
    dead prophet, Samuel, in 1 Sam. 28:13–15. The rich man, Abraham,
    and Lazarus conversing after death in Luke 16:19–31. Finally, Mark
    9:2–5 tells of the transfiguration, where Moses and Elijah engage in
    dialogue with Jesus. Coogan, *New Oxford Annotated Bible*, 442 [OT],
    74, 129 [NT].

rousing at a later point. In the case of Daniel 12:1–2, the use of "sleep" appears as a gentle or reverent way of describing the cessation of life.

The Teaching of Jesus

The four Gospels reveal the life of Jesus Christ, including his virgin birth, life teachings, death, and resurrection. The purpose of the accounts is to make known a way of salvation. The high point of the narratives is death by crucifixion, where Jesus makes atonement for all the past, present, and future sin of humankind. The resurrection of Christ provides for a new and everlasting covenant for all who believe in him. After rising from the dead, Jesus appears to many people, including a crowd of more than five hundred. Believing in the atoning sacrifice and resurrection points toward a rebirth of the spirit, which is the renewing of a person's mind.

John the Baptist was the prophet who paved the way for the arrival of Jesus. His ministry focus was on preaching repentance to the multitude and then performing water baptism. In his confrontation with Jewish religious leaders, he was quick to expose their hypocrisy and self-righteous attitudes. In one encounter, John gave a prophetic warning to the impenitent. In Matthew 3:12, he declares about Jesus, "His winnowing fork is in his hand, and he will clear his threshing floor and will gather his wheat into the granary; but the chaff he will burn with unquenchable fire."

John's discourse frequently contains warnings about judgment directed to the religiously pretentious of his day. In the passage, John envisions a futuristic time when Jesus Christ will come to judge the world. It will be an occasion to sift and sort the righteous from the unrighteous. The figurative language is appropriate for the agrarian-based Palestinian culture. Cultivating and harvesting wheat was common in the eastern Mediterranean. The grains are precious, but the husk surrounding the cereal has a light, worthless character. Chaff was normally disposed of through incineration.

The teaching of Jesus is ultimately responsible for the unveiling of hell as an eternal place of separation, suffering, and loss. In Matthew 7:13, the Lord states, "Enter through the narrow gate; for the gate is wide and the road is easy that leads to destruction, and there are many who take it." In Matthew 10:28, Jesus tells the disciples, "Do not fear those who kill the body but cannot kill the soul; rather fear him who can destroy both soul and body in hell [Gk. *gehenna*]." Gehenna was a dumping site situated near Jerusalem and was a visual reminder of what associates with hell.

The many warnings about perdition given by Jesus during his ministry led to a heightening of people's awareness, as well as instilling a healthy sense of fear and concern. God knows the human condition is one of indifference, resulting in spiritual neglect. Without overt warnings, many in a self-seeking and materialistic world would overlook the grace, goodness, and continual love of God. This is why Jesus alerted people to separation and destruction in hell with a plethora of verses throughout his ministry.

In Mark 9:43–48, Jesus speaks about taking heed not to commit sin and ruin your own soul. The passage mentions the atrocious deed of cutting off a hand or foot, or tearing out an eye if it causes you to sin. A maimed body with one hand or one foot is better than eternal separation. The tearing out of an eye would be horrible. Not meant literally, you can see the seriousness of hell as the substitute for performing this grizzly act. Sin is toxic and will result in the soul being condemned. Transgression is a grave matter before God, not to be taken lightly.[23]

---

23 Equating the severity of sin to cutting off body parts demands our attention. Temptation should be kept in check, with no provision made for bad behavior. Coogan, *New Oxford Annotated Bible*, 75 [NT].

In speaking to an unrepentant community, Jesus states in Matthew 11:23, "And you, Capernaum, will you be exalted to heaven? No, you will be brought down to Hades. For if the deeds of power done in you had been done in Sodom, it would have remained until this day." Capernaum was a primary dwelling place for Jesus and the disciples, and the site of many public miracles. A city blessed by his presence will ultimately face a heavy price of collective judgment because of its unbelief. The city inhabitants are culpable, due to their exposure to the truth. As a result, many souls will be condemned to Hades, just as those from the morally corrupt Sodom.

When you depart from this world, you will continue to exist, and where you exist in eternity depends on the choices made in the here and now. If anyone discounts this notion, then consider Jesus' parable of the rich man and Lazarus in Luke 16:19–31. The story brings reality to life after death. The narrative portrays dead men in conversation with one another. The audience for the parable was the Pharisees, but the disciples were likely listening. The complete scripture bears repeating for its weightiness and value to understanding Hades.

> There was a rich man who was dressed in purple and fine linen and who feasted sumptuously every day. And at his gate lay a poor man named Lazarus, covered with sores, who longed to satisfy his hunger with what fell from the rich man's table; even the dogs would come and lick his sores.
>
> The poor man died and was carried away by the angels to be with Abraham. The rich man also died and was buried. In Hades, where he was being tormented, he looked up and saw

Abraham far away with Lazarus by his side. He called out, "Father Abraham, have mercy on me, and send Lazarus to dip the tip of his finger in water and cool my tongue; for I am in agony in these flames."

But Abraham said, "Child, remember that during your lifetime you received your good things, and Lazarus in like manner evil things; but now he is comforted here, and you are in agony. Besides all this, between you and us a great chasm has been fixed, so that those who might want to pass from here to you cannot do so, and no one can cross from there to us."

He said, "Then, father, I beg you to send him to my father's house—for I have five brothers—that he may warn them, so that they will not also come into this place of torment." Abraham replied, "They have Moses and the prophets; they should listen to them."

He said, "No, father Abraham; but if someone goes to them from the dead, they will repent." He said to him, "If they do not listen to Moses and the prophets, neither will they be convinced even if someone rises from the dead."

Analyzing the Parable

Parables were a common form of teaching. Parables of Jesus are not only instructive; they convey a profound truth with penetrating ethical implications. I will use the parable to draw attention to several pertinent points. The exercise is not intended to extract every aspect of the teaching.

- The use of the word "Hades" equates to Sheol, which is in the lower regions of the earth. As noted earlier, Hades is the Greek word corresponding to Sheol.
- Jesus, a man of impeccable integrity, teaches that there is life after death. He introduces two separate compartments within Sheol–Hades, a concept unfamiliar to his Jewish contemporaries.
- In the underworld is a great divide between the righteous and the unrighteous. Lazarus is in Abraham's bosom, a term associated with heaven or paradise. The rich man is on the torment side of Hades.
- The rich man's fate is primarily due to his lack of compassion for the destitute. He never showed mercy toward the needs of others. While feasting lavishly, he ignores the poor, who waste away outside the entrance to his home.
- There is a sense of irreversibility to the damnation of the rich man and the blessedness of Lazarus. It is too late for the rich man to show shame or contrition for his stingy and heartless attitude.
- The flames cause the rich man to suffer with no relief. Without the shielding of Abraham's bosom, the soul in Hades experiences high temperatures.
- The desire for water is so severe on the torment side of Hades that a mere drop from a dangling finger can bring satisfaction.
- The five living brothers have to rely on the testimony of Moses and the prophets, or the "law and the prophets." In other words, the evidence from Scripture and the witness of faithful believers are sufficient proofs of God.

In the parable, human dialogue follows physical death. The theme points to the reality of an afterlife. Using the term "Hades" instead of "Sheol" puts the two worlds in one integrated place, pointing to a location beneath the earth. Jesus unveils a separation that exists in Hades, where the righteous soul resides apart from the unrighteous. The division is a paradigm shift. The righteous find comfort in Abraham's bosom, while the unrighteous are in a place of distress. The teaching emphasizes eternal consequences associated with choices made during a person's life.

Many people are uneasy with the idea of an eternal hell. No one experiences the situation more fully than the rich man in Hades. He knew his sin was set within an ordinary lifespan. Yet, he does not protest the unending state of affairs. He never cries out, "This is an extreme penalty!" Readers need to ask, "Why?" One possible answer is the expanded mind of the rich man. He knew his sin was deserving of the punishment. It is important to note his rigid feelings. While managing to express concern for his immediate family, he shows no sign of remorse toward Lazarus. The character from his mortal life remains the same in immortality.

In John 3:13, Jesus tells Nicodemus, "No one has ascended into heaven except the one who descended from heaven, the Son of Man." Jesus is telling Nicodemus his ancestry directly links to heaven (because he was conceived in Mary's womb by the Holy Spirit). The passage also reveals that up until Jesus' ministry, no one had gone to heaven. As such, it adds credence to Abraham's bosom not being in heaven. Abraham's bosom was an area under the earth, adjacent to Hades. It is essential to understand heaven's lack of human habitation before the crucifixion. At the time of Jesus' ministry, all souls in the intermediate state were in an underworld location.

The souls of faithful individuals who pass away no longer depart for the underworld. Paul tells believers in 2 Corinthians 5:6–8 that being physically alive means we are at home in the body, but when we are away from the body, we are at home with the Lord. The timing of Paul's message to the Corinthians is after the resurrection of Jesus. We can deduce that because of the atoning work of the cross, direct admission into heaven is possible without first going to Abraham's bosom. When believers die today, they have the privilege of promptly entering God's presence in heaven.

The payment for sin at the cross of Calvary was an event of cosmic proportions with one result being the emptying of Abraham's bosom. In receiving the final payment for their sin through the blood of Jesus, millions of believing souls were allowed to depart from under the earth and enter God's presence in the third heaven. The relocation may have taken place in the short time interval between the death of Jesus and his resurrection. The passage referring to the transfer is in Ephesians 4:8–10, which states,

> When he ascended on high, he made captivity itself a captive; he gave gifts to his people." (When it says, "He ascended," what does it mean but that he had also descended into the lower parts of the earth? He who descended is the same one who ascended far above all the heavens, so that he might fill all things.)"

In the New Testament, writers often allude to the Hebrew Scriptures. In this case, Paul's words are a cross-reference to Psalm 68:18. It reads, "You ascended the high mount, leading captives in your train and receiving gifts from people, even from those who rebel against the Lord God's abiding there." A proper understanding of verse 18 first requires understanding the entire psalm. Psalm 68 uses imagery: a victorious military leader and his traditional right to give prisoners as gifts. In this case, Christ has liberated people through his redemptive act.

As the victor, Jesus has the privilege to give those who are captive in Hades (Abraham's bosom) as gifts to the kingdom of God.[24] In order to rescue everyone, Jesus descends into the heart of the earth to gain access to them. The righteous souls depart from the underworld, being raised by Christ in glory to dwell in heaven. The condemned souls of the faithless remain behind. At this point, Abraham's bosom becomes an empty cavity. What remains behind is the netherworld of Hades. It becomes a complete place of darkness and separation from God.

The primary purpose of Jesus' ministry was to announce the arrival of God's kingdom and the good news about repentance and salvation. Beginning with the forerunner, John the Baptist, and continuing afterward with the apostles' teachings, the good news is spread throughout the land. An underlying problem emerges when ignoring or not listening to the message. People will ultimately find themselves in a bad situation. The warnings about going to hell are about a permanent exile. The alerts are clear about the impending suffering and loss in the spiritual afterlife. The decision to pay attention is in the hands of every individual.

Warning from Paul in the Epistles

The book of Romans is a formal and systematic epistle. Paul's letter places emphasis on a believer's "right standing" with God—a right standing coming by faith in Christ. But Romans doesn't begin that way. After a salutation and prayer of thanksgiving, the apostle presents a record of human vices. Paul finds people fully responsible for a long list of transgressions because everyone has a built-in sense of right and wrong. The instinctive sense of a higher authority is

---

24 John F. Walvoord and Roy B. Zuck, *The Bible Knowledge Commentary*, (Colorado Springs, CO: David C. Cook, 2002).

what makes everyone guilty. Therefore, individuals don't have a valid excuse for a life of unbelief, rebellion, and sin.

In the body of the epistle, Paul speaks about the peace, honor, and grace given to those who live by faith. He also addresses a day of wrath coming to those who are defiant. The apostle writes about the consequences of hell, without explicitly addressing hell itself. The approach is consistent in all of his letters. Paul portrays perdition as a state of chastisement and exclusion from the presence of the Lord. The warnings appear frequently. Every person ignoring the plan of salvation will receive recompense for his or her deeds. No one will "skate by" the judgment of God.

In two letters to the Corinthians, Paul writes to a troubled church. He sees the struggles of an emerging Christian movement in a big metropolis. His letters address the problems of an assembly exposed to secular thinking that was widespread and influential. The belief systems, careless speech, and bad behavior of the surrounding city had entered the church and were affecting the body of believers. The city of Corinth was a seaport prospering as a commercial success, but the value system of the residents was infectious and filled with moral decay.

The ancient seaport was a Roman colony located on the Isthmus of Corinth. An isthmus is a narrow strip of land bordered on each side by a large body of water. In this case, the Isthmus of Corinth joins the northern mainland of Greece with the southern peninsula of Peloponnesus. Travelers from around the known world came to the Isthmus of Corinth, which was centrally located between (modern) Italy and Turkey. The sojourners were a problem to the residents. The debauchery in Corinth was acknowledged to the point where the word *korinthiazomai* ("to act like a Corinthian") was coined as a synonym for sexual immorality.[25]

A young church in a corrupt city needed encouragement and reminding of their position in Christ. Paul addresses the reckless mindset of worldly wisdom in 1 Corinthians 1:18 when stating, "For the message about the cross is foolishness to those who are *perishing*, but to us who are being saved it is the power of God." The apostle contrasts two groups: one having attained salvation and the other on the path to ruin. Paving the way to ruin is rejecting a Savior who has undergone crucifixion for the sake of human sin. Today, pervasive unbelief in one true God saturates society. It is a place where individualism and self-sufficiency rule with a prideful attitude.

In the passage, the word "perishing" comes from the Greek verb *apollumi* and means "on the way to destruction." The same term, "perish," finds use in the oft-quoted John 3:16, "For God so loved the world that he gave his only Son, so that everyone who believes in him may not *perish* but may have eternal life." Perishing is in sharp contrast to eternal life. The meaning of the word goes beyond the point of physical death. Perishing is more than expiring, cashing in your chips, or kicking the bucket. The true usage brings a sense of continual devastation and loss in the next world.

In his letter to the Thessalonians, Paul speaks about a day of reckoning for humankind. In 2 Thessalonians 1:9, he states, "These will suffer the punishment of eternal destruction, separated from the presence of the Lord and from the glory of his might." The word destruction (Gk. *olethros*) does not mean obliteration or extinction. As both a conscious and eternal outcome, destruction involves the

---

25 Aristophanes of ancient Athens was a comic playwright with the power of ridicule. He receives the credit for coining the Greek word *"korinthiazomai."* J. Hampton Keathley, "The Pauline Epistles," http://bible.org/seriespage/pauline-epistles (accessed Sept. 28, 2020).

loss of everything worthwhile. An earthly parallel would be the ruin of a person's life and property following an overwhelming tsunami. The trigger for destruction will be the final judgment, where nothing will be hidden. The exposure of sin without repentance results in irrevocable banishment.

In the letter to the Philippians, the apostle speaks of Christ's exaltation in 2:9–11, saying, "Therefore God also highly exalted him and gave him the name that is above every name, so that at the name of Jesus every knee should bend, in heaven and on earth and under the earth, and every tongue should confess that Jesus Christ is Lord, to the glory of God the Father." Inhabitants of heaven, Hades, and all the peoples of the earth will at some point pay homage to God for Jesus Christ. The act will be done by some in joyful faith, but for others with hesitancy or resentment.

A final warning from the Pauline epistles relates to the distraction of wealth. The apostle raises concern with those who are attached to money. In 1 Timothy 6:10, he says, "The love of money is a root of all kinds of evil." A focus on a big bank account, or more stocks, bonds, and property, is a deterrent to centering on God. Warnings overflow about being stingy, ignoring the needy, and adoring money. The Bible urges people to be thankful and generous, directing attention to spiritual matters. In Matthew 6:24, Jesus cautions about not being able to serve both God and money because undue emphasis on obtaining wealth distorts judgment. An excessive desire for money and possessions creates a mindset toward the temporal, leaving little or no room for eternal considerations.

Final Judgment in Revelation

The great white throne judgment, or final judgment, occurs after the resurrection of the dead. It is when both the small and the great face a final reckoning before God. Prior to the final judgment, two other judgments appear in the Bible. The first is for the faithful believer and is called the "judgment seat of Christ." The judgment seat (Gk. *bema*) is the raised chair of a Roman governor or judge. Pilate tried Jesus at the bema in Jerusalem. The Lord's bema will be a judgment of the righteous, which determines eternal gifts in proportion to one's good works. The time and place for the event will be in the third heaven, prior to the second coming of Christ to the earth.

The "judgment seat of Christ" comes from 2 Corinthians 5:10, where Paul states, "For all of us must appear before the judgment seat of Christ, so that each may receive recompense for what has been done in the body, whether good or evil." The apostle reminds the faithful that they are on their way to both eternal glory and an evaluation. Deeds akin to wood, hay, and straw will burn in a fire while undertakings of gold, silver, and precious stone will survive to receive an imperishable reward. How one invests his or her time, talent, and financial resources in the temporal realm becomes the testing ground for making or marring a destiny, winning or losing a crown.

A second judgment is the "judgment of the nations" in Matthew 25:31–46. "Nations" is a reference to the Gentiles. A Gentile is someone belonging to any nation or group other than the Jewish people. The judgment comes up at the end of an expository of parables and prophecies by Jesus concerning the end of the age. The actual timing of the judgment occurs immediately after the second coming when Christ gloriously appears on the earth. The purpose for the judgment centers on how people treated "the least of these," or those in great material, emotional, or financial need. In the rendering of verdicts, a division unfolds between righteous sheep and unrighteous goats.

The sheep perform good deeds by helping needy

individuals, whom Christ considers his brethren. The sheep are given a place of honor and blessing on the right-hand side of the king. These people were faithful in feeding and clothing the poor, nurturing the sick, and visiting the elderly. The blessing for helping those in need is an inheritance in the eternal kingdom. A quintessential example of such a person is Mother Theresa. She spent a lifetime helping the poor and destitute in Calcutta, India. Not everyone will have such dedication, but even doing small acts of charity for the less fortunate carries weight with God.

On the other hand, the goats are found guilty of disregarding those lacking food, clothing, shelter, or in need of cash assistance. Like the rich man in the parable that mentions Lazarus, these individuals were stingy toward others. The last thing on their mind was helping the needy. The goats display selfishness in failing to help others. An important takeaway from the parable is the degree to which Christ empathizes with the broken. He puts himself in the very place of the person in desperate need. As a result, the disobedient goats are given a place of dishonor on the left-hand side of the king. These workers of iniquity go on to suffer eternal separation from God.

The theological significance of the "judgment of the nations" is in its support of good works. James 2:26 teaches that it is always proper to consider that "faith without works is also dead." This does not mean a person is saved by doing good works. Helping others is not the basis for salvation. Works show evidence of a person's gratitude for God's forgiveness, blessings, grace, and gift of eternal life. Thankfulness best expresses itself by looking beyond ourselves and reaching out to others. Appreciation manifests itself in a willingness to give back. Ignoring the teaching of being charitable means taking the risk of significant loss in the world to come.

The final end-times event is the great white throne judgment. This judgment occurs after Satan is cast into the lake of fire. In Revelation 20:11–12, John describes a great white throne, where he states:

> Then I saw a great white throne and the one who sat on it; the earth and the heaven fled from his presence, and no place was found for them. And I saw the dead, great and small, standing before the throne, and books were opened. Also, another book was opened, the book of life. And the dead were judged according to their works, as recorded in the books.

The appearance of "the dead, great and small, standing before the throne" requires that souls in Hades be clothed in a resurrected body before arrival. The body is similar to that of the risen Christ. The soul is only a transitional state. The final state is the resurrected body, which the text sometimes refers to as the immortal spiritual body. God resurrects the individual soul coming out of Hades into an immortal spiritual body for final judgment. Whether God deems a person righteous or unrighteous does not change the fact that a resurrection awaits every individual.

Because Hades is a temporary underground prison, it will empty out entirely. Even with billions of souls in the queue, cases are heard one at a time. The makeup of the immortal spiritual body facilitates walking up to the throne. Arriving are individuals from every level of society. Preference or favorable treatment will not be available to those of rank, authority, financial status, or intellectual achievement. The white color of the throne reflects the purity and holiness of the One who sits on the throne. It is also an indication of the fair and impartial hearing each person will receive.

The opening of various books, which record the thoughts, words, and deeds of every person provides evidence for charges of misconduct and law-breaking. Individuals who have heard the gospel and rejected the message must stand alone in attempting to justify various actions. The findings of any evil or wrongdoing will result in condemnation. After the proceedings, the basis for conviction and sentencing is finding a person's name not written in the book of life.

Individuals found guilty at the great white throne judgment are to be thrown into the lake of fire. The offenders will have to face an eternal penalty for transgressions. Without an intercessor, lost humans will join Satan, his demonic army, the beast, and the false prophet in the lake of fire. During the judgment, souls from Hades will get a fresh glimpse of a beautifully renewed Earth—an independent, quick look at a stunning and magnificently refurbished planet. Once banished from God's presence, these people will face an abysmal change of venue. The final destination is a hot, desolate, and sulfur-filled planet with vast lava fields and countless volcanoes.

Annihilationism and Universalism

The idea of eternal separation has biblical foundation, but for many, it raises unsettling ethical questions. Why would a good, benevolent, and loving God allow individuals to experience such a fate? How can wrongdoing or spiritual neglect in a short lifetime turn into permanent exile? Are there theological understandings of the Bible that provide a better fate for unrepentant people?

Theologians primarily utilize the content of the scriptures to develop perspectives on God. Contributing factors to the process include reason, experience, and religious tradition. Together with the Bible, these perspectives allow for an overall understanding of God and facilitate the pursuit of "faith seeking understanding." In examining the primacy of Scripture, it is imperative to do *exegesis*. Exegesis requires a thorough analysis of biblical content to clarify meaning and discover the author's original intent. A discussion about the methods of exegesis will follow in the next chapter.

To be avoided is *eisegesis*, which is the practice of reading the interpreter's own personal opinion into the Bible. Eisegesis is contrary to letting textual analysis rule. Driven by feelings, individuals put their own personal ideas into passages. A poor interpretative technique, it has been the cause of many problems in Christianity. In the field of personal eschatology, this faulty approach gives rise to the concepts of annihilationism and universalism. These stand-in theologies have always existed in one form or another over the centuries. Unfortunately, these false viewpoints continue to gain prominence in the church.

Annihilationism

Annihilationism is the belief that those who die without faith will ultimately face a complete end with no chance of an afterlife. One form of annihilationism, known as conditional immortality, conceives of a total end to existence immediately after physical death. Guilty souls are extinguished before going to Hades. Another form sees a universal resurrection before final judgment and sentencing, where the resurrected bodies of lost people will disintegrate or be completely terminated upon arrival at the lake of fire.

The doctrine of annihilationism has existed as a minority view throughout church history, but it underwent a resurgence in the 1980s among some theologians. Annihilationism sees the traditional view of hell or the lake of fire as morally repulsive. It rejects the idea of the lost suffering conscious separation and punishment. Clark Pinnock sums up the view best:

> Obviously, I am rejecting the traditional
> view of hell in part out of a sense of moral

and theological revulsion to it. The idea that a conscious creature should have to undergo physical and mental torture through unending time is profoundly disturbing, and the thought that this is inflicted upon them by divine decree offends my conviction about God's love. This is probably the primary reason why people question the tradition so vehemently in the first place. They are not first of all impressed by its lack of a good scriptural basis but are appalled by its awful moral implications.[26]

Pinnock claims that the case for eternal punishment does not have a strong biblical basis. Let's cite two passages countering his assertion.

In Matthew 25:46, a division occurs between the sheep and the goats. The righteous sheep go on to "eternal life," while the unrighteous goats move on to "eternal punishment." In the passage, the Greek term *aionios* is the source for the translation "eternal," which modifies both the word "life" and the word "punishment." The meaning of *aionios* pertains to an everlasting state or condition. Grammatical consistency in translating Greek into English demands that *aionios* apply to the eternal condition of both the sheep, who inherit the kingdom, and the goats, who depart into the eternal fire.

A second passage is from Romans, where the apostle Paul provides a warning about an everlasting sentence. He portrays perdition as an unending state of punishment and exclusion from the presence of the Lord. Romans 2:6–11 states:

---

26 Pinnock's statement leads to his final position of favoring annihilationism. William Crockett ed., *Four Views on Hell* (Grand Rapids, MI: Zondervan, 1992), 164–65.

For he will repay according to each one's deeds:
to those who by patiently doing good seek for
glory and honor and immortality, he will give
eternal life; while for those who are self-seeking
and who obey not the truth but wickedness,
there will be wrath and fury. There will be
anguish and distress for everyone who does evil,
the Jew first and also the Greek, but glory and
honor and peace for everyone who does good,
the Jew first and also the Greek. For God shows
no partiality.

You see a parallel existence for both the righteous and
unrighteous in eternity. The faithful person will find glory
and honor when stepping into the next world. For those who
shun the truth of the gospel, God's wrath will lead to anguish
and distress. According to Paul, eternity for some will be a
negative experience.

After a nearly eight-year study, the Church of England
published a change to its doctrinal position on the idea of
final judgment that ends in everlasting banishment. The
commission believes that professing such a theology turns
God into a sadistic monster that psychologically affects both
believers and those without Christian faith. Driving the
change is a moral protest to such a merciless fate. In order
to preserve each person's human freedom, the committee
rejects the idea of universalism. Instead, it settles for
annihilationism, which it holds to be a more trustworthy
picture of damnation than any of the traditional images of
hell and the lake of fire.[27]

Pinnock and the Church of England provide two

---

27 According to the commission, the only reasonable end for unsaved
    people is complete non-being. Doctrine Commission of the Church of
    England, *The Mystery of Salvation: The Story of God's Gift* (London:
    Church House Publishing, 1996), 199.

different reasons for accepting a personal eschatology of annihilationism. Pinnock believes the assurance of God's love will diminish when Bible readers accept a vague, unending punishment. The Church of England considers God's love in Christ far distant from the idea of eternal torment.

Of course, it is natural for theologians and church bodies to have genuine concern for the fate of the lost. One goal of this book is to help alleviate the worst thoughts about perdition. The idea of unquenchable fire conjures up all sorts of terrifying scenes of eternal suffering and agony. Although not good, places such as Venus or exoplanets provide a better understanding of hell. A clearer grasp about hell alleviates a number of irrational perspectives on the afterlife.

The vignette in chapter 7 will tackle the afterlife conditions on Venus. The story brings clarity to biblical phrases such as "the worm never dies" and "the fire is never quenched," or even where "there will be weeping and gnashing of teeth." In that short fictional drama, Venus is seen as an unpleasant place. It is a planet that is completely obnoxious and disagreeable. Unsaved people will suffer distress inhabiting a lifeless volcanic domain. Any place designed for banishment from God will have poor living conditions and maintain a sinful and corrupt state of affairs. Still, it is a reasonable location where resurrected beings can function and think clearly.

Universalism

The second questionable view of the hereafter is universalism. Universalists believe that every departed soul achieves restoration to a right relationship with God, thereby obtaining entry into the kingdom of heaven. The common thread among various types of universalism is the final salvation of all humanity. The basis for this belief lies in emphasizing the love and compassion of God. These attributes were clearly on display in the life and ministry of Jesus of Nazareth. Universalists say that no one can minimize Jesus' care and concern for every human being. Consequently, universalism proposes that God's final victory over evil comes through the reconciliation of all humanity.

As with annihilationism, the motivation for reconciliation is with hating endless punishment. Universalism finds support at the grassroots level, as well as with pastors and theologians who come to embrace the doctrine as a pious hope. Having love for all individuals, I understand the yearning for universal salvation. Who can find fault with desiring every person to be heaven-bound? Everyone wants deceased friends and family members to be in a better place than life on Earth afforded. All people share a common vision of a blissful heaven for departed ones. Yet, universalism is not a clear or evident teaching in the Bible.

Universalism has a long history of prominent supporters. Entering the twenty-first century, it sustains a minor but growing position in Christianity. It appears as a topic of discussion in many seminaries. One current sponsor of a universal type of reconciliation is author, speaker, and former pastor Rob Bell, who has written the popular book *Love Wins: A Book about Heaven, Hell, and the Fate of Every Person Who Ever Lived.* Bell believes unsaved people will have the opportunity to say yes to God over an indefinite period. He writes:

> Telling a story in which billions of people spend forever somewhere in the universe trapped in a *black hole of endless torment* and misery with no way out is not a very good story. Telling a story about a God who inflicts unrelenting punishment on people because they did not do or say or believe the correct things in a brief

window of time called life is not a very good story.[28]

The use of the expression "black hole of endless torment" reveals that Bell has no clear concept about the state of perdition. He draws a parallel between biblical images of hell and black holes in space, which have no correspondence. As noted earlier, a black hole exerts an extremely powerful gravitational pull. Beyond the event horizon, the spaghettification of objects is likely to make the environment an unlivable place, even for spiritual beings. When you consider another celestial body such as a planet, the idea of hell as a realistic place becomes more acceptable.

In his book, Bell accepts the existence of hell, but not as a final resting place. In his view, there is a "period of pruning" or "time of trimming," where impenitent individuals experience a change of heart. He believes the grace of God brings unceasing evangelical dialogue until a correction occurs. The confinement of Hades or hell is for restorative purposes, even for the worst offenders. Bell's view is in contrast with passages such as Hebrews 9:27, which states, "It is appointed for mortals to die once, and after that the judgment." This verse does not suggest an intervening second chance, but instead has a sense of permanence.

Bell finds hope with the lack of specifics about perdition. The Bible is vague on the details of Hades, hell, and the lake of fire. Nonetheless, his idea to discredit the entire doctrine of eternal separation lacks a solid foundation. The absence of specifics is not a license to diminish the reality of such an existence. Appealing to an irrational place such as a black hole does not help his case. In the end, he rejects eternal

---

28 Bell envisions God's unconditional love to be greater than bad choices made by people. Rob Bell, *Love Wins: A Book about Heaven, Hell, and the Fate of Every Person Who Ever Lived* (New York: HarperCollins, 2011), 110–11.

banishment for the unrighteous and couches it as "suffocating church dogma." But the church was merely reading the Bible.

Those favoring the doctrine of universalism found in *Love Wins* are using the love of God to supplant the justice of God. On the one hand, God's divine nature does have love toward human beings. On the other, God has justice toward choices and actions. Bell presents an imbalance of love and justice by emphasizing only the eternal love and compassion of God. He ignores the justice and "wrath of God," which the apostle Paul repeatedly warns about in the epistles. The wrath comes to bear not only in the Old Testament but in the apocalyptic events of Revelation, where God's anger and judgment pour out on the earth.

The refusal to assent to perdition is a growing problem in the church. One goal of this book is to address the issue. In the final analysis, the idea of eternal punishment needs to be accepted because the concept is fully evident in the scriptures. The free will choice of a person will determine their final destiny. The white throne judgment gives good indication that salvation is not available by way of evangelism beyond someone's mortal life. If what the Bible says about hell is taken at face value, then no pastor, Bible scholar, or theologian has enough evidence to gainsay the text. If someone distrusts the scriptures, then they are free to accept universalism.

Chapter 3

Science and the Creation Sciences

Science is both a theoretical and real-world pursuit of understanding the structure and behavior of the physical world. The discipline requires observation and systematic experimentation to uncover bodies of fact leading to general truths. Through this pursuit, fundamental natural laws of universal workings unfold. Being a methodical enterprise, science builds and organizes knowledge in a logical manner to explain and predict the world around us.

Science began as a mandate from God to humankind. Genesis 1:28 directs humans to dress, till, keep, replenish, subdue, and have dominion over the earth. The effort expresses itself historically in the progressive tool-making technologies of the Stone Age, the Bronze Age, and the Iron Age. The ability to effectively carry out daily tasks comes through the development, establishment, and implementation of the natural sciences. The body of information gathered by the sciences helps humanity to understand the makeup and meaning of the physical world.

Science addresses *only* the natural world, while religious faith addresses *both* the natural and the spiritual domains. The discipline of science assesses observable data within the limits of space and time. Scientific coverage does not go beyond the boundaries of the observable universe. Neither does it recognize supernatural forces or events such as miracles. Science will rationally search for an answer to the unknown, while attempting (at its best) to maintain an objective treatment of subject matter.

The churchgoer will encounter assertions by the sciences in the area of natural evolution that go against biblical teaching. Science attempts to show that biological life came to the planet through natural means and without the assistance of a divine being. When these claims occur, it is best to draw lines of distinction between ambitious assumption and fact. You must assess the real evidence coming into play. It is not wise for Christians to agree with the speculations of modern science offered by the experts. Still, we are called to honor and appreciate the scientific endeavor as an important discipline, existing for the health and well-being of creation.

The Old and New Testaments do not specifically teach about the sciences. The Bible is an invaluable text of history, poetry, prophesy, salvation, and wisdom. The book contains the essentials for living a sanctified life and does not directly address fields such as biology or physical cosmology. Passages will speak to certain processes and conditions in nature, but not in a scientific manner. As such, fully comprehending the Genesis creation is not possible with stand-alone use of the biblical text. Even science has its own limitations when it comes to grasping cosmic events. Still, God willingly provides humanity with avenues of inquiry in the natural world. A proper scientific understanding works in cooperation with the scriptures in order to help answer questions.

Scientism and Church Dogma

Scientism

Albert Einstein and Isaac Newton were able to contribute greatly to the field of physics while retaining a belief in God. Science did not deter the minds of these prominent intellectuals from having faith or religious belief. But in today's world, few scientists believe in God or even consider an afterlife. Scientific communities bathe in the philosophy of humanism and are filled with skepticism toward religious matters. Having roots firmly planted in non-belief, technical experts disregard whatever is spiritual or sacred. With high cynicism among professionals in the field comes the dreaded transformation of science to scientism.

What is scientism? Scientism is a philosophy that promotes excessive belief in the power of scientific knowledge. It is a conviction dating back to the Age of Enlightenment of eighteenth-century Europe. It was a time when intellectuals were using reason as the primary source of legitimacy and authority. From that time forward, scholars have had a love affair with natural science and the power of thought, while casting doubt on orthodox religion. In today's world of physical cosmology, scientism retains a level of authority. Yet, astrophysicists cannot even provide basic answers about the source of the Big Bang expansion. They can only speculate.

History regards August Comte as the first philosopher of modern science. When Comte brought forth the worldview of positivism in the nineteenth century, academia came to embrace scientism in a formal and enduring manner. Positivism is the belief that scientific knowledge is the only worthwhile and practical knowledge. All other philosophical approaches are not valid for explaining life as we know it. The twentieth century brought the development of logical positivism. Logical positivism considers anything not verifiable through logical analysis to be trivial and irrelevant. This system of thought renders religious concepts such as "God" to be meaningless.

Materialism works alongside scientism and logical positivism. Materialism is the philosophy that nothing is important or even exists outside of matter. The basic construct sees the physical universe consisting of matter, energy, space, and time. God, angels, demons, souls, and resurrected beings are imaginary because they are not physical, measurable, or observable. Matter is so basic to life that all phenomena, including mental thought and sensation, link to material exchanges.[29] The outlook excludes the possibility of the supernatural. As a result, materialism supports scientism and logical positivism.

Advocates of scientism, such as the late Stephen Hawking, decree that science alone is capable of seeing truth and reality. As such, his writings make a bid to corner knowledge. In his book, *The Grand Design*, the astrophysicist attempts to answer basic questions about life and the universe. Early in the text, he dismisses philosophy, claiming it is dead.[30] He then moves forward to ignore all religious input. The Bible does not count, and philosophy is empty, so both are cast off. As a result, only science is left to explain our entire existence. If you are set back by his position, remind yourself that you are rejecting the worldview of *scientism* and not science itself.

Another example of scientism comes from the popular book called *A Universe from Nothing* by best-selling author and

---

29 Bernardo Kastrup, *Why Materialism is Bologna* (Alresford, UK: John Hunt Publishing Ltd., 2014), 13.

30 Stephen W. Hawking and Leonard Mlodinow, *The Grand Design* (New York: Bantam Books, 2010), 5.

astrophysicist Lawrence Krauss. In the book, Krauss makes a rare attempt to show that without God, the cosmos could have arisen from nothing. He endeavors to use "relativistic quantum field theory" to explain his case. In the theory, particle fields are understood by their arrangement, rather than physical existence. Some arrangements called "vacuum states" consist of a zero-particle count. Krauss seems to think of these compositions as a state of *nothing*. One glaring problem with the theory is the existence of the energy field itself, which is actually *something*.

Church Dogma

The word "religion" comes from the Latin *religare*, meaning to bind or tie together. It represents the intrinsic power of religious organizations. Catholic, Protestant, and Orthodox institutions alike have held dogmatic beliefs that challenge the sciences. Theological doctrines, having been set firmly in place, can be hard to alter, regardless of evidence and facts. As such, the church (both medieval and modern) does not have a stellar history when dealing with the sciences. One primary example goes back almost five centuries to the Polish astronomer Nicolaus Copernicus, who modeled the night sky in his 1543 groundbreaking book, *On the Revolutions of the Celestial Spheres*.

Copernicus is the father of heliocentrism, meaning his map of the sky had the sun at the center of planetary motion. His observations concerning our planet were twofold. First, the earth rotates on its axis. Second, the earth orbits about the sun. His new theory of the cosmos dethroned geocentrism, wherein the universe's center is the earth. Original naysayers of the theory included prominent Christians, who were opposed to the teaching. Apparently, dethroning Earth at the heart of the universe was counter to the scriptures. As a result, Copernicus' charting of the solar system became an affront to Christian theology.

Before his death in 1546, the great Protestant reformer, Martin Luther, spoke against Copernicus and his findings, saying, "This fool wishes to reverse the entire science of astronomy; but sacred Scripture tells us that Joshua commanded the sun to stand still, and not the earth." A second cynic of the time was reformer and theologian, John Calvin. He affirmingly states, "Who will venture to place the authority of Copernicus above that of the Holy Spirit?" These two prominent Protestant clergymen, relying solely on their interpretation of the Bible, made errant and negative conclusions about scientific discovery.

The Galileo affair of the seventeenth century was a faith and science clash brought on by the earth-centric error of the Catholic church. Galileo Galilei was a highly educated man of the sciences who made major contributions as a philosopher, mathematician, and astronomer. Galileo's observation of the heavens began in 1609, following his development of a telescope. After seeing the moonlike phases of Venus, he became an advocate of heliocentrism. Galileo understood the earth and planets as rotating around the sun, with the sun being the center of the solar system.

Galileo's observations conflicted with accepted wisdom. Like the Protestants, unseating the Ptolemaic system did not sit well with the Roman Catholics. The ancient Ptolemaic system relies on the earth being central in the cosmos, with some of the church's doctrine resting on the theory. However, the Bible never states the earth is at the center of the universe. Misread scriptures in support of the Ptolemaic system were Psalm 104:5, "You set the earth on its foundations, so that it shall never be shaken" and Isaiah 40:22, "It is he who sits above the circle of the earth..." Ancient naked eye observation by science had led the church to accept an Earth-centered universe.

Galileo's teaching led to a Roman Catholic inquisition in 1633, which ended with his house arrest. The fate of Galileo did not stop the scientific world from adopting the heliocentric theory. The episode, however, cast the church in a bad light for centuries. The reign of scholarly-minded Pope Benedict XIV (ruler of the Papal States, 1740–1758) brought some easing to the Galileo sanction. In 1822, a major concession from the College of Cardinals paved the way for full acceptance of heliocentricity. In 1835, Galileo's book on heliocentrism, *Dialogue Concerning the Two Chief World Systems*, was removed from the list of banned books by the Vatican.

In order to reconcile faith with science and gain a better understanding of the Galileo affair, Pope John Paul II requested an in-depth study of the incident by the Vatican in 1979. The Pope was an advocate for the sovereignty of science and realized that faith and science, if properly interpreting the truth, could never be at odds. In 1992, the concluding report to the Pontiff cited mutual misconceptions, giving equal blame to Galileo and the church. The Vatican made the results of the inquiry public at a news conference. Contained in the announcement was a reinforcing statement on heliocentrism, which the College of Cardinals had adopted over a century earlier.

The news media was quick to jump on the occasion, incorrectly concluding that the Roman Catholic Church was finally, after 350 years, accepting that the earth moves around the sun.[31] As one can construe from the incident, "fake news" was alive and well back in the twentieth century. Such reports make religion look foolish and out of touch, leading to division in our society. In this case, people of faith are brought into question by being portrayed as unreasonable

31 New York Times, "After 350 Years, Vatican Says Galileo Was Right: It Moves," http://www.nytimes.com/1992/10/31/world/after-350-years-vatican-says-galileo-was-right-it-moves.html (accessed Nov. 13, 2020).

and extreme. Journalistic writing that unfairly belittles religious institutions can only serve to stir up the flames of controversy.

The last two sections have shown excesses in scientific and religious thinking. First, you see the negative development of scientism, which is widespread today. As a result, godless rhetoric comes from prominent astrophysicists. Little credence is given to philosophy or religious faith as scientists attempt to monopolize knowledge. Then, you see the dogmatic thinking from Christendom in attacking heliocentrism. Unfortunately, negative views about science still exist in the church today. In the next section, a current issue unfolds regarding the age of the universe. Although not universally held, the church's belief in a Young Earth creation theology (from the Genesis narrative) has led to a division between people of faith and those within science.

Discerning the Creation Story in Genesis

Reading the book of Genesis, or any part of the Bible, requires the application of personal theology. Theology is from the Greek word *theologia* (*theos*, meaning "God," and *logos*, meaning "word"). Studying the word of God is a mindful, organized approach that leads to understanding the nature of God. Coming into play are individual beliefs, spiritual practices, and religious traditions. Biblical theology attempts to arrange the many teachings of the Bible into a logical, coherent structure while placing metaphors and imagery in proper context. The influence of personal experiences and worldviews goes into the development of our theology.

When we think about a teaching in the Bible, or strive to understand God in any way, we are engaging in theology. Some people react negatively to the word "theology," believing it involves boring discussion about minor points of doctrine. This is a false idea. The personal development of our theology helps to reveal the character of God, allowing Christians to recognize his ways and better glorify him in their lives. Bible believers use faith as a motivator to seek a greater understanding of God and to put their theology into practice. So, in essence, every follower of Christ operates as a theologian.[32] The question to ask is, "Are we good theologians?"

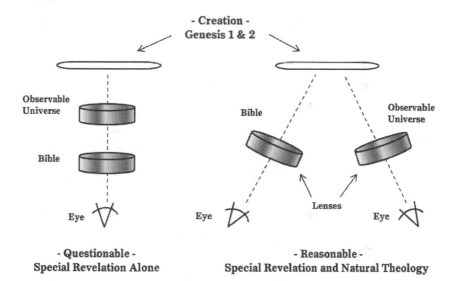

Figure 1
Special Revelation and Natural Theology in Genesis

The two methods for seeing the creation story are in Figure 1. The eyes of the Bible reader are at the bottom. The questionable approach to theology is on the left side. It relies on special revelation alone, which limits the reader to the things of God known through the lens of the Bible. By not separating the two lenses, the method distorts the observable world. You cannot effectively use the biblical text alone to fully grasp the creation of the universe. Special revelation

---

32 R. C. Sproul, *Everyone's a Theologian: An Introduction to Systematic Theology* (Sanford, FL: Reformation Trust Publishing, 2014), 12.

works best using two lenses independently—the Bible lens and the observable universe lens. Seeing God in the material world requires a stand-alone look at the material world, apart from the Bible. A person's theology requires input from the natural sciences when dealing with physical surroundings.

Relying on special revelation alone to understand and interpret the acts of God in creation is problematic. The Bible may be divinely inspired, but it is not a far-reaching guide on every subject. The scriptures are a historical account of fallen humankind, the plight of the Jewish nation, and the essentials of repentance, salvation, and sanctification through Jesus Christ. The beginning of Genesis is a stirring guide of the power of God, but uncovering details about the creation in its entirety requires more than the Bible. It requires juxtaposition between faith and science. Mental consideration of observable facts brings truth regarding the universe's creation.

The reasonable use of both special revelation and natural theology is on the right side of the diagram and will steer toward higher truth. The all-inclusive approach allows you to function scientifically. The earlier section, "The Nature of Revelation," addresses special revelation, which brings specific truths about God, sourcing from the Bible. That section took up natural theology, which gives rise to a worldview that contains the fingerprint of God. Natural theology uses observation of the surroundings, seeing God's handiwork in creation. The physical realm gives evidence for an all-powerful, all-knowing, and ever-present God.

The Figure 1 use of special revelation and the worldview of natural theology will work with observation and human reason to understand God's creation. The biblical text can then provide better insight into the creation story. To be able to think optimally, a person must use the basic source of wisdom, which is the word of God. At the same time, however, you must review surrounding physical evidence. It means including scientific thinking for the origin of the universe, galaxies, stars, and planets. The reasonable approach provides an all-inclusive review of the Genesis creation narrative and will be useful in the Fruitful Integration model of biblical faith and science.

Francis Bacon was a philosopher and English statesman who made a great impact in regard to the sciences. This parliamentarian of the sixteenth century is regarded as the father of both empiricism and the scientific method. Bacon contends that God reveals himself in two books: the book of nature and the book of Scripture. He brings the point across when writing, "There are two books laid before us to study, to prevent our falling into error; first, the volume of the Scriptures, which reveal the will of God; then the volume of the Creatures, which express his power."[33] His words show the need for special revelation and natural theology to work together in order to avoid mistakes.

Some Christians see faith and science at odds, so using special revelation and natural theology together can be uncomfortable. These people fear science will dominate faith because accepting physical cosmology as true might allow for importing speculative biological findings, such as humans evolving from microorganisms. This may lead to having less trust in the accuracy of the Bible. This worry should be put to rest. As will be discussed in the next section, when a conflict exists between the Bible and scientific evidence, there is a reason. It is due to failing to follow the established processes of scientific investigation.

The use of the Bible lens in Figure 1 involves proper textual analysis. Textual analysis requires words and phrases within biblical passages to undergo a full assessment. The text of the Old Testament was originally written in Hebrew before

---

33 Libquotes, "Francis Bacon Quote," https://libquotes.com/francis-bacon/quote/lbk3m3m (accessed Feb. 17, 2021).

translation into English. Translating can be a subjective process. Understanding how to deal with the translation is a critical part of the study. An end-to-end textual analysis of Genesis chapters 1 and 2 will include the etymology of words and a dissecting of phrases. Scholars come to understand verses in the Bible using three methods: (1) exegesis, (2) hermeneutics, and (3) scripture interpreting scripture.

Exegesis is the process of examining text to learn the original intent, in order to find meaning with the modern reader. The process utilizes the three-pronged approach of (a) historical–critical study, (b) literary interpretation, and (c) reader self-awareness. Historical–critical study addresses the author's original intent and how the text came to be. It encompasses the ancient setting and culture. Literary interpretation examines the text and includes genre, grammar, sentence structure, and vocabulary. Finally, self-awareness looks at you, the reader, to determine cultural bias, worldview, presuppositions, and attitudes.

The next level in gaining understanding is hermeneutics, which is the principles of interpretation. Hermeneutics sits at a controlling level above exegesis. It deals with the standards of interpretation and creates the baseline thinking for use in exegetical practice. It contains the formal rules one applies when using exegesis and incorporates all the techniques that make up the process of biblical interpretation. In other words, hermeneutics puts the specific tools in the toolbox that are going to come into play when analyzing the written text. Exegesis concerns itself with actually using the tools to interpret a specific Bible passage.

Scripture interpreting scripture is the ability of one part of the Bible to lend clarity to another part of the Bible. From beginning to end, the authors of the sixty-six canonical books create a unifying disclosure. In reading the scriptures, you see a passage in one book finding support by being referenced in an earlier or later book. For example, quotes from (and allusions to) prophets in the Old Testament are sprinkled throughout the New Testament. In the teachings of Jesus, he often restates the Old Testament for emphasis. It shows the Holy Scriptures deliver a consistent truth in regard to subject matter. The knitting together of passages over time provides for a harmonious Bible that will not contradict itself.

The methods of exegesis, hermeneutics, and scripture interpreting scripture are theologically sound but can fall short in grasping the creation narrative if the Bible alone is in use. For example, Genesis 2:4b states, "In the **day** that the Lord God made the earth and the heavens." The Hebrew word for day is *yôm*. The word *yôm* can be translated as a short twenty-four-hour day or as a very long period of time. Without the proper, independent scientific input for the age of the universe, a reader is inclined to go with a short period of time. Impartiality can only come by using the reasonable approach in Figure 1, which separates the Bible lens from the observable universe lens. The judicious practice results in scientific facts not being blurred out of the analysis.

In summarizing the section, the mandate for Christians is to use special revelation from the Bible while also considering the world around them. Truth comes by the Holy Spirit after an honest and open evaluation of all the evidence. In order to do this, people of faith are to study the scriptures and maintain a realistic outlook about the observable domain. This requires using the sciences. Rational thought then guides the believer toward a proper interpretation. Using the separate views of special revelation and natural theology places trust in both the biblical text and the observable universe. It will aid in leading to a proper timeline for God's work in the Genesis creation narrative.

Various Views of Creation Science

In the beginning, there was God's eternal realm. It is where he initiates the Big Bang expansion of energy, which comes out of nothing (*ex nihilo*). From the energy burst, the heavens and the earth expand out. Chapter 1 of Genesis gives the first account of creation. Chapter 2 gives a second account. Each rendition shows that all things originate from an all-powerful deity. Chapter 1 provides an overview of God's work, guiding the reader through a six-day creation story. Genesis 2:4b begins the second story, providing a close-up view that focuses more on humanity. Here, the newly formed Adam finds home in the garden of Eden, where he names the animals and receives his wife Eve.

God's creation of human beings brings to light a major difference between faith and science, because science includes the field of biological evolution. When hearing the term "evolution," you think of natural evolution. Natural evolution is a science accepting that random change over long time periods will advance the design of large-scale anatomies, persevering through natural selection. One species evolves to the next higher level of species through a macroevolutionary process. Macroevolution is a major evolutionary transition from one type of organism to another, occurring over time within the taxonomy of biological groupings.

In 1859, Charles Darwin's book, *On the Origin of Species*, became the first systematic explanation of natural evolutionary theory. Further work by paleontologists brought forth a consensus that the fossil record reveals macroevolution. By the early 1900s, most of the scientific community had accepted some form of natural evolution. Life first began as a primordial soup of amino acids on the early earth, which led to the formation of a single shared ancestor. Scientists now call this progenitor the Last Universal Common Ancestor (LUCA). It is recognized as the source of all complex life.

LUCA is not the first living organism on Earth, but the one to survive from many original organisms.

Theories of natural evolution continued to develop until science and religious faith finally clashed in the schoolroom. The famous Scopes Trial (a.k.a. "Scopes Monkey Trial") of 1925 brought the creation/evolution conflict to a political and legal climax. John T. Scopes was charged with violating Tennessee state law by teaching Charles Darwin's theory of evolution. The state had declared unlawful the teaching of any doctrine denying the divine creation of man, as taught by the Bible. Entering the debate were theological differences between liberal and fundamental interpretations of the scriptures, as well as the teaching of modern science in school.

Scopes was found guilty, but the verdict was overturned on a technicality. In analyzing the aftermath of the trial, historians note the schism between the men of science and the men of religion, who emerged strongly at odds. Driven by the philosophy of humanism, educational institutions went on to fully accept scientific theories of natural evolution while ignoring faith-based claims of creation. The end result was the teaching of natural evolution in public school. At the government level, the National Science Foundation, a taxpayer-funded organization, began to back claims about humans evolving from a universal common ancestor.

The middle part of the twentieth century was a time of religious response. Various churches and ministries ramped up stances on divine creationism. The formal structure of "creation science" teaching appeared in the 1960s. Creation science attempts to validate the biblical creation story using scientific backing. Four main organizations exist to provide an overall faith-based approach. One current release, *Four Views on Creation, Evolution and Intelligent Design*, contains contributions from today's organizational leaders. It is useful to know the people who represent these groups, as well as to study the reasons for their beliefs.[34]

The creation sciences and supporting ministries include:

(1) Intelligent Design (ID); The Discovery Institute
(2) Theistic evolution (TE); BioLogos Foundation
(3) Young Earth creationism (YEC); Answers in Genesis
(4) Old Earth creationism (OEC); Reasons to Believe

Table 1 contains a summary of each group's position. The synopsis requires breaking down the cosmological, geological, and biological aspects of creation. The chart appears before the general discussion in order to give the reader an overview of each element. Science is given as the first item, so one can draw a direct comparison between natural evolution and the creation sciences. Intelligent Design does not formally consider itself a creation science movement, but it does oppose evolution by providing insightful, academic responses about an intelligent designer.

---

34 Contributors to the book are Stephen C. Meyer (Intelligent Design), Deborah B. Haarsma (Theistic evolution), Ken Ham (Young Earth creationism) and Hugh Ross (Old Earth creationism). J. B. Stump, ed., *Four Views on Creation, Evolution and Intelligent Design* (Grand Rapids, MI: Zondervan, 2017), 7–8.

Domain	Cosmological	Geological	Biological		
	Age of Universe 13.8 B yrs.	Age of Earth 4.5 B yrs.	Natural Evolution	Progressive Creation	Adam & Eve as Parents of all Humans
1 Science	X	X	X^a		
2 Intelligent Design	NP	NP	X^b		NP
3 Theistic Evolution	X	X	X^c		
4 Young Earth Creationism					X
5 Old Earth Creationism	X	X		X	X

X - Accepts the column position
X^a - Accepts random mutation, natural selection, and LUCA
X^b - Intervention by an Intelligent Designer
X^c - Accepts random mutation, natural selection, and LUCA overseen by God
NP - No position

Table 1
Stance of Science and the Creation Sciences

Science

As shown in the table, modern science fully supports natural evolution. Evolution accepts abiogenesis. Abiogenesis is the basic mechanism thought to be responsible for the origin of life. It is the *unproven* natural process by which life arises from nonliving matter, such as amino acids and simple organic compounds. The laboratory environment has never been able to create a single cell, such as an amoeba, from nonliving matter. Yet, scientists insist on claiming abiogenesis is self-evident, even though the process is unexplained and unverified. Pre-life chemical reactions that give rise to life have no basis in fact.

Evolution accepts large-scale changes in the hereditary traits of biological organisms over long periods of time due to random mutation and natural selection. Evolutionary biology and paleontology are collaborative areas of study that engage in investigating the history of evolutionary life on Earth. Valid concepts can arise from their studies. One is microevolution, which is minor changes in one or more species. Another is extinction, which is the total loss of a species, family, or other grouping of plants and animals. Unfortunately, questionable claims are also made. The primary one is macroevolution, where new types of species arise from previously existing species.

Darwinian evolution has become a forgone conclusion in the scientific community. Nevertheless, efforts by scientists, educational institutes, and the news media to persuade the masses have not been effective. Even in secular America, more than four in ten adults believe God created humans in their present form.[35] Natural evolution continues to come into question, as it requires the application of time and chance to elemental mishmash in order to create a common ancestor and higher-order life. Further questions arise because solid evidence is lacking in the fossil record for higher-order species transitions.[36] Macroevolution, or speciation, has a limited listening audience.

Let's overview the two main branches of natural evolution, which are evolutionary biology and paleontology. Evolutionary biology concerns itself with the processes and patterns of biological evolution. Special attention is given to the diversity of organisms and how they change over time. Current research covers topics such as mutation, natural selection, genetic drift, divergence, speciation, and extinction.

Paleontology deals with the fossil record. Paleontologists infer the lineages of species by associating the anatomies of modern species with past species that have left records of their evolutionary history. In the earth layering, fossils are

---

35   In a poll of Americans, 42% accept the creation of human beings. Gallup News, https://news.gallup.com/poll/170822/believe-creationist-view-human-origins.aspx (accessed Jan. 27, 2021).

36   Reasons to Believe, "Does Macroevolution Fit the Fossil Record," http://www.reasons.org/explore/topic/evolution (accessed Nov. 29, 2020).

dug out using shovels, hammers, drills, and chisels. Coming into play is geological mapping, radiometric dating, chemical testing, microscopic examination, and comparative studies. Fossilization is a rare event because erosion destroys most bone and shell specimens. Soft tissue findings are almost nonexistent. As such, for every acceptable small specimen that is found, a billion are lost from the fossil record.

Finding transitional fossils to prove evolution of one species to the next is a major problem due to the heavy loss. As a result, the process of macroevolution is normally upheld by Darwin and his followers using the concept of gradualism. Gradualism is the accumulation of infinitesimally small genetic modifications that are profitable to the species. Yet, many organs, such as the eye, require an intricate combination of complex parts to perform their function—and many of them need to appear at the same time. How is the orchestration and formation of separate and simultaneous elements possible? What explainable process is driving gradualism?

In the popular book, *Darwin on Trial*, author Philip Johnson sees natural evolution in trouble because it defines common ancestry not as a hypothesis, but as a certain and logical outcome.[37] His findings uncover that scientific organizations are devoted to protecting the concept of evolution, rather than testing for it. Disturbing is the fact that the basic rules of scientific investigation have been reshaped to help evolutionary biologists and paleontologists succeed in the safeguarding campaign. The rule changes allow scientists to get away with not using benchmark scientific methodology, which can open the door to pseudoscientific practices.[38]

Karl Popper (1902–94) was a leading philosopher of science and a distinguished expert when it came to differentiating

---

37 Phillip E. Johnson, *Darwin on Trial*, (Downers Grove, IL: InterVarsity Press, 2010) 187.

38 Johnson, *Darwin on Trial*, 189.

between science and pseudoscience. He believed in pure scientific research needing to have the ability to test, refute, and falsify claims.[39] Popper states that theories need to be subject to rigorous empirical testing. He views the falsification criterion as the way for discerning science from other intellectual pursuits. In applying falsification, he had a negative view about natural evolution because it is a field where claims cannot be proven to be false. Rather than science, he sees evolution as a tautology that "attempts to explain everything, but actually explains nothing." He went on to soften his position when confronted by indignant Darwinists.[40]

The gradualism process of macroevolution has proven difficult to support using the fossil record. If evolution is meant to be the gradual change of one kind of organism into another kind of organism, then its validation would come through unearthing lots and lots of transitional fossils showing gradualism. But the limited fossil finds reveal quite the contrary. Most species exhibit little or no fundamental changes in appearance during their time on the earth. Known as stasis, it is the restrained and directionless morphological change expressed by a species. Some species, which have been traced for more than a million years, have been found to remain unchanged.

In order to construct *plausible* microevolutionary theories, evolutionary biologists analyze the DNA string for elements such as gene sequencing, timing, intensity, and on/off switching. The mechanisms are shown to work together, so laboratory findings are valid. When it comes to constructing *implausible* macroevolutionary theories, the work expands beyond the laboratory and becomes the job of paleontology. In their duty, the paleontologists have failed entirely. The digs do

---

39 Karl Popper, *Conjectures and Refutations: The Growth of Scientific Knowledge*, 2nd ed., (London: Butler & Tanner Limited, 1965), 256.

40 Johnson, *Darwin on Trial*, 180.

not find enough bone and tissue to validate macroevolution. When comparing the lab work of microevolution to the field work of macroevolution, it is clear that macroevolution does not deliver.

Although the acceptance of natural evolution is mainline thinking in the scientific community, it falls short in actual evidence that is necessary to establish factual data. Transitional fossils from one order of species to a higher order are desperately lacking, as is the evidence for gradualism. In terms of findings, natural evolution as a science fails in its ability to test, refute, and falsify its claims. In the laboratory, the concept of abiogenesis—where life arises from simple, nonliving, organic compounds—remains completely unverified. Given the shortcomings, the scientific view of human origin through natural evolution does not fit the Fruitful Integration model.

Intelligent Design (ID)

Intelligent Design works to counter the natural evolution theory that living organisms evolved as a result of random mutation and natural selection. The ID movement does not directly promote God as Creator, or accept supernatural acts, or even use the Bible. ID bases its belief on scientific evidence about the origin and development of life on Earth. Advocates speak to the complexity of living organisms, which require an intelligent source. Promotors of the research program realize that biological complexity and intricacy require input from a designer. As such, the view challenges both natural evolution and theistic evolution.

> ID contends that the information-rich sequences in DNA and RNA behave like a highly developed processer. The technology is similar to functional software in a laptop computer, a

smartphone, or their applications. The DNA instruction contains an inherent design logic and is capable of information storage. Natural mechanisms of evolution will not account for the algorithmic nature of biochemical information in the genetic code. Amazingly, each new species comes equipped with a new operating system. Similar to Microsoft and Apple products, it is not difficult to believe the "software coding" must derive from an intelligent source.

PLUSES:

- ID offers compelling scientific reasons for the coding and sequencing of all life's biochemical information to come from an intelligent designer.

MINUSES:

- ID proponents do not credit the God of the Bible as the intelligent designer.

Theistic Evolution (TE)

According to TE, the science of natural evolution explains the way God designs, creates, and sustains life. While disavowing the godless aspect, theistic evolution accepts macroevolution and the minimal evidence for it. At some point in the early earth, God steps back from direct involvement. He becomes an overseer of the biological process, letting natural evolution take over. God allowed nonliving matter to do what it was designed to do, and life emerged through abiogenesis. TE takes materialism under its wing by looking to natural causes for all evolutionary processes. As such, scientific reasoning is sufficient to fully explain God's role in biological evolution.

The TE hope is for audiences to marvel at the complexity of biological evolution and then perceive this as a witness to God the Creator, who apparently works miracles elsewhere. One reason for this harmonizing approach to science is to avoid God-of-the-gaps arguments. These are claims wherein "God" is invoked to cover mysterious or unsolved evolutionary steps that science cannot explain. In the past, using God to fill the gap has proven erroneous because scientific knowledge advances to explain the condition. To avoid a reoccurrence, TE enforces the idea of no supernatural acts of God in creation.

The approval of natural evolution by TE causes problems because LUCA becomes the source of all life. Turning into a falsehood is the foundational account of Adam and Eve being the biological parents of all humanity. Significant theological issues arise. A historical Adam is necessary for a historical fall. A historical fall verifies man's creation was originally sinless and good, which follows from a holy Creator. After disobeying God and eating the forbidden fruit, the nature of Adam changes for the worse. By using TE's progression for natural evolution, we see humanity coming into existence in a fallen state. What does this say about a holy God, who is overseeing the process?

Many Christian scientists and theologians give a warm reception to TE due to its settling effects. Faith and science can finally be brought together in the Complementary model in order to accept natural evolution, which is actually TE. Discord is thought to cease between the scriptures and science. As a bonus to educators, TE opens up new theological thought, which has special attraction in seminary circles. Students can write enlightening papers on how God and the Bible relate to natural evolution. As the accepted creation science of higher education, TE provides great fodder for scholars in formulating theses and dissertations.

PLUSES:

- TE agrees with the cosmological, geological, and biological timetables of mainstream scientific thought.
- Harmony exists between faith and science in the research and analysis of natural evolution.

MINUSES:

- TE undermines the integrity of God and the Bible by relegating Adam and Eve to something less than the biological parents of the human race.
- It is a logical necessity for abiogenesis to be a miraculous act. TE refuses to accept this truth, believing science can provide an answer.
- TE accepts poor scientific methodology in the field of evolution and the unclear evidence of gradualism, leading to macroevolution.
- TE claims the computer coding of organisms is built into the chemistry of the evolutionary system. Strong evidence from ID disagrees.
- TE provides misleading concepts. God cannot step away from the process of random mutation and natural selection while still controlling the outcome.

Young Earth Creationism (YEC)

YEC believes the Genesis creation story takes six literal days, with each day lasting twenty-four hours. The idea derives from the questionable use of special revelation alone (see Figure 1). The word "day" (Heb. *yôm*) has translational choices. It can be a twenty-four-hour day, or extend to an unspecified duration of eons in length. YEC accepts the twenty-four-hour day interpretation as the correct one. Yet even apart from science, a problem persists in the biblical text with this rendering. In the sixth day of creation, God brings forth the male and the female in his image (Gen. 1:27). The day is broken down into segments in the second creation story.

The second creation story begins in Genesis 2:4b and provides a close-up view of humanity. In focusing in on Adam's *day*, we see he was created in verse 2:7. Direction is given for him to till and keep the garden of Eden in verse 2:15, which is a large expanse. It includes a river and four branching tributaries. Later in the day, Adam labors in verse 2:20 to name *every living creature*, which at the time includes thousands of bird and mammal species. His long day concludes with a lingering loneliness, which requires the creation of Eve in verse 2:22. It is reasonable to conclude from the events of these passages that the use of the word "day" is not meant to be a literal twenty-four-hour day.

The biblical position of a twenty-four-hour day creation leads YEC to accept that the universe, and all life on the earth, was made 6,000 to 10,000 years ago. In defense of the short period of time, YEC comes up with a strange stance against scientific study by claiming that a really old-looking Earth is actually quite young. The reasons are because of the dramatic effects of Noah's flood and the Gen. 3:17–18 passage. In the verse, the Lord God curses the ground after Adam's fall. According to YEC, the curse of the soil expands beyond the thistles and thorns of the harvesting process. It includes the entire physical universe, which is untrustworthy and must be viewed with suspicion.

Wariness about the surrounding environment is difficult to support biblically. In the Psalms, King David spoke of the heavens declaring the glory of God and of a firmament proclaiming his handiwork.[41] During his ministry, Jesus gave many warnings to the disciples, but never about the deceitfulness of nature. The apostle Paul follows up by writing of a visible creation that reveals the truth about God.[42] Being cautious about observing our earthly domain is not part of biblical thinking. Ultimately, YEC finds itself in a struggle with the world around them. Disagreeing with baseline scientific facts promotes the Conflict model and is viewed with skepticism.

PLUSES:

- YEC accepts Adam and Eve as the biological parents of all humanity.
- In terms of eschatology, YEC supports an end-of-the-age rather than an end-of-the-world theology.

MINUSES:

- Accepting the Genesis creation occurs over six literal days means discounting both the second creation story and valid scientific findings.
- By bringing questionable theological "truth" to bear on the church, YEC creates tension and a loss of authority in Christian evangelism.
- The 1961 YEC foundational book, *The Genesis Flood*, has lost credibility. In 2011, the fiftieth-year edition came out with no changes. As such, it fails to address

---

41 David speaks to the glory of nature in Ps. 19:1. Coogan, *New Oxford Annotated Bible*, 790 [OT].

42 Paul speaks to the truth of nature in Rom. 1:20. Coogan, *New Oxford Annotated Bible*, 244 [NT].

a half century of geological discovery working against Young Earth theory.

- YEC criticizes evidence for an Old Earth theory, yet it does not present its own comprehensive model that fits known science.

Old Earth Creationism (OEC)

Old Earth, day-age creationism is at the forefront of creation science. OEC sees creation "days" in Genesis as very long periods of time. The timeline begins 13.8 billion years ago with the universe's creation. About 4.5 billion years ago, a molecular cloud formed the sun, and the accretion of the planets followed. The six days of creation are spread over geological eras, with some overlaps of time between the eras. The OEC model fully agrees with physical cosmology, the geological time scale, and the earliest discoveries of biological life found in the fossil record.

OEC considers the cataloging of the fossil record as generally accurate but rejects the idea of random mutation and natural selection for advancing species. Foremost in OEC thinking is progressive creation, which accepts God's supernatural involvement in the creation of life on Earth. Creation events occur over a six-day period, with great lengths of time filling each creation day. The new appearance of higher-order species in each stage represents moments of direct intervention by God. In opposing theistic and natural evolution, Old Earth creationism rejects the LUCA concept, while accepting in its place Adam and Eve to be the biological parents of the human race.

The Cambrian explosion serves as a tangible example of a day-age creation event. The Cambrian explosion was the unparalleled emergence of organisms between 540 and 480 million years ago.[43] Highlighting the event was the sudden appearance of 25 to 35 major phyla. It suggests that animals with incredible complexity appeared on Earth in a relatively short time period without any evolutionary predecessors. The higher life forms did not evolve from primitive life because there is no evidence for transitional fossils. To the extent possible, the fossil record supports the Cambrian findings. The episode suggests spontaneous creation by God, highly favoring the progressive creation model.

PLUSES:

- OEC agrees with the cosmological, geological, and biological timetables of mainstream scientific thought.
- Sees no clear evidence in paleontology for random mutation and natural selection to advance species.
- OEC does not agree that gradualism will lead to macroevolution, as suggested by natural evolution.
- Maintains the integrity of the Bible by accepting Adam and Eve as the biological parent of the human race.
- Progressive creation in OEC connects God's creative acts to known speciation events such as the Cambrian explosion.

MINUSES:

- In terms of eschatology, OEC supports an end-of-the-world rather than an end-of-the-age theology.

OEC exemplifies the effort to align the creation narrative with the sciences without undermining the integrity of

---

43 The Cambrian Explosion let loose a plethora of complex organisms. It is the quintessential biological event of the planet, paralleling the first formation of life itself. Peter D. Ward and Donald Brownlee, *Rare Earth: Why Complex Life is Uncommon in the Universe* (New York: Copernicus Books, 2004), 131.

God and the Bible. Unlike TE, OEC sees the impossibility of abiogenesis without God. OEC advocates for divine intervention for originating life on the earth. Natural and theistic evolution disapprove of God's participation, with both rejecting Adam and Eve as the biological parents of all humanity. By using progressive creation, OEC accepts God's involvement in the origin of life, and the creation of a vast array of species on Earth. OEC also denies YEC concepts by accepting the scientific findings for the age of the universe and the earth. The creation science provides strong input into the Fruitful Integration model.

Table 1 conveys the *differences* between science, Intelligent Design, and the three creation sciences. The next chapter will shift gears to show the *similarities* that exist between science and the Bible, with special emphasis on the areas of physical cosmology and geology. The scriptures work with the sciences because people of faith accept the truth about the universe being 13.8 billion years old. Going beyond this current age and into the future age, the chapter will discuss the possibilities of a healthy cosmic structure for eons to come. The viewpoint will align with accepting an end-of-the-age theology, rather than an end-of-the-world theology.

Chapter 4

Faith and Science as Synergistic

*Lead me in your truth, and teach me,
for you are the God of my salvation;
for you I wait all day long.*

Psalm 25:5

Using past, present, and future events, this chapter will show how physical cosmology and geology associate with the biblical creation narrative. Science assists in the divine command for humans to be involved in the sustaining and advancing of the created order. When God formed Adam and Eve, he provided direction to till and keep the garden. Keeping the garden requires know-how. It comes through the experience gained by seeing what works and doesn't work in horticulture. As such, faith and science are ordained by God to work together for the common good in order to guide humankind toward a bright and productive future.

Astronomy is the study of phenomena outside Earth's atmosphere. The field deals with the nature and motion of various heavenly bodies such as galaxies, nebulas, stars, planets, black holes, comets, and asteroids. The astronomer's desire is to search for, and ultimately find, life-harboring places in the universe. In the solar system, one current focus is on the icy moons Titan, Europa, and Enceladus. The planet Mars draws interest as well, while serving as a future destination for human spaceflight. An adjoining field, theoretical astronomy, uses analytical or numerical models to study areas such as dark matter and dark energy, and to evaluate cosmic events.

One branch of theoretical astronomy is physical cosmology, which seeks to understand the origin, evolution, structure, and fate of the universe. It considers the entire makeup of outer space and the workings of natural laws that keep it in order. Physical cosmology builds upon Albert Einstein's theory of general relativity. Over the last century, advances in optical and radio telescopes have aided greatly in verifying his math models. As a science, physical cosmology measures and maps the cosmos, while developing evolutionary theories for the universe.

Bridging Faith and Science

Belief in the Bible can work together with physical cosmology. The relationship begins with the universe's creation, continues today, and will remain far into the future. At their best, faith and science seek to find ultimate truth. The pursuit of this common goal allows the disciplines to be brought together in a meaningful manner. Each school of thought can grasp the history and future possibilities of the human experience. As a practical, systematic, and intellectually based enterprise, physical cosmology builds and organizes knowledge through observation of the universe.

Christians anticipate Jesus returning to the earth in order to rule and reign forever. The second coming of Christ is a major theme of the New Testament. But in a cosmic sense, what does this mean? A healthy planet cannot stand alone in outer space. The earth requires a sun to orbit about for stability and warmth. The sun itself is circling around a supermassive black hole in the center of the galaxy. The Milky Way is part of the Virgo Supercluster of galaxies, which is moving rapidly through space due to the expanding universe. Cosmic stability depends both on celestial body motion and interaction. After the Lord returns, these bodies will continue to behave the same way.

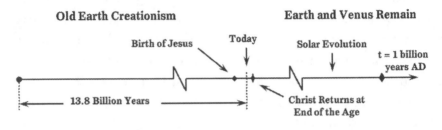

Figure 2
Biblical Theology in Accord with Physical Cosmology

Three elements cover creation's progression. There is (1) the origin of the universe and establishment of celestial bodies (cosmological), (2) the formation of the earth (geological), and (3) the origin and development of life on the earth (biological). The text uses the Figure 2 timeline to cover the cosmological and geological aspects. The timeline shows that biblical views such as Old Earth creationism and the "end of the age" can work well with physical cosmology. In putting the picture together, readers will come to know the cohesive truth that exists in the world around them. You should plan on referencing the timeline when reading the remainder of the chapter.

Astrophysics and the Bible give strong evidence for time itself, represented by the letter "t," having a start, which occurs at "t = 0." The creation clock begins at the Big Bang. The pure energy expansion moves out with time underway to create matter and space. At the incipient stage of creation, the energy was in an extremely small, hot, and incalculably dense state. This "singularity" contains all the mass-energy in the universe. Energy is able to convert directly to matter. The matter leads to the formation of subatomic particles that become the building blocks for hydrogen and helium. The "t = 0" point initiates the universe's formation.[44]

The timeline from Figure 2 moves along to place the universe's age at 13.8 billion years. Over the period, the cosmos expands out immeasurably, forming untold numbers of galaxies. Several Old Testament verses reinforce one another when describing the heavens as "stretching out."[45] The stretching correlates with the Big Bang expansion. In Jeremiah 51:15, the passage reads, "It is he who made the earth by his power, who established the world by his wisdom, and by his understanding *stretched out* the heavens." The Hebrew verb *natah* means to "stretch out" or "extend out." The continual movement of galaxies away from the Milky Way is evidence of this expansion.

The timeline then moves to the present. It centers on the birth and second coming of Jesus Christ, which occurs at the end of the age. In this present age, we look back to acknowledge a universe that is 13.8 billion years old. It requires a review of astrophysical and geological evidence and then accepting known facts about physical laws set in place by God. Humans are given the privilege through biblical study, and the observation of the physical world, to explore and grasp the history of the cosmos, while attempting to fill in the details. You can take comfort in knowing that life is in harmony because the Holy Scriptures and the findings of science are consistent with one another.

---

44 Robert John Russell, *Cosmology: From Alpha to Omega* (Minneapolis, MN: Fortress Press, 2008), 77.

45 The following passages contain reference to stretching out of the heavens: Job 9:8, Ps. 104:2, Isa. 42:5, Isa. 51:13, Jer. 10:12, Jer. 51:15, and Zech. 12:1. Coogan, *New Oxford Annotated Bible*, 736, 865, 1035, 1050, 1095, 1161, 1367 [OT].

Further synergy between faith and science arises from the continuation of the planets, stars, galaxies, and universe after Christ's return. The solar evolution of the sun is a critical phase of the timeline. Over the eons, the sun will grow older. The sun still has five billion years left in the main sequence phase, but it grows hotter over the next one billion years due to a projected 10% increase in solar luminosity. Since Christ's return to the earth is likely within a thousand years, his reign will exist for many hundreds of millions of years before problems occur. The return of the heavenly armies will bring paradise to Earth, while Venus could serve as an alternative location for the lake of fire.

Correlating biblical faith and physical cosmology will lead to a fruitful integration that unfolds higher truth. Having truth means being in alignment with proven or indisputable fact. The inspiration, the authority, the trustworthiness, and the power of Scripture will lead Christians in truth. Given as a gift by God for understanding and safeguarding the earth, the sciences provide humanity with observable and verifiable truths. What is shown true in one field will ultimately be true in the other. All truth is God's truth and results in one accord. Contradictions do not exist at the summit of knowledge and wisdom, which is in the mind and thoughts of the Creator.

The Beginning of Time and Creatio ex Nihilo

This section explains how Old Earth creationism and science work together on the left side of Figure 2. The section also gives a brief review of how physics sees a beginning of time (t = 0) and reflects upon both biblical and theological support for a beginning of time. Each field of study sees the universe as billions of years old. We next turn to the development of physical cosmology up to the twenty-first century.

History of Physical Cosmology

For a major part of human history, cosmology was not well-developed. Before the advent of the telescope, cosmology was a philosophy as much as it was a science. Plato was the first to express theories about the universe to explain the deeper realities of life. Unable to envision the rotating Earth as a planet orbiting about the sun, it was Platonists who first modeled the earth as a fixed object in space. Being at the universe's center, the earth was surrounded by a moving celestial sky. Early depictions were made on a 2-D plane, with heavenly bodies moving around the earth in a circle.

Aristotle, a student of Plato, is credited with creating the first 3-D geocentric model with Earth being at the center of concentric spheres.[46] The ensuing philosophers of Greece agreed with the depiction. In AD 150, astronomer Claudius Ptolemaeus brought together an explicit cosmology. The Ptolemaeus model called for spheres of various sizes representing the sun, moon, planets, and stars rotating around our fixed, central world. The Ptolemaic system held great precedence, receiving no challenges until the Renaissance period over fourteen hundred years later.

In the mid-1500s, Nicolaus Copernicus brought forth a novel idea, believing that the planet itself was in motion. It was the earth that both spins on its axis and orbits around the sun. These two rotations could account for all the motion of the sun, moon, planets, and stars. The publication of his book, *On the Revolutions of the Celestial Spheres*, just before his death in 1543, was a major event in the history

---

46 The idea of educated people and European scholars of the Middle Ages believing in a flat Earth is a modern historical misconception. Acceptance of a spherical Earth dates back to the ancient Greeks.

of science. The groundbreaking research on the heliocentric system became known as the "Copernican Revolution." The advent and use of the telescope by Galileo, as well as other astronomers, confirmed the Copernican model.

Advances in physical cosmology also came from Johannes Kepler. He improved the heliocentric system of Copernicus by replacing circular orbits with elliptical ones. Released between 1609 and 1619, his three laws of planetary motion provided backing for the law of universal gravitation, brought forth later by Sir Isaac Newton. In a 1687 release, Newton laid the foundation for classical mechanics. The work includes descriptions of planetary orbits due to gravity effects. His scientific findings were valid for bodies in the night sky and objects on the earth. His work went on to dominate ideas about physical cosmology for the next two centuries.

By the early 1900s, improved optical telescope technology resolved opposing theories about the cosmos. The first idea was long-standing; it was of a static universe where space was inactive, and stars were fixed in place. The second idea was of a dynamic universe where space was expanding, and stars were moving away from one another. Between 1912 and 1925, at the Lowell Observatory in Flagstaff, Arizona, astronomer Vesto Slipher detected and measured radial velocities in several spiral galaxies. Situated beyond the Milky Way, the moving clusters meant the cosmos was not static. The discovery provides evidence for an expanding universe.

George Lemaître and Edwin Hubble

In 1927 Monsignor George Lemaître, a Belgian priest, astronomer, and professor of physics at the Catholic University of Louvain, published an obscure paper written in French documenting "red shift" in the cosmos. The phenomenon explains that the farther away a galaxy is, the greater the light is shifted toward the red end of the electromagnetic spectrum.[47] Red or infrared is just beyond the visible range, where the wavelength begins to widen out, suggesting an "opening up" of stellar space. The discovery provides evidence for galaxies moving away from our vantage point on the earth. It gave support to a stretching or enlarging universe.

Paralleling Monsignor Lemaître's work in Europe, American astronomer Edwin Hubble published a paper in 1929 showing a linear velocity-distance relationship in the motion of galaxies. The findings reveal that the farther away a star cluster is from the earth, the greater its departure speed from the earth. The "recessional velocity" concept was born using the same red-shift phenomenon published by Lemaître. The condition became known as Hubble's law or Lemaître's law. The awareness of galactic speeds increasing with increasing distance from the earth gave evidence of an acceleration to the expanding universe.

Another significant issue under debate at the time was how the expansion of the cosmos was actually happening. One theory being tossed about was called the steady state universe. A steady state universe has expansive motion from an energy source that has existed forever and ever. It had no single point of origin and no beginning of time. Supporters envision the cosmos to be like a growing balloon. It was once a small balloon of unknown origin, which is growing to become a larger and larger one. New galaxies are thought to emerge within the swell of the expanding space. The origin of such a strange universe was anybody's guess.

In 1931, Lemaître countered the idea of a steady state theory, officially proposing the cosmos to have a beginning

---

47 The electromagnetic spectrum contains all radiation frequencies. From shortest to longest wavelength, the list includes gamma, x-ray, ultraviolet, visible, infrared, microwave, and radio/TV. Joseph A. Angelo, *Encyclopedia of Space and Astronomy* (New York, NY: Facts on File, 2006), 212.

as a "single quantum." The single quantum is a distinct point of infinite density. The singularity contains all of the mass, energy, and space-time in the universe. In 1949, the theory was coined "big bang" by one of its opponents. Within two decades, the discovery of cosmic microwave background radiation (CMBR) would solidify Lemaître's theory. CMBR finds its source from the Big Bang expansion. As a result, the Big Bang became the accepted standard of the scientific community. This paradigm shift led to the concept of a beginning of time for the universe.

Einstein's Physics Leads to a Beginning of Time

Theoretical physicists apply high-level math to physical systems to explain and predict natural phenomena. Albert Einstein gets credit for the complex calculus that reshaped the study of physical cosmology. His theory of special relativity, expanding later to general relativity, forms the basic model for the universe's structure. Physical cosmology continues to center on the work of Einstein. In the 1960s, finding a real beginning of time came from astrophysicists who were attempting to solve his field equations. Dissemination to the technical community came through journals. The effort legitimizes the left side of Figure 2 beginning at time zero.

Let's examine the concept of "time" within the boundaries of our planet. Living on the earth dictates that every person sees time and space as detached from each other. Analog and digital clocks, cell phones, watches, calendars, and planning schedules draw our attention to the progression of time (t). Time is absolute, being split off from both physical matter and the space (x, y, z) surrounding us. We see people, spaces, and places as physically separate from one another. Daily life demands the dimensions of time (t) and space (x, y, z) work together, but as separate entities. Neither affects the other directly, as they remain unchanged in basic construct.

Outer space presents an entirely different story. The brilliant work by Einstein highlights an interdependence between time (t) and space (x, y, z). Examining the light path of distant objects throughout the universe shows how time and space connect to each other. The notion of non-separate space and time is known as "space-time." Space-time is woven together into a single fabric, which can undergo distortion. In examining the effects closely, gravity appears to play a part in the phenomenon by causing measurable warping to the space-time fabric. When passing by large celestial bodies, light rays will bend around them due to gravitational effects.

Einstein based his 1905 theory of special relativity on two key principles. The first idea was about relativity, which states the laws of physics don't change when comparing two non-accelerating (inertial) frames of reference, which can be traveling at different velocities. The second principle relates to the constant known as the speed of light. The speed of light (represented by the symbol "c") is the same for all observers, regardless of the observer's motion relative to the light source. In other words, the speed of light in a vacuum maintains 186,282 miles per second. In spite of any movement between the light source and the onlooker, the measured speed cannot be sped up or slowed down.

Mass-energy equivalence is a second outcome of special relativity. It means mass and energy can be converted back and forth between each other. This brings rise to the well-known equation: $E = mc^2$. The expression shows pure energy, E (in joules), is equal to the mass, m (in kilograms), of an object multiplied by the squared speed of light, c^2 (in meters per second). It is interesting to note that the speed of light (c) is measured using the distance (in meters) divided by time (in seconds). The meters represent a spatial distance in the numerator and the seconds represents time in the denominator. It reveals the equation's complete incorporation of space, time, matter, and energy.

Einstein Advances Relativity a Second Time

Following the publication of special relativity, Einstein began formulating how to take gravity into account. By including gravity into the calculus, a huge step forward was made in discovering how the universe works. In 1915, he issued the theory of general relativity, which provides a cohesive description of gravity as an integral part of the space-time fabric. Under general relativity, Einstein was able to predict the effects of gravity to be the bending of light in the universe. In other words, gravity becomes evident when studying the effects that light and space have on each other.[48]

In later years, British astrophysicists Stephen Hawking, Roger Penrose, and George Ellis did important work to provide solutions to Einstein's equations beyond matter and energy to include space and time. In 1965, Penrose first gave credence to a gravitational singularity being contained within a black hole region of space. A singularity places titanic amounts of mass into a very small area. A gravity collapse following a supernova can eventually form a black hole or singularity. Density and gravity are so extreme in the singularity that basic laws of physics do not apply. The singularity theorem draws a comparison to the energy source moments before the Big Bang event.

Then in 1968, Hawking and Ellis issued a joint paper studying the motion of time and light. The publication documents with certainty that time and light "geodesics" will converge toward a singularity.[49] A geodesic is the

---

48 The total solar eclipse of May 29, 1919, gave scientists the opportunity to detect starlight bending around the sun due of gravity, confirming Einstein's theory. Space.com, "How a Total Solar Eclipse Helped Prove Einstein Right about Relativity," https://www.space.com/37018-solar-eclipse-proved-einstein-relativity-right.html (accessed Aug. 25, 2020)

49 Stephen W. Hawking and George F. R. Ellis, "The Cosmic Black-Body Radiation and the Existence of Singularities in Our Universe," *Astrophysical Journal*, 152 (1968): 25–36.

curvature of light in space-time. Along the surface of our spherical world, a geodesic is the shortest distance between two points, represented by a curved path. It would be the most efficient route that a commercial airliner takes on a long flight between cities. The unveiling of time and light geodesic convergence in space-time implies that space and time move toward an origin, just as matter and energy do. The origin is at the start of the universe.

A second paper published by Hawking and Penrose in 1970 completed the work of what is now called the space-time theorems of general relativity. The development reaffirms the idea of geodesic convergences in a past light cone.[50] So, what is a past light cone? In astrophysics, light cones follow the path of light rays moving backward and forward in time. It depicts in a graphical plot called a Minkowski diagram. Hermann Minkowski was one of Einstein's teachers and is best known for his work in relativity. The graph appears to follow the Cartesian coordinate system (x, y, z). The diagram has three axes, with the triplet of perpendicular lines meeting at a common point, or origin.

Figure 3 is a 3-D graph of a Minkowski diagram. It illustrates the path of a light source in space and time, radiating in all directions. The present event (A) is the light source. In order to see space and time on the same plot, one of the space axes is replaced by a time axis, which is where the present event (A) originates. Drawn in a conical shape, the past and future light cones are outward projections of light paths, which bring space and time together along the time axis. Adding the third spatial dimension back in would make the graph four-dimensional. The complete 4-D depiction would have the cones jumping off the page of the book and becoming spheres.

---

50 Stephen Hawking and Roger Penrose, "The Singularities of Gravitational Collapse and Cosmology," *Proceedings of the Royal Society of London,* Series A 314 (1970): 529–548.

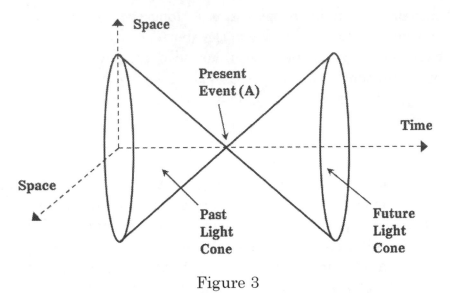

Figure 3
Light Cone Convergence to the Beginning of Time

Following the past light cone back from present event A, the light spreads out to great distances as the cone area increases into light-years of travel (1 light-year = 5.88 trillion miles). In going back billions of years into the universe's history, the light paths will be bent into geodesics by space-time. An expanded pictorial would then show the continuing straight lines of the past light cone becoming curved in shape. The theoretical notion of the bending of light in times past is validated by the previously mentioned 1970 Hawking-Penrose publication, which analyzes the path of past light cones. The bending or curving of the light is the start of a convergence toward an origin.

If there is sufficient matter and energy in the cosmos, the light ray bending continues. The matter and energy come from lots and lots of particulates situating in the cosmos. The particulate provides the gravity necessary to further light convergence. As gravity from the energized particles continues, the light rays bend and concentrate, ultimately focusing toward a single point. The convergence toward one spot unveils an origin to the universe. Providing evidence of this single point helps to support the theory of the Big Bang expansion. The light-cone convergence will also include a beginning of time, or a moment when t = 0.[51]

An important answer was already in place with the 1970 release of the Hawking-Penrose publication. The question dealt with the amount of matter and energy available in outer space. The dominance of gravity can only come into play when there is sufficient matter and energy available. Large amounts of particulate are critical for providing the gravity necessary to curve and focus the past light cone back to a single point. Yet, when we examine the night sky, there is a vast, empty vacuum between stars that are hundreds of light-years apart. How can there be enough of anything within the vacuum of space to bend and refocus a light beam?

The response is that the emptiness of space is not a perfect vacuum. In order to do a thorough review, you need to consider invisible energy, which is part of the plasma of space. The 1964 discovery of cosmic microwave background radiation (CMBR) was historical. Robert Wilson and Arno Penzias were testing a sensitive antenna when CMBR was detected in the microwave frequency range. The input was like a noise in the test setup. The disturbance is akin to an electrical problem on a television screen, which visually appears as "snow." The scientists thought the noise was coming from one location in outer space, but moving their antenna around didn't help matters. The same signal level was coming in from all directions in space.

What is CMBR, and what does it consist of? Essentially, CMBR is omnipresent thermal radiation in the universe. It exists in the form of ionized hydrogen and energized subatomic particles. The plasma fills the cosmos in every direction with

---

51 Stephen W. Hawking, *A Brief History of Time* (New York: Bantam Books, 1998), 53.

thermal radiation or heat. The actual temperature of the heat is cold by human standards, sitting at 2.73° Kelvin, or minus 454.75° Fahrenheit. Truly, a temperature of minus 454.75°F is extremely cold. Still, the frigid temperature is 4.92°F above 459.67°F, which is absolute zero.[52] In the thermodynamics of space, scientists see a temperature of 4.92°F above absolute zero to be a storehouse of residual heat.

CMBR sits at the temperature to which the universe has cooled since the Big Bang expansion. Close study of the energy source has given scientific validity to the universe's age of 13.8 billion years. Scientists consider CMBR to be left over from the very hot and rapid creation of the universe. The remaining heat source of charged particles blankets deep space. With scientists understanding CMBR particulate from the Big Bang to blanket the universe, it became easy to accept the gravitational convergence to a single point of beginning. So, the physics given by the 1970 Hawking and Penrose paper clearly points to a beginning of time, or a moment when t = 0.

In summary, the theory of general relativity by Einstein presents the basic calculus for understanding the cosmos. In later decades, the solution to his equations by prominent astrophysicists shows a convergence of the Figure 3 past light cone. The converge is back to the single point of origin or Big Bang event. The convergence is possible because of CMBR, wherein countless numbers of energized particles exist in the vacuum of space to create the necessary gravity to curve the light. The convergence includes space, time, matter, and energy. Therefore, the Figure 2 timeline, beginning at t = 0, is given credibility by the work of astrophysicists and fits in with the physical cosmology model.

52　Absolute zero is the temperature at which molecules and atoms become motionless. Angelo, *Encyclopedia of Space and Astronomy*, 14.

Theological Support to a Beginning of Time

Biblical review for the left-hand side of Figure 2 cannot begin without again looking at the work of Belgian clergyman and scientist George Lemaître. Being a Roman Catholic priest did not slow Lemaître's dedication to studying Einstein's theory of general relativity. In 1931, his proposal for an expanding universe meant that matter, energy, space, and time had a localized beginning. Initially, his "single quantum" concept of physical cosmology did not go over well with the scientific community. After all, the universe having a starting point is suggestive of a higher power.

The academic research of Monsignor Lemaître did attract the attention of Pope Pius XII, who announced in 1952 that the Big Bang was in harmony with the scriptures because it affirms the notion of a transcendent Creator. In other words, it was a scientific concept that makes sense to Bible believers. Lemaître was the brainchild behind the Big Bang theory. Yet, the priest and scientist would not find satisfaction until acceptance of his theory came from the technical field. The big break came in 1964 with the detection of CMBR. Thankfully, Lemaître, who has become known as the "father of the Big Bang," was told about the discovery of CMBR just days prior to his death in 1966.

From a biblical viewpoint, Genesis speaks directly to a creation beginning, which implicitly reveals a beginning of time. The declaration of Genesis 1:1 reads, "In the beginning when God created the heavens and the earth." In searching for meaning to the statement, you can raise a deeper question: "In the beginning of what?" An applicable response would be "in the beginning of time." Creating the heavens and the earth requires initiating the dimension of time. It means bringing a real $t = 0$ starting point to our physical universe from the eternal realm. From there, time moves forward with the burst of energy from the Big Bang expansion.

Several scriptures imply a previous period or "beforehand" to the beginning of time. In his eternal realm, God considers making the creation. In 2 Timothy 1:9b we read, "This grace was given to us in Christ Jesus before the ages began." The phrase, *before the ages began*, suggests divine activity before the launch of time. The verse has several cross-references, validating its robustness.[53] It implies divine activity, even before time arrives on the scene. The collaborating passages give the Creator's plan for humanity either "before the ages began" or "before the foundation of the world." In God's eternal realm, preceding time, God thought through his purpose for humankind.

So, the question becomes, "Is there really 'time in eternity,' and does it connect to the dimension of 'time' in our material universe?" The answer is yes. It makes practical sense for a higher time dimension to be in eternity and for a portion of it to stream into our world. Time in eternity has to be synchronized with our time in order for God to deal with those he creates in his image. As Robert Russell explains in his book, *Time in Eternity*, parts of eternal time contain elements of ordinary time in its design. Eternity operates in a higher dimension, time-integrated state with no start or finish. Time in eternity consists of a past-present-future makeup, which Russell calls *co-presence.*[54]

The arrival of eternity's co-presence in the universe originally comes from the co-presence found in God's eternal realm before the Big Bang event. The past-present-future makeup of this co-presence is what Russell considers extra-dimensional time. Before creation, God's eternal realm was

53   The verses collaborating 2 Tim. 1:9b include 1 Cor. 2:7, Eph. 1:4, Titus 1:2, and 1 Pet. 1:20. Coogan, *New Oxford Annotated Bible*, 271, 321, 363, 396 [NT].

54   Robert John Russell, *Time in Eternity: Pannenberg, Physics and Eschatology in Creative Mutual Interaction* (Notre Dame, IN: University of Notre Dame Press, 2012), 13–14.

operating in co-presence. After creation, eternity flows into the physical universe operating in co-presence. Eternity then synchronizes with the material realm by giving it a portion called "time." It becomes the ticking on the clock that moves steadily forward in one direction. As time moves forward, the co-presence of eternity holds time and the history of all events together. The text adopts the metaphysical term "co-presence" to define the extra time dimensions in eternity.

God's eternal realm was in existence when he initiated the Big Bang expansion from nothing. The Latin expression *creatio ex nihilo* means "creation out of nothing." It is the theological term whereby God creates the world out of nothing. The Bible does not directly state that God made everything from nothing, but Hebrews 11:3 states, "By faith we understand that the worlds were prepared by the word of God, so that what is seen was made from things that are not visible." What is not visible can directly relate to nothing. Merriam-Webster defines "nothing" as "something that does not exist" or "the absence of all magnitude or quantity."

In a scientific sense, we can define nothing in four ways. It is the absence of: (1) matter, (2) matter and energy, (3) matter, energy, and space, or (4) matter, energy, space, and time. Biblical *creatio ex nihilo* means God creates matter, energy, space, and time out of nothing. Prior to the $t = 0$ creation out of nothing, there was a complete lack of matter, energy, space, and time.

Coming forth out of nothing was energy for the Big Bang. The energy expansion initiates time while making physical space. The energy converts to matter and forms the visible universe. At the same instant, God's eternal realm moves to become part of the physical universe. What the universe is expanding into is speculation in the field of science, but I suggest a realm of nothing that replicates the nothing from the initial point of biblical creation. This study calls the domain the "ethereal," which lies beyond the edge of the universe.

One can envision the vastness of outer space as an ever-increasing expansion. It is a volume that continues to grow today. The observable universe extends out to a radial distance of 46.5 billion light-years. It is not possible to see beyond this point. So, if the entire observable universe is 93 billion light-years across, what lies beyond? The best-guess answer made by some astrophysicists is more universe and by others, more universe until reaching the point of nothing. This text agrees with the latter proposal, calling the nothing the "ethereal" realm.

Saint Augustine of Hippo considered the Genesis 1:1 passage to give credence to a creation out of nothing. He believed original matter was made from nothing and that the matter was made apart from God. Ordinary matter did not come from the composition of a holy God because all substance would then be holy. In Augustine's *Confessions*, the Roman Catholic theologian and philosopher states:

> In the beginning, that is from yourself, in your wisdom which is begotten of your substance, you made something and made it out of nothing. For you made heaven and earth not out of your own self, or it would be equal to your Son and therefore to yourself . . . That is why you made heaven and earth out of nothing, a great thing and a little thing, since you, both omnipotent and good, make all things good, a great heaven and a little earth.[55]

For Augustine, creation out of nothing (*creatio ex nihilo*)

---

55 The creation of the heavens and the earth comes out of nothing. It is not part of the holy being of God. Henry Chadwick, trans., *Saint Augustine Confessions* (New York: Oxford University Press, 1998), 249.

includes the creation of time, which he believes comes from eternity.[56] His writing in *Confessions* tells the reader God is everlasting, and as human beings, we cannot comprehend the eternal. As such, time is part of the initial creation story, being uniquely fashioned to operate in the universe. To speak about ordinary time before the creation is pointless.

Augustine believes that being in eternity means realizing past memories and future expectations in a time-integrated state. The idea is similar to that brought forth by co-presence or extra time dimensions. It is amazing for an early church father to grasp such a relativistic theory of time.

When the Genesis creation incorporates known physical cosmology, you can envision the Big Bang starting the universe. As seen earlier, the passage "before the ages began" (2 Timothy 1:9b) suggests there was God's eternal realm before the beginning of time. The initial energy comes out of nothing (*ex nihilo*) because the singularity originates from God. The sudden expansion of the concentrated energy source begins the creation event. It allows time and space to come into existence. The cooling of the energy forms matter. So clearly, a proper synthesis of the Bible and science can work together to declare a time when t = 0.

Thirteen billion years is mind-blowing to the ordinary person, but it is not a problem for an eternal being in extra-dimensional time. From the very beginning, the Lord God involves himself in the creation processes of the cosmos. He did not get weary waiting for nebulas to congeal into stars, overseeing black hole and galaxy formation, watching countless supernovae events, or hovering over our 4.5-billion-year-old planet when it was a sea of hot lava with no atmosphere. In Psalm 90:4 and 2 Peter 3:8, the reader is

---

56 Ted Peters, "On Creating the Cosmos," in *Physics, Philosophy and Theology: A Common Quest for Understanding*, ed. Robert John Russell; William R. Stoeger, SJ; and George V. Coyre, SJ (Vatican City State: Vatican Observatory Publications, 1988), 279.

told that "with the Lord one day is like a thousand years." These passages imply that God exists in a time domain that goes beyond our understanding.

The Big Bang model merits Christian acceptance because it has been verified using proper scientific methods. The theory has rebuked every attempt at its falsification. Stepping back before the Big Bang event is the realization that the physical universe has not always been in existence. Out of necessity, its beginning is grounded in a transcendent being. One of the basic tenets of philosophy and science is that "nothing comes out of nothing." It was God who created the cosmos out of nothing. Nothing by itself before a Big Bang expansion would only create nothing. The creation is therefore a causal event of divine agency, with the agency being the God of the Bible.[57]

In summary, the left-hand side of Figure 2 provides for a fruitful integration between the Bible and science for a beginning of time. Several scriptures give witness to a time in God's eternal realm that was "before the foundation of the world." This time is known as co-presence, which consists of a past-present-future makeup. Genesis 1:1 gives witness to a beginning of time for all matter, energy, and space, which is initiated by God from nothing. The theology of Augustine concerning *creatio ex nihilo* gives support to the arrival of time with the creation of the heavens and the earth. One can accept the timeline starting at t = 0 as being in harmony with the scriptures.

---

57 Reasonable Faith, "The Ultimate Question of Origins: God and the Beginning of the Universe," http://www.reasonablefaith.org/the-ultimate-question-of-origins-god-and-the-beginning-of-the-universe (accessed Oct. 12, 2020).

Earth and Venus Remain

This section clarifies how the Bible and science work together for the right-hand side of Figure 2. The discussion supports the continuation of life on Earth and gives evidence for a long-term solar system, galaxy, and universe. The scientific assessment leads to believing in enduring longevity for the planetary bodies of Earth and Venus. The biblical portion discusses two end-time scenarios: the questionable view about the "end of the world," and the reasonable view about the "end of the age."

Evidence for a Continuing Earth and Lasting Universe

What does the future of the cosmos look like? To what extent will the sun be stable and maintain a healthy solar system? Can the planets Earth and Venus last long enough to legitimately be the final resting spot for heaven and hell respectively? The current thinking in physical cosmology is for the observable universe and multitude of galaxies to remain functioning for hundreds of billions, perhaps trillions of years. Accepting a positive celestial future allows for a partnership between the Bible and science, since both areas anticipate a vibrant creation lasting for eons of time.

To support the idea of life enduring on the earth, this study will review two human-induced catastrophes and four cosmic threats that could end the world. The first five hazards will be shown to be incapable of terminating intelligent life on the planet. The sixth cosmic threat of a growing Sun is scheduled to begin more than one billion years into the future. The findings will verify the accuracy of the right side portion of the Figure 2 timeline.

To begin with, what could humans do that would end life on Earth? The first threat is climate change, which manifests itself in both global and regional climate variations. Climate change has become an interchangeable term with global warming and is attributed to human influence. Burning fossil fuels is a potential cause for global warming. Fossil fuels can contribute to the greenhouse effect, which results in increasing levels of carbon dioxide in the atmosphere. The climb in levels began in the mid- to late- twentieth-century. Other contributors to global temperature fluctuations include changes in solar output, Earth's orbital variations, and volcanism.

Burning fossil fuels and the deforestation process act together to increase carbon dioxide levels. Other gases besides CO_2 contribute to greenhouse effects. These include water vapor, methane, and ozone. These gases tend to absorb the sun's radiant energy, leading to a warming of the planet's atmosphere. Temperature increases can cause the melting of glaciers and lead to a sea level rise, threatening coastal areas. Additional impacts are variations in agricultural yield, the possible extinction of some species, and changes in atmospheric circulation patterns, resulting in extreme weather patterns.

In the book *Global Catastrophic Risks*, editor Nick Bostrom addresses cosmic threats, which might bring a disastrous end to the world. As the director of the Future of Humanity Institute at Oxford University, he performs extensive research into the probability of natural disasters, as well as short-term and long-term catastrophes induced by human activity and cosmic events. He sees climate change as a disturbing and harmful trend but finds it difficult to quantify the extent of future risks.[58]

His reasoning is straightforward. Normal weather models are mathematically chaotic, and the history of meteorology is

---

58 Nick Bostrom and Milan M. Cirkovic, eds., *Global Catastrophic Risks* (New York: Oxford University Press, 2008), 282.

filled with abnormal events. Strange weather patterns emerge and then retract without our understanding. Meteorologists are technically unable to precisely forecast weather systems. From a scientific viewpoint, this unpredictability translates into the inability to delineate a future global climate model. The fuzziness results in Bostrom listing the probability of human extinction due to long-term climate change as very low. Still, he believes global warming requires national attention and mitigating steps to be put in place.

The second human-induced threat to survival is all-out nuclear war. Could a nuclear conflict end life on our planet? Interestingly, the response is no. The impact of a global nuclear war is survivable by millions of people. The fact book, *Nuclear War Survival Skills*, states:

> Researchers who have spent much time and effort learning the facts about effects of nuclear weapons now know that all-out nuclear war would not be the end of humanity or of civilization. Even if the United States remained unprepared and was to be subjected to an all-out nuclear attack, many millions of Americans would survive and could live through the difficult post-attack years.[59]

The handbook published by the Oregon Institute of Science and Medicine dispels the myth that high radiation from nuclear fallout would kill everyone by poisoning the air and environment. In reality, the amount of radiation emitted per hour drops exponentially from the time of a nuclear explosion. Within forty-eight hours, the potency of radiation release from the fallout of nuclear weapons drops to

---

59 Cresson H. Kearny, *Nuclear War Survival Skills* (Cave Junction, OR: Oregon Institute of Science and Medicine, 1987), 5.

1% of the initial amount. Within two weeks, it shrinks down to 0.1%, allowing people to leave shelters.[60]

Bostrom's study of the post-effects of a nuclear war discusses both black-carbon emission and Sun blockage. The consequence of each would result in lower temperatures globally.[61] Although the effect would trigger massive crop failures, the human species would manage to survive.

In studying the four primary extraterrestrial risks that could cause an end to the world, Bostrom brings up a distinctive point about astrophysics: factors for measuring the processes are very accurate. As one small example, the velocity calculation for galaxies moving away from the earth is exact. In Bostrom's field of cataclysmic studies, precise measurement ability is very important. This cherished fact is available in the field of physical cosmology. Unlike weather patterns that are unpredictable, a high reliability is in place for Bostrom's future projections of cosmic events. High reliability leads to high confidence in predicting final outcomes.[62]

To begin, we examine the primary threat to the universe, which is its own termination. In examining cosmic longevity, one needs to grasp dark matter and dark energy. The term "dark" simply means that the matter and energy are nonluminous and have no known interaction with light. Dark matter acts like gravity and restrains the expansion of the universe. Working in the opposite direction is dark energy. It is the antigravity force, acting to increase the expansion of the cosmos. Albert Einstein did consider antigravity in his theory of general relativity and called it the "cosmological

---

60 Kearny, *Nuclear War Survival Skills*, 13.

61 Bostrom, *Global Catastrophic Risks*, 392.

62 The projections are based on the current understanding of dark matter and dark energy, as well as the laws of physics. Increasing scientific knowledge could result in a revision to the estimates. Bostrom, *Global Catastrophic Risks*, 33–34.

constant." Dark energy replaces the cosmological constant as the antigravity force.

Dark energy contains the pressure to grow the universe. It opposes the compressive forces of dark matter and gravity. The interaction between dark energy and dark matter will ultimately determine what happens to the cosmos. Depending on the density of the dark energy, the universe will have a different future. There are three options, which include an open, closed, or flat universe:

> **Open**—There is sufficient energy density to overpower gravity and continue the expansion, so the universe will expand forever.

> **Flat**—There is barely enough energy density to overcome gravity, so the expansion continues slowly, making for a modestly open universe.

> **Closed**—There is insufficient energy density, so gravity will halt the expansion. The universe will eventually collapse back to a singularity.

Astronomical evidence gathered over the years shows the cosmos is expanding. It is an ever-increasing outer space, which leads to accepting either an open or flat model. In 2001, scientists began reporting on the precise expansion rate for the universe and decided to name it the "Hubble constant." The latest estimate for the Hubble constant is 74 kilometers per second per megaparsec. In layman's terms, it means that for every 3.3 million light-years farther away a galaxy is from the earth, it appears to be moving at a speed of 74 kilometers (46 miles) per second faster.[63] At this rate, dark energy is clearly overcoming dark matter and gravity.

The question of longevity now turns to the field of thermodynamics. Thermodynamics deals with the relationship (back and forth conversion) of heat to mechanical energy or work. An expanding universe is losing heat and will have less thermal energy available for work. This eventually means the birthing of no new stars. The universe moving to thermal equilibrium and preventing new stars from forming will result in a slow heat death. With thermal degradation taken into consideration, the modeling still leads to the universe's life expectancy being over ten trillion years. Most of the long-lasting stars will be of the red dwarf variety.[64]

A second cosmic danger is the intergalactic collision of the Milky Way galaxy with the large, spiral-shaped Andromeda galaxy. The Andromeda galaxy is 2.5 million light-years away and contains around a trillion stars, which scientists consider to be about twice as many as in the Milky Way. Andromeda is moving rapidly in our direction and will make contact in about 4.5 billion years. Galaxy mergers are a common event in the cosmos. It is part of galaxy formation, evolution, and growth.

The expectation is for the "collision" to combine the two spiral galaxies and create a much larger galaxy. Typically, mergers occur with little chance of stars hitting one another, due to the light-year distances between them. The likelihood of disrupting our Sun and planetary system will remain low, while the unifying assembly of stars will gently sweep our solar system farther from the galactic center. The additional

---

63 NASA, "Mystery of the Universe's Expansion Rate Widens with New Hubble Data," https://www.nasa.gov/feature/goddard/2019/mystery-of-the-universe-s-expansion-rate-widens-with-new-hubble-data, (accessed May 4, 2020).

64 Bostrom, *Global Catastrophic Risks*, 39.

stars in the galactic mix will lead to a night sky that is twice the current brightness.[65]

A third cosmic threat is from a large asteroid or comet striking the earth. The lethality of a meteorite collision depends on its size, velocity, composition, angle of incidence, and whether the impact is on land or water. The Chicxulub event was a large strike on the tip of Mexico's Yucatán Peninsula sixty-five million years ago. The devastating hit led to the loss of the dinosaurs as well as the extinction of many other plant and animal species. The diameter of the Chicxulub crater is about ninety-three miles, which calculates back to an incoming asteroid or comet diameter of greater than six miles.

The following chart includes both the Chicxulub event and the recent Tunguska event of 1908 that occurred in a remote part of Siberia. In that incident, meteorite samples were spread over eight hundred square miles, indicating the asteroid burst in the air prior to impact. The graph plots frequency of impact against asteroid size. It includes energy release in megatons of TNT along the top.

---

65 Bostrom, *Global Catastrophic Risks*, 37.

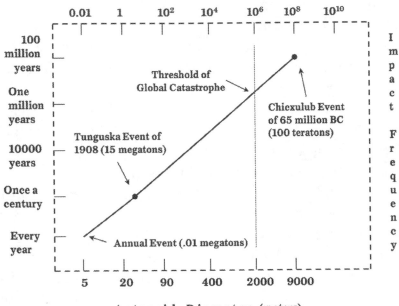

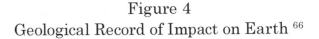

Figure 4
Geological Record of Impact on Earth [66]

In looking at Figure 4, the threshold for a worldwide, catastrophic asteroid strike is on the vertical dotted line. An incoming projectile striking the earth would have a 1.24 mile or 6,560-foot diameter. This is a "best-guess" estimate and correlates to an occurrence of once every million years. During such a strike, dust in the atmosphere could circle the globe and reduce sunlight for plant growth. Burning embers falling from the blast would ignite fires in multiple locations. If the meteorite struck water, a large-scale tsunami would hit the shores of many nations. Tribulation and death would

---

66 Two asteroid strikes plotted linearly over time create a record of impact. Astr 1210 (O'Connell) Study Guide, "Impacts and Bio-Extinctions," http://www.faculty.virginia.edu/rwoclass/astr1210/guide22.html (accessed Jan. 4, 2020).

continue for years. Ultimately, evidence points to the human population surviving.

The fourth cosmic threat that could end Earth's population is the life cycle of our Sun. The sun is a ball of white-hot plasma, which classifies as a G-type main sequence star. The sun has changed little since reaching this phase 4.5 billion years ago, but it will not last forever. The sun generates energy by the process of nuclear fusion, which changes hydrogen to helium. As nuclear reactions continue to convert more hydrogen to helium, the sun will increase in diameter and begin to get brighter and hotter. The change will affect the planets in the solar system.

The composition of the sun is about 73% hydrogen and 25% helium, with the remainder being heavier elements or metals. The layering is roughly in four sections: the core, the radiative zone, the convective zone, and the photosphere (surface). Looking at the sun directly, you see the photosphere. The central core makes up about 20% of the solar radius. That is where the nuclear fusion occurs, with radiative and convective effects bringing the heat to the surface. Scientists estimate that only 10% of the sun's entire hydrogen content is for burning, with the rest lying outside the core.[67]

As the sun continues to burn, thermal changes will be seen in the solar system. In 1.2 billion years, a rise in solar heat will begin to affect the inner planets. On Earth, it will bring a slow end to complex life. At the 2-billion-year point, the seas of Earth will evaporate from the increase in temperature. At the 5-billion-year point, the hydrogen in the core will exhaust and the sun will increase greatly in size, becoming a red giant. The girth of the red giant will be large

---

67   The 10% estimate is from Dr. Paul M. Sutter, Researcher Professor at the Institute for Advanced Computational Science at SUNY Stony Brook. Science Channel, *How the Universe Works*, "Death of the Last Stars," https://www.sciencechannel.com/tv-shows/how-the-universe-works/full-episodes/death-of-the-last-stars (accessed Feb. 13, 2020)

enough to consume Mercury, Venus, and possibly Earth, as measured by current orbits. Ultimately, the sun will collapse from the red giant state and become a white dwarf star.

The timeline for the loss of the sun should be put into perspective. The written records of human history date back about five thousand years. How does this number compare to the demise of intelligent life in 1.2 billion years? Well, five thousand years fits into 1.2 billion years 240,000 times. If you believe the return of Jesus Christ will be in the next one thousand years, then the time span will complete only one-fifth of one of the 240,000 remaining periods. One can see that the records of human history and the future arrival of God's kingdom to the earth are mere "drops in the bucket" on the celestial timetable. A billion-plus years of normal sunshine is in store for the paradisical planet.

For eons to come, the earth will exist as a paradisical planet, while under the control of God. Jesus Christ, resurrected humans, angels, and the animal kingdom will live peacefully in a perfectly restored and globally safe environment. Free access to the throne of God will allow for questions regarding the longevity of the sun. One answer to the dilemma of the sun's longevity may rest within the sun itself. Since 90% of the sun's hydrogen is outside the core, it is not accessible for burning. Extending the life cycle could be a simple one. Hydrogen in the outer layers of the sun could undergo redistribution to the central core and be made available for fusion reaction.[68]

In summary, a long future is in store for Earth after reviewing potential threats. Global warming, nuclear war, and three of the four leading cosmic disasters do not bring a

---

68   It would not be unusual for a star to burn endlessly. Scientific estimates for the life of a red dwarf star range from one to ten trillion years. Michael Richmond, "Late Stages of Evolution for Low Mass Stars," http://spiff.rit.edu/classes/phys230/lectures/planneb/planneb.html (accessed April 14, 2021)

foreseeable end to planetary habitation. Despite the loss of species and substantial loss of life and property, humans will continue to survive in the environment. Star formation will remain in place beyond a trillion years, with galaxies moving through the expanding universe. The limiting cosmic factor is the sun's stellar evolution, which still brings longevity to planets such as Earth and Venus beyond one billion years. As such, this review allows the reader to scientifically accept the Figure 2 timeline.

Overview of Biblical End-Time Scenarios

Astronomical evidence points toward Earth and Venus remaining healthy in the solar system for a long time. Since the Bible addresses eschatology or end-time events, what do the scriptures have to say on the subject? Do biblical prophecies make reference to the longevity of the earth and the future of the cosmos? What does the coming of the kingdom of God to the planet have in store for God's people? If the return of Christ were to unfold in the next one thousand years, would Earth and the present physical universe remain the same, be totally changed, or vanish completely?

People of faith await the appearance of Christ to set up his kingdom on Earth. The second coming is commonly referred to as the second advent, or *parousia*, a Greek word meaning arrival or presence. In discussing the end-times with his disciples, Jesus states in Matthew 24:30 that all people of the earth "will see 'the Son of Man coming on the clouds of heaven' with power and great glory." It is a biblical mandate to be ready for the Lord's coming. Sermons containing prophetic or apocalyptic scenarios often include the Lord's return. Eschatology produces much excitement in Christianity, due to the potential and imminent nature of events.

How one interprets the approaching end of the church age

will draw a person into accepting a timeline of events. The differences in Christianity generally hinge on the meaning of the "millennium," which is a thousand-year period. Revelation 20:1–10 brings the millennium period into focus by using the phrase "thousand years" in six verses. The thousand-year period talks about Christ's reign on the earth prior to final judgment. Some consider that his reign is physically on the planet, while others believe the reign is spiritual from heaven. Depending on how one understands final events, the three main views unfolding are: (1) premillennialism, (2) postmillennialism and (3) amillennialism.

This text will utilize the premillennial belief, which is accepted in large parts of Christianity. Premillennialists believe faithful followers of Christ will be taken up to heaven before the seven-year period of tribulation. The tribulation is an apocalyptic period that brings seven years of plagues and suffering upon the earth. The taking of believers involves the material removal of the body from the planet and is called the rapture.[69] After the seven-year period, the wrath of God is complete. Christ physically returns with his saints to rule over the nations of the earth for one thousand years. The place of rule is from the holy city, New Jerusalem.

The millennium brings an idyllic age to the earth, where Christ maintains a theocratic rule of all nations. The blissful period occurs prior to the final judgment and will include the peaceful coexistence of angels, human beings, resurrected spiritual beings, and the animal kingdom. The thousand years will be a time when physical and immortal bodies

---

69 Biblical support for the rapture is in 1 Thess. 4:16–7. The passage reads, "For the Lord himself, with a cry of command, with the archangel's call and with the sound of God's trumpet, will descend from heaven, and the dead in Christ will rise first. Then we who are alive, who are left, will be caught up in the clouds together with them to meet the Lord in the air; and so we will be with the Lord forever." Coogan, *New Oxford Annotated Bible*, 343 [NT]

walk the earth, existing together in a glorious supernatural manner. It is the quintessential example of the intertwining of the physical universe and eternity, which will coexist mutually in a visible manner.

During the millennium, the influence of Satan is eliminated from the earth, because the ruler of darkness endures confinement in Hades. Revelation 20:2–3 tells of an angel who "seized the dragon, that ancient serpent, who is the Devil and Satan, and bound him for a thousand years, and threw him into the pit, and locked and sealed it over him, so that he would deceive the nations no more, until the thousand years were ended."

Satan is in confinement when Christ reigns on the earth, but after the thousand years is over, he is set free "for a little while" (Rev. 20:3b) to once again deceive. He will gather an army of rebellious people to take up battle against the Lord. The clash is futile and will end with Satan and his minions banished to the lake of fire. Then, all of humanity occupying Hades will come up from the underworld in resurrected bodies to God's throne for final judgment. A review of thought, word, and deed must pass against biblical law and moral code. Following the arraignment, the book of life is opened. If the person's name is not found written in the book, they are banished to the lake of fire.

According to the scriptures, joyfulness prevails after final judgment, with the righteous being in eternal glory. A key question then comes up. Jesus Christ and all saints are in eternal glory, but where is eternal glory? Whether one accepts premillennialism, postmillennialism, or amillennialism doesn't matter. All of the views flow into either an end-of-the-world or an end-of-the-age scenario. Some maintain eternal glory requires an "end to the world," as the righteous enter an unimaginable paradise. Others believe in an "end of the age," which provides for an enduring paradisical world around them. In the latter case, Earth remains in place.

A Questionable View of the "End of the World"

The end-of-the-world scenario is an event bringing about a physical termination of our world. The planets, moons, and Sun of our solar system, the stars of the Milky Way, other distant galaxies, and the universe at large are thought to disappear right before final judgment (Rev. 20:11). God executes a cataclysmic finish to what is familiar to the eye in order to establish his heavenly kingdom. This theological view espouses a physical end to Earth itself, where little, if any, familiarity with our time-honored planet and celestial sky remain. It is paradise in a realm completely unfamiliar to humans.

The evidence of the worldview is in today's end-time prophecies. Bible teachers regularly promote the idea of Earth's eradication after the second coming of Christ. The material domain is unnecessary in light of the spiritual kingdom of God. Apparently, God and the heavenly throne descending from the sky does not mix well with our planet, which has become obsolete. The timing of the cataclysmic event varies. Most believe the end of the world will occur immediately before final judgment. In any of the scenarios, the entire expanse of the universe is made unfashionable by the presence of God, with no further need of celestial bodies anywhere in the universe.

This type of earth-shattering prediction finds place in persuasive books such as *The Popular Encyclopedia of Biblical Prophecy*, coedited by Tim LaHaye, creator and coauthor of the *Left Behind* series. The text provides extensive material relating to eschatology. In his view, the second coming of Christ with the heavenly armies is made out to be an earth-shattering event. According to the text, "In the presence of this divine majesty, the earth and its immediate atmosphere vanish."[70] The end-of-the-world scenario has the planet and firmament completely disappearing. Any and all experience in the current world of existence has come to a close.

A cataclysmic ending to everything that human beings have come to love seems like an indifferent way to transition to a new heaven. The eradication of cities, towns, shorelines, state and national parks, and all the planet's natural beauty invalidates our most cherished memories. What scriptures do theologians and Bible scholars use to support such a disheartening view? The first passage is in Revelation 21:1–2, where the apostle John testifies to seeing a new heaven and a new earth:

> Then I saw a new heaven and a new earth; for the first heaven and the first earth had passed away, and the sea was no more. And I saw the holy city, the new Jerusalem, coming down out of heaven from God, prepared as a bride adorned for her husband.

The "new" in "a new heaven and a new earth" is the Greek adjective *kainos*, rather than *neos*. If John the apostle, the writer of Revelation, had made use of the adjective *neos*, then it would mean heaven and earth are brand new in origin. But *kainos* is found in the original language. The meaning of *kainos* is applied to something already there. It means giving freshness and renewal to an existing object. It does not refer to a completely new item. The selection of *kainos*, instead of *neos*, tells the reader that John does not have something brand new in mind. The passing away of the earth is a visual revitalization, refreshing, and beautification of the planet.

Another point of clarification is with the phrase "the sea was no more" (Rev. 21:1). John's wording does not mean the

---

70 Tim LaHaye and Ed Hindson, eds., *The Popular Encyclopedia of Bible Prophecy* (Eugene, OR: Harvest House, 2004), 126.

oceans of the world have dried up and that aquatic life has disappeared. The reader must grasp the verse in the context of the apostle being shown the New Jerusalem. The holy city has become an immense edifice encased by solid walls. According to the scriptures, the new city comes down out of heaven fully prepared. It is arriving intact to the earth's surface. Revelation 21:16 tells of the outer-wall casing being fifteen hundred miles in length, width, and height. Further, the metropolis walls are made of solid jasper that is 144 cubits or 72 yards thick.[71] Jasper is a hard, opaque, and finely polished gemstone with a reddish-brown hue.

The holy city would seem upon first reading to be in the shape of a cube, but further analysis allows one to accept a pyramid structure. In the case of a pyramid, the length and width of fifteen hundred miles would be at the base of a four-sided pyramid. The four walls of the pyramid would then taper up toward each other, touching at the highest point. A plumb bob from the top of the pyramid to a central point in the base would form the last dimension: a height of fifteen hundred miles. Other than having an extremely small base, the Transamerica building in San Francisco has a similar shape. Except for having three sides, the ancient pyramids of Egypt offer another model of the New Jerusalem.

The pyramid structure of the New Jerusalem would come down and sit on top of the existing site of Jerusalem in Israel. As the crow flies, Jerusalem is only forty miles from the sea. As such, the large structure coming down out of heaven would cover the entire nation of Israel and extend out into the Mediterranean Sea by over seven hundred miles. The holy city would sit on solid ground, requiring the waters of the eastern Mediterranean to dry up and be replaced

---

71 The apostle John's report of a rigid wall thickness of seventy-two feet is imprecise by civil engineering standards. For structural support of a fifteen-hundred-mile length to the side of the city, the walls would have to be much thicker.

by a large sediment buildup. It is easy to understand why John perceives of "no more sea." His observation is a local reference to the Israeli coast. It does not mean the oceans and waterways of planet Earth are gone.

A second passage that appears to connect the New Jerusalem to the "end of the world" is found in Revelation 21:23-26. It states:

> And the city has no need of sun or moon to shine on it, for the glory of God is its light, and its lamp is the Lamb. The nations will walk by its light, and the kings of the earth will bring their glory into it. Its gates will never be shut by day—and there will be no night there.

John's location must be taken into account when reading the verse. The apostle's vision is within the walls of the New Jerusalem. The city is a fully enclosed facility with opaque walls. In order for people to see and enjoy the surroundings, there needs to be a light source. A shining light of glory coming from God the Father and the Lamb will bring sufficient lighting to the city streets—and the lights will not go out. Yet it does not change the situation when someone is outside the city walls. The solar system will still be in place. As the third rock from the sun, the paradisiacal earth will still see sunshine by day and the moon will bring its light at night.

A third passage theologians use to support an end-of-the-world scenario is found in 2 Peter 3:6–7 and its continuation in verse 10. The first passage reads:

> through which the world of that time was deluged with water and perished. But by the same word the present heavens and earth have

been reserved for fire, being kept until the day
of judgment and destruction of the godless.

In looking closely at verses 6–7, the apostle is addressing Noah's flood, where the deluge of water causes disobedient people to perish. The reason for Noah's flood was primarily to destroy the godless and not the earth. By the same word [of God], he then sees the present heavens and earth reserved for fire, with the same goal of bringing ruin to the godless. So then, if the fire mirrors the same purpose as the water, why would it destroy the earth? If there are destructive blazes around the planet, the godless will perish, and the surroundings will remain as it did after the flood. The planet will then be eligible to undergo a renewing and refreshing.

Turning to 2 Peter 3:10, we read:

> But the day of the Lord will come like a thief, and then the heavens will pass away with a loud noise, and the elements will be dissolved with fire, and the earth and everything that is done on it will be disclosed.

The passage is very unusual because of the two phrases "the heavens will pass away with a loud noise" and "the elements will be dissolved with fire." In dealing with atypical expressions, it is best to find a cross-reference in another part of the Bible. A second reference is critical because end-of-the-world theology is at stake. Scripture interpreting scripture will help to understand the passage content. In searching the entire Bible, no similar phrase is found. As such, 2 Peter 3:10 lacks additional scriptural support. The two phrases contained in the passage become problematic. Scripture standing alone should never be a basis for formulating theological doctrine.

In summary, a review of passages supporting the

end-of-the-world scenario shows that it lacks convincing evidence. Fruitful integration cannot be achieved with this questionable theology. Though foreseen by some biblical scholars, the termination of the cosmos is presumptuous. God has no requirement set in place for destruction of the planet, the closing down of the Milky Way galaxy, or ending the universe at large. Over a billion years will remain for the Sun-Earth system to function normally. There is no valid reason for the heavens and the earth to suddenly disappear at the return of Christ in order to bring the saints into an unfamiliar heavenly environment.

A Reasonable View of the "End of the Age"

The earlier review of two human-induced catastrophes and four cosmic threats was shown to provide for a robust and enduring planet. A biblical end-of-the-age theology fully agrees with the science and allows for the continuation of a healthy, beautiful, and inviting world. It sees the new heaven and the new earth undergoing a renewing and refreshing after the apocalypse. The end result is the establishment of a long-lasting planet. The solar system, the Milky Way galaxy, and the entire cosmos will remain intact after the return of Christ. Safeguarding the very fabric of our creation plays a key role in the realization of an eternal paradise for all to enjoy.

Reasoning is the ability to formulate inferences, correlations, conclusions, and even judgments. It requires having convincing evidence. Reason will triumph when recognizing an end of the age, which brings forth the orderly and recognizable furtherance of our ecosystem. The destiny of the planet is one of recovery, renewal, and regeneration, following the institution of the kingdom of God on Earth. The removal of sinful behavior and banishment of the unrighteous results in an eternity of sinless perfection on Earth, which underscores the new age.

The records of human history provide evidence for a division of the ages. The earmarking for "ages" follows a definable pattern. It is when certain realities about life are present, and then a transition occurs, where new realities about life become clear and begin to flourish. Following the conversion to a new age, fresh ideas, worldviews, preferences, and pursuits become available to the peoples of the world, leading to new types of interests and activities for its citizens.

The three ages of Western history divide into (1) classical antiquity, (2) the Middle Ages, and (3) the modern era. The Middle Ages, or medieval period, provides a bridge between the ancient world and the modern world. The Middle Ages began in the fifth century with the fall of the Roman Empire. One of the highlights of the period was the isolation of Europe from the rest of the known world. The result was a society lax in general awareness, where superstition, rather than perception, ruled the thought life. The printing press as a means for circulating information had not come into being. As a result, the opinions, values, and activities of others could not be known.

Historical evidence is abundant for the conversion from the medieval to the modern era. It provides a clear example of an end to an age. The dawn of the new age came in the fifteenth century with the Renaissance, a long and complex cultural development affecting European life. Further maturation and enrichment would follow during the Age of Enlightenment. These movements had dramatic effects on the sciences, philosophy, religious thought, literature, and fine arts such as architecture, music, painting, and dance. Because lives and lifestyles changed dramatically in the transition, and then continued in a new social construct, the phrase "end of the age" applies.

The Bible presents an example of a spiritual "end of the

age" in the coming of Christ. 1 Peter 1:20, reads, "He was destined before the foundation of the world, but was revealed at the end of the ages for your sake." The life, death, and resurrection of Jesus Christ made an indelible mark in human history two thousand years ago. God's revelation of himself through the Son brought fulfillment to Hebrew Scriptures and paved the way for spiritual clarity and right relationship. The mercy, grace, and forgiveness offered through the cross brought the beginning of a new age. As a result, lives, hearts, and thinking processes altered throughout the known world.

The first passage supporting the end of the age is in the Great Commission of Matthew 28:16–20. These verses give the basic principles of Christian service by emphasizing baptism, ministry, and evangelism. In his final remark in Matthew 28:20, the Lord assures the disciples that he is always with them, even to the "end of the age." The Greek phrase, *sunteleías toú aioónós*, translates as "end of the age." The original KJV erroneously states the phrase as "end of the world," which is a source of concern. Fortunately, the NKJV translators provide a correction, saying "end of the age." The Greek word *aioónós* properly translates "age" and not "world."

The Lord's mention of the end of the age refers to the second coming. The appearing of Jesus will occur at the end of the modern era, ushering in sweeping changes around the globe. His arrival will be instantaneous and worldwide; visible to everyone living on the earth at the time. God's sovereign rule will change people's lives and bring permanent renewal to the surroundings. Following the final judgment, the new earth will form on our home planet, where immortal beings can enjoy family, friends, oceans, forests, flowers, animals, and the presence of God.

The Bible addresses the idea of the earth being a never-ending place in both the Old and New Testaments. The following six passages provide suitable cross-reference to one another, reinforcing the prophetic declaration of a continuation to our world. The end of the age is a transition into a fully restored planet, which becomes a lasting inheritance to the faithful. The following group of passages provides assurance to the reader of a proper interpretation:

> **Ps. 37:29**—"The righteous shall inherit the land, and live in it forever."

> **Eccl. 1:4**—"A generation goes, and a generation comes, but the earth remains forever."

> **Matt. 5:5**—"Blessed are the meek, for they will inherit the earth."

> **Matt. 6:10**—"Your kingdom come. Your will be done, on earth as it is in heaven."

> **Matt. 25:34**—"Then the king will say to those at his right hand, 'Come, you that are blessed by my Father, inherit the kingdom prepared for you from the foundation of the world;'"

> **Rev. 5:10**—"You have made them to be a kingdom and priests serving our God, and they will reign on earth."

Matthew 5:5 is taken from the Beatitudes, which is the introductory portion of the Sermon on the Mount. The blessings direct toward the disciples of Jesus. These individuals will share in final salvation. In the passage, the Lord is giving assurance of an inheritance to those who act meekly or are of a gentle spirit. An inheritance is a possession coming to an heir. The act of inheriting through succession means receiving a gift or some type of financial benefit. Jesus is pledging that his faithful followers will receive a permanent endowment on the earth. He does not elaborate whether it will be land, property, or a prominent administrative role.

Matthew 6:10 is part of the Lord's Prayer or "Our Father," which Jesus taught as a way of supplication to God. The petition is central to Christianity. It begins in verse 9 with the address, "Our Father in heaven, hallowed be your name" and continues with verse 10, "Your kingdom come. Your will be done, on earth as it is in heaven." Verse 10 asks the Father for two things. The first request is for God's kingdom to come to the earth. Second, it asks for God's will to be done on the earth. As such, the Father is hearing a request for his kingdom to show up on our home planet. Fully incorporated into church liturgy and voiced countless times, it is likely that God's kingdom will permanently come to the earth.

Revelation 5:10 is part of a chant being sung in heaven by twenty-four elders, who are standing before the Lamb. The apostle John witnesses the scene because he has been taken up into paradise and has a view of the throne of God. The verse points to the authority of redeemed people, who are consecrated as priests and given dominion over the earth. Righteous individuals will hold offices of trust and responsibility on the paradisical planet, helping to direct various affairs. Similar to an endowment, the declaration does not indicate a specific length of time for the rule, such as a millennium, but suggests an open-ended and enduring administrative position.

In summary, we go back to the beginning of the chapter, where we first looked at the left-hand side of Figure 2. The Bible and science work together to find truth in the creation timeline. The declaration of "In the beginning" (Gen. 1:1) implies a start to time itself. Astrophysics provides evidence for time having a start, which occurs at "t = 0." The Genesis creation story uses the Hebrew word *yôm* for "day," which can translate as a great length of time, such as an eon. Old Earth creationism accepts these day-ages, which works in step with the Big Bang expansion and physical cosmology. The findings show that God ordains science to aid in the understanding of biblical scriptures.

In looking at the right-hand side of Figure 2, a scientific review of human-induced and cosmic threats helps one to accept life on Earth surviving beyond a billion years. After that, God could maintain an existing state of affairs. One idea would involve keeping the sun in perpetuity by reallocating hydrogen to the core for use in fusion reactions. The biblical support for a continuing world comes from end-of-the-age theology. Jesus' statement that "the meek will inherit the earth," can be accepted as true. A key verse in Revelation 21:1 about "a new heaven and new earth" uses the Greek word *kainos* for new, implying the renewing and refreshing of an ongoing planet.

The entirety of Figure 2, which includes end-of-the-age theology, shows that the Bible and science can work together in fruitful integration to explain the world around us. Redeemed people can expect to live in a cosmic structure that will be long-lasting after the return of Christ. With the kingdom of God on the planet, you see the end of the church age and the beginning of a new age. God's kingdom and sovereign rule on a renewed Earth provides for the continuation and safeguarding of the environment. The restoration of our world will bring believers a place of future paradise. Venus and exoplanets will remain intact as well, making them available as places of banishment.

Chapter 5

The Soul and the Eternal Domain

For God alone my soul waits in silence,
for my hope is from him.

Psalm 62:5

Have you ever seen a painting with soul? In this regard, having soul means putting emotional and intellectual energy into an artistic project. The portrait or landscape is both inspirational and imaginative. Another meaning for soul is the nonmaterial or spiritual part of a human being, which is considered either temporal or immortal. This chapter examines the latter aspect—seeing the person as having an eternal soul. At death, the body becomes a cadaver, allowing the soul to depart into the next world in one of two directions. The paths contrast with one another and are irreversible in destiny.

A departing soul will move into a domain that expands his or her known universe. Interestingly, the soul does not leave the material universe, but goes into a higher existence within the cosmic structure. Eternity is the new home for a departing soul, but the eternal domain is not outside of space and time. It is not beyond the edge of the universe but is interactive with the physical domain. The soul experiences time as an integration of past, present, and future events. It experiences extra-dimensional space that is hidden and adjoining our three-dimensional world. The extra dimensions are tangible and play an active role in theoretical particle physics.

You can better believe that a departing soul remains connected to the universe if the soul permanently retains an aspect of the creation. In order to give evidence about this feature, the chapter will review the experimental work of Dr. Duncan MacDougall. His experiment shows how the departing soul retains measurable weight. Weight measured on the earth is mass subject to the force of gravity. The ability to reliably measure a soul's weight means the soul has a physical mass. Souls will have mass leaving the corpse because physical matter is necessary in the eternal domain. The soul having mass verifies eternity is an interactive part of the material universe.

The Soul and Resurrected Spiritual Body

A nonvisible soul residing inside a physical body is an idea that comes from both the secular and sacred realms. The secular concept originates from the earliest study of philosophy. The sacred originates in the Bible. The soul has a beginning with the creation of the first man, Adam. Genesis 2:7 reads, "Then the Lord God formed man from the dust of the ground, and breathed into his nostrils the breath of life; and the man became a living being." The word "being" (Heb. *nephesh*) can translate as "soul," which in the biblical context means a "living being," having vitality and life. In the passage, the soul appears to be the life-giving force for the body.

In regard to "the dust of the ground," the substance for the first man essentially comes from star dust. The nebula forming our Sun brought the basic elements to the planets. Earth's soil composition finds use as building blocks for the human body. God amasses the biological assembly through the molecular rearrangement of elements into complex organic compounds. Forming Adam into flesh did not create any life. Initially, he was a motionless corpse. God infused a vibrant soul into his lifeless body in order to create a living, breathing being. The soul contains the nonphysical aspects of the person, consisting of your mind, thoughts, character, and feelings.

In pursuit of the fundamental issues of life, philosophers have engaged in the analysis of our inner being. Important Greek thinkers such as Socrates and Plato taught about the existence of a soul, which contains the real and transcendent person. Each man held to the belief that a soul continues on after death. Aristotle thought the soul to be an integral part of the body, while considering the human intellect to be never-ending. Through systematic and rational argument, these intellectuals considered the soul to be the incorporeal essence of a person or living creature.

Ideas by later philosophers serve as the secular foundation for assigning a temporal existence to a person's soul. In exploring the dilemmas of the human mind, the field of psychology looks to natural philosophy. It is common in the study of the human psyche to reference the soul as the distinct, nonphysical, yet mortal aspect of an individual. In their work, a psychologist will allude to a patient having a soul. In part, the soul is the complex of human attributes, contributing to thoughts, attitudes, behaviors, and feelings, which can, at times, require professional support to function normally. According to secular psychology, the soul will ultimately expire with the death of the person.

The concept of a soul in the sacred and secular realms differs primarily because of the soul's longevity. In the secular view, the nonspiritual soul directs one's conscious and life functions. The soul remains a life-limited entity that cannot live on after physical death. The sacred view assigns awareness and life functions to the soul as well but adds in an everlasting feature, allowing the soul to spiritually depart the body after death. In both views, the soul references the mental underpinning and emotional makeup of the person. It contains the seat of the deepest and truest nature, giving a unique personality to the individual.

Regarding the sacred aspects, the Bible views the soul as eternal. It contains the mind or thoughts of an individual, their willpower or resolve, and the emotions behind a person's physical feelings. Every person born into the world arrives with an active inner soul. An extrapolation back in time would have the soul entering the world at the union of sperm and egg, assigning itself to the embryo. In calling the prophet Jeremiah, the Lord God proclaims in Jeremiah 1:5, "Before I formed you in the womb I knew you." The forming process includes the entire gestation period of nine months. Even during pregnancy, God knows the soul in the womb.

Scripture suggests a division of the human being into three distinct spheres: the body, the soul, and the spirit. In 1 Thessalonians 5:23, Paul gives a final exhortation to his fellow brothers and sisters, saying, "May the God of peace himself sanctify you entirely; and may your *spirit and soul and body* be kept sound and blameless at the coming of our Lord Jesus Christ." According to Paul, the spirit, the soul, and the body—each as a functioning entity—constitute the complete individual. The spirit is capable of being aware of God, while the soul has self-consciousness, and the body, working through the senses, has connectivity to the surrounding environment.

A living, breathing human being is a unity of body, soul, and spirit. When speaking about the body, this study considers the person from a temporal standpoint. When speaking of the soul or spirit, the text addresses the eternal aspects of the individual. The following illustration of concentric circles serves to illustrate a biblical view about the essence of a person. The temporal body is in gray, and the eternal soul and spirit are in white.

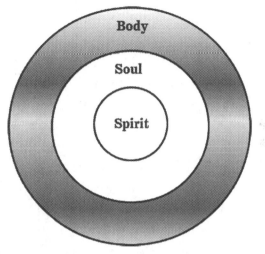

Figure 5
Depiction of Body, Soul, and Spirit

The inner circle represents the spirit, which has direct input into the operation of the soul. The spirit governs conscience, which instructs a person in judgment. It makes rulings toward particular thoughts, actions, and behaviors. The conscience governs the person by performing ethical functions, such as determining right from wrong. The spirit can act in an intuitive role as well, helping to discern the actions of others. The spirit or conscience of a believer can have awareness of God and be indwelled by the Holy Spirit. Paul brings this understanding to bear in Romans 9:1, saying, "I am speaking the truth in Christ—I am not lying; my conscience confirms it by the Holy Spirit."

The middle circle represents the aforementioned soul. In being the same shade of white, the soul and spirit are able to work in juxtaposition with one another. In one story about the early patriarchs of Israel (Abraham, Isaac, and Jacob) there is a mention of the soul leaving the body. In the life of Jacob, you read about the untimely death of his wife, Rachel, who passes during childbirth. The verse in Genesis 35:18 states, "As her soul was departing (for she died), she named him Ben-oni, but his father called him Benjamin." An important idea to remember from the tragic incident is the timing of the departure of Rachel's soul. It leaves precisely at her death.

The Hebrew Scriptures suggest a material form or physical outline to the soul. The natural appearance of the soul may exactly mirror or closely resemble the physical body of the person. When the first king of Israel, Saul, goes to the medium of Endor, he has a goal in mind. It is to call up the dead prophet Samuel in order to obtain information about his dire circumstances. When Saul asks the psychic to describe what she sees, 1 Samuel 28:13–14 gives her reply: "I see a divine being coming up out of the ground. . . An old man is coming up; he is wrapped in a robe." To the medium, the soul of the prophet Samuel emerges in the shape of a human body.

The outer gray circle represents the corporal aspects of an individual, containing the five senses of sight, hearing, smell, taste, and touch. The senses make contact with the material realm. Numerous biological systems operate within a person to ensure continual life and health. It is the job of the soul to nurture and care for the body. Still, the structure of a human anatomy, with its internal organs and extremities, will eventually grow old and die, returning to dust. A person is dualistic in the sense of having a temporal body but housing an eternal soul and spirit.

In discussing life after death and the eternal realm, the text will use the word "soul" to represent both "soul and spirit." As shown in Figure 6, the souls of the righteous and the unrighteous will depart the earthly surroundings, heading for either the celestial heaven or Hades. These two physical locations can accommodate the spiritual essence of the soul. The soul is an intermediate state of existence after death. In other words, it is our temporary mode of actuality after physical death, but before universal resurrection.

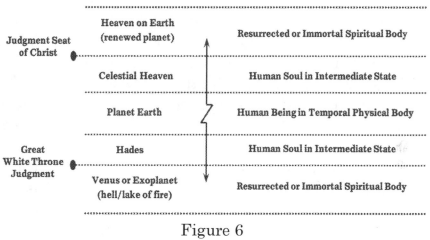

Figure 6
Dual Paths of the Spiritual World

The dual paths of the spiritual world are laid out vertically in Figure 6. Following the up arrow, the diagram shows the righteous soul in the intermediate state, residing in the celestial heaven. The term "celestial heaven" equates to the "third heaven" or paradise. In 2 Corinthians 12:2–4, Paul discusses being caught up in the third heaven and hearing things that no mortal should repeat. Most likely, Paul is describing an experience where he was brought up into the presence of God and his angels. The apostle John was also taken to heaven in Revelation and experienced seeing the throne of God. In all likelihood, Paul and John made these journeys to a material location in the universe.

The down arrow has the unrighteous soul going to Hades. In comparison to heaven, the dark netherworld of gloom is a diametrically opposed state of affairs. Hades is a place of separation from God. It is a form of incarceration that lacks any satisfaction or contentment. While awaiting final sentencing, human souls remain under detention in a dark and dreary world. As will be discussed in the next chapter, Hades is a physical location that likely situates in the center of the earth.

The return of Christ to Earth will bring an end to the intermediate state. It will be a time when every soul receives a promotion and is clothed with a resurrected spiritual body. Whether God will deem a person righteous or unrighteous does not change the fact that every soul will undergo transformation to an immortal body. For all human beings, final resurrection will result in either eternal life or eternal condemnation. As shown in Figure 6, the righteous will receive rewards at the judgment seat of Christ before traveling to the paradisical earth, while the unrighteous will face the great white throne judgment.

Resurrection is the process of going from a soul to an immortal spiritual body. It is the eternal destiny for all humanity. The resurrected body is the quintessential expression of being. Its design is fully functional and in perfect harmony with the surrounding physical environment. The essence is *immortal* in the ability to live on forever and ever. The essence is *spiritual* in the sense of retaining the attributes of the individual's soul and spirit. The essence is a *body* because it has the physical appearance and anatomical members appropriate for a human being. Paul's description of the resurrected spiritual body in 1 Corinthians 15:42–44 is as a superhuman body.

Following the resurrection, Jesus verifies his physical presence by allowing himself to be touched, and then later, by eating a piece of broiled fish. These and other activities fully authenticate his bodily resurrection, which is in the form of an immortal spiritual body. Jesus' resurrection brings with it a prototypical body for the afterlife. The body is made for habitation on a planet, whether it be Earth, Venus, or an exoplanet. For the saved, the provision of a resurrected spiritual body (following the up arrow) will make possible a joyous life on Earth. For the unsaved, the provision of a resurrected spiritual body (following the down arrow) will result in either a gloomy existence on Venus or an unspecified exoplanet.

Jesus validates the physical resurrection by using gravity. In full equilibrium, he stands and walks forward like a mortal being. Walking by his immortal spiritual body shows that it has balance and weight in a field of gravity provided by the earth and that it is biomechanically able to cooperate with the physics of a material environment. For life on other terrestrial worlds, the dynamics of having to walk around on the surface should not be a problem. For example, Venus has 90% of Earth's gravity, which will facilitate balance and easy forward motion. The high atmospheric pressure at the surface will compensate for the slightly lower force of gravity.

The Interactive Domain of Eternity

It is possible to view eternity and the physical universe as closely interactive with each other. Before the beginning of the cosmos, there was God's eternal realm. God then brought forth the Big Bang out of nothing. It began at t = 0 as an extremely small and infinitely dense point called the initial singularity, which was a concentrated energy source. With the energy expansion, the time, space, and matter of the material universe came into being. Along with the creation of the physical universe came eternity, wherein God and the spiritual world reside. The nothing was at the instant prior to creation and now moves to become the nothing that lies beyond the edge of the universe. The following flow in Figure 7 depicts the event.

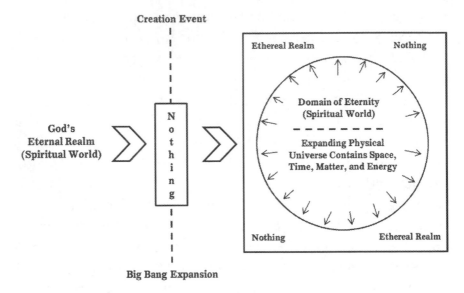

Figure 7
Flow of God's Eternal Realm during Creation Event

The meaning of "eternal" is from the Greek word *aionios*, which simply means "without beginning or end." As such, eternity does not suggest a distinct place. During the Big Bang's expansion out of nothing (*ex nihilo*), God's eternal realm enters the universe. God and spiritual beings come into our physical world, along with the properties of co-presence and higher spatial dimensions. The domain of eternity is now interactive with the material universe. Lying dormant beyond the edge of the universe is the ethereal realm of nothing.

The concept of eternity being integral to the material world has a biblical basis. Let's examine the following two passages:

> **Acts 17:26–27**—"From one ancestor he made
> all nations to inhabit the whole earth. . . so that
> they would search for God and perhaps grope

for him and find him—though indeed he is not far from each one of us."

Eph 1:9–10—"He has made known to us the mystery of his will, according to his good pleasure that he set forth in Christ, as a plan for the fullness of time, to gather up all things in him, things in heaven and things on earth."

The apostle Paul tells Greek idol worshippers in Acts 17:26–27 that they can grope for God because of his close proximity. The statement implies an adjoining connection between eternity and the physical universe. Later, in Ephesians 1:10, Paul reveals God's plans to gather together all things in Christ—the spiritual things of heaven and the material things of the earth. The passage indicates a confluence of the visible and invisible worlds, where all things are finally revealed. The following table shows how the properties of eternity and the physical universe work together.

	Properties of the Physical Universe, Eternity, and Ethereal Domains				
	Dimension of Space	Dimension of Time	Property of Mass	Force of Gravity	Additional Comments
Physical Universe	Three dimensional space (x, y, z)	Fourth dimension of time (t)	Yes	Yes	Miracles of Jesus and supernatural events of the Bible are due to intertwining of physical universe and eternity.
Eternity	Extra-dimensional space	Past-present-future of co-presence	Yes	Yes	
Ethereal	Outside spatial dimensions	Independent of time	No	No	No connection to physical universe

Table 2
Comparison of Physical Universe,
Eternity, and the Ethereal

A review of Table 2 begins with the domain of the physical universe (first row). The absolutes in our world are the dimensions of space and time, as well as the property of mass and the force of gravity. In the second row, eternity connects with the creation via extra-dimensional space and the past-present-future makeup of co-presence. It will also contain the property of mass and the force of gravity. Eternity ties into our world in these four tangible ways. The concept is essential for a God who is part of our lives. As will be shown, the miracles and supernatural events of the Bible can be due to the intertwining of the material universe and eternity.

The ethereal is the third domain in the chart (third row). Before the creation event, God's eternal realm was the spiritual domain. After the Big Bang energy burst out of nothing (*ex nihilo*), eternity became part of the expanding universe, leaving the ethereal to situate beyond the edge of the universe. The Big Bang results in an observable universe 93 billion light-years across. Going many billions of light-years beyond this point will result in possibly reaching the edge of the universe. If an edge exists, then going past the edge will reach the ethereal realm or the nothing. The state will have no spatial dimensions, no flow of time, no material substance, and no force of gravity.

When Bible teachers declare God to be "outside the universe," they are unintentionally proclaiming him to be in the nothingness of the ethereal. The ethereal is not a domain for either a physical or a spiritual being because it lacks properties. If spiritual beings or habitations were in the ethereal, they would have no ability to consider time and be without mass and space. When looking at the domains of eternity and the ethereal, one sees a clear-cut divide, showing what conditions are like either inside or outside the material universe. This section will show that the best place for the eternal realm to exist is as an intricate part of the cosmos.

God has freely chosen to enter the universe and be part of his creation.

The domain of eternity contains co-presence, with its past-present-future makeup. The physical universe receives a portion of the higher dimensional time as ordinary time. The material universe is chronological, directly aligning with ordinary time. Time flows forward in one direction, locking history in its place. The present moves from moment to moment with a past and an impending future. In eternity, ordinary time is part of co-presence, which integrates events into a past-present-future framework. If spiritual beings were in the ethereal, rather than eternity, no connection between time and co-presence could be made.

Why is "time in eternity" shown as co-presence? Shouldn't a past-present-future makeup be strictly thought of as a "higher time dimension," which aligns with higher spatial dimensions? While this seems reasonable, a shortcoming exists. Science cannot work with extra-dimensional time. String theory physicists have looked for extra time dimensions, but without positive results.[72] Unlike extra spatial dimensions, extra time dimensions are not part of current theoretical research. So, the spiritual term of co-presence is a relevant term for higher time dimensions. As discussed earlier, co-presence is a theological construct providing the basis for time in eternity.

Science may not utilize extra-dimensional time, but the idea of a "higher time" in eternity finds evidence in the life of the believer. Christians conceive of co-presence in the very act of praying. How can God listen to and sort out thousands of prayer requests arriving at once? The answer lies in the

---

72 Brian Greene, *The Elegant Universe: Superstrings, Hidden Dimensions, and the Quest for the Ultimate Theory, 2ⁿᵈ ed.* (W. W. Norton & Company, 2010), chap. 8, Kindle.

ability of God to operate in at least one extra time dimension.[73] Otherwise, it would be an impossible task. Going further, the Bible speaks of God allowing all humans to have free will. In accepting this truth, how can God foresee a confluence of people's actions leading to outcomes he chooses to control by his providence? The activity would require a third time dimension to be at work.

In Revelation 1:8 one reads, "'I am the Alpha and the Omega,'" says the Lord God, "'who is and who was and who is to come, the Almighty.'" The passage is a prelude to the predictive nature of the book of Revelation. It suggests that as the great "I AM," the Lord God can work freely within any dimension of time. As such, the past-present-future makeup of the Almighty allows him to maintain the truth of the Word, while making room for individual self-determination. These concepts attest to the spiritual significance of extra time dimensions.

In terms of extra or higher spatial dimensions, there seems to be both biblical and scientific support. To begin with, everyone can understand and appreciate physical space. It is the ability to have some elbow room. The Big Bang event began the creation of three-dimensional space, which houses galaxies, stars, and planets. In our world, tangible space creates discrete habitations for humans to grow up and flourish. We live, breathe, and move about because of available 3-D space. At the same time, the realm of eternity exists spatially in our world by way of extra-dimensional space.

So, in what ways are the extra dimensions of space evident in the world around us? This text will work with examples from the Bible first, then science. In terms of the scriptures, one can look at the supernatural acts of Jesus to see how

---

73 Two dimensions of time give God the ability to hear prayers simultaneously. Hugh Ross, *Beyond the Cosmos: The Transdimensionality of God,* 3rd ed. (Covina, CA: RTB Press, 2017), chap. 13, Kindle.

the higher spatial dimensions of eternity function in our universe. In the next section, the focus will be on quantum mechanics, where extra spatial dimensions are active, but hidden in the universe. Being hidden means the dimensions are obscure to the observer, but fully present and operative. The dimensions are not visibly perceptible except by noting the influences and outcomes they have in particle physics.

A reader can pick out certain acts of Jesus during his ministry that reveal hidden spatial dimensions. The Lord is in a body of flesh and bone, yet he is able to access the dimensions when necessary. In his hometown of Nazareth, Jesus preaches a sermon on the Sabbath that is offensive to those in the synagogue. The crowd becomes angry and decides to lead Jesus to the edge of a cliff and throw him off. In that moment, Luke 4:30 says, "He passed through the midst of them and went on his way." Jesus seems to move into the higher spatial dimensions of eternity and walk through the mob, avoiding contact with bodies in the physical world.

Following the resurrection, Jesus continues to have access to the higher dimensions of eternity while modeling a resurrected spiritual body. On the road to Emmaus, he walks with two grief-stricken men traveling to a village. In the dialogue, he teaches from the scriptures as to why the Messiah had to suffer before entering into glory. After sitting down to have dinner with the men, Jesus takes bread, blesses it, breaks it, and gives it to eat. Luke 24:31 then tells the reader, "he vanished from their sight." The Lord's disappearance was instantaneous. An explanation could be his moving into the higher spatial dimensions of eternity.

A second example of extra spatial dimension access after the resurrection is shown in John 20:19 and 20:26. In the first passage, the disciples gather behind locked doors without Thomas. In the next passage, a week later, the disciples gather behind locked doors with Thomas. In each case, Jesus suddenly appears by coming through doors that are shut tight in order to stand among them. The Lord appears in material form without any entrance available. Coming from the hidden, higher spatial dimensions of eternity into the 3-D physical space of a locked home can explain why Jesus does not have a problem going through walls or obstacles.

Let's apply the properties of mass and gravity to a biblical scenario. During the transfiguration, Jesus turns radiantly white upon a mountain top, with the spiritual bodies of Moses and Elijah next to him. Moses and Elijah appear to have bodily weight, subject to the law of gravity. The gravity acts on their mass, allowing their spiritual body to stand firmly next to Jesus. The figures are not floating in air. The men have material substance, and the mass is held in place by gravity. The question becomes, "Do Moses and Elijah have the same bodily mass in the eternal state?" In an upcoming section, the discovery of soul substance will bring clear evidence for mass being in eternity.

A final point regards what will happen at the end of the age. At that time, the second coming of Christ occurs with the saints. All spiritual beings returning with the Lord will be seen by the human eye, with the extra dimensions of eternity becoming visible in the physical world. The uniting will include all properties. Ordinary time will move into time as co-presence, with its past-present-future makeup. Angels and resurrected people alike will be made visible and retain material substance, just as the risen Christ displayed. Having mass means being subject to gravity, which will hold all entities firmly to the earth's surface.

In summarizing Figure 7 and Table 2, one can consider the universe and the eternal realm as intertwining. The idea of eternity being part of the physical world and having a space, time, and mass-gravity connection provides input into the Fruitful Integration model. The miracles of Jesus give a hint to the metaphysical insight of extra-dimensional space. He came in the flesh but had access to the space and time of eternity. During his ministry, he was able to walk through crowds. After the resurrection, he could appear and disappear at will and was able to traverse solid objects. During the entire time, Jesus had mass and was subject to the gravity of the planet.

The teaching of heaven or hell being outside the universe is not rational because the ethereal realm does not contain space, time, matter, or energy. The ethereal is by definition outside of spatial dimensions, free of time, and lacking in mass and gravity. Any domain lacking in these features cannot reasonably connect or interact with the physical world. One should expect eternal locations to be in tangible places that are within the confines of the Big Bang expansion; that is, within the observable and "yet to be observed" material universe. As such, the third heaven, the confinement of Hades, the lake of fire, and the future paradisical earth can situate in the cosmos.

If the universe and eternity coexist mutually and share properties, then it allows us to rethink matters. It suggests that planetary bodies in the night sky, which contain mass and gravity, can become habitations for spiritual beings. This is true for both righteous and unrighteous individuals, each of whom has physical mass. Two objects—one being the spiritual entity and the other being a planetary body—will be linked to each other by the force of gravity. Within the space-time continuum, our world can contain the current Hades and the future paradisical earth. Additionally, other planets in the solar system, or even exoplanets, can house the third heaven and the lake of fire.

Extra-Dimensional Space in Quantum Physics

This section provides background for why science considers extra-dimensional space as real, yet hidden from the world. Current research in particle physics is using extra spatial dimensions to understand the small and the invisible. Higher spatial dimensions are not imaginary, but rather are a concept physicists use in attempting to solve real-world quantum mechanics problems. While extra spatial dimensions find acceptance in modeling the world of subatomic particles, no parallel path can be found for using extra time dimensions.

The discipline of particle physics began in the early twentieth century with the discovery of the atom and its most notable constituents; the proton, neutron, and electron. The three particles were originally thought to be the basic building blocks of the atom. As it turns out, these components were only the tip of the iceberg. In the 1930s, scientists began examining metal plates hit by cosmic rays from outer space. Bursting out of the impact were fragments that were even smaller than protons, neutrons, and electrons. These fundamental or elementary particles required further investigation.

In order to carry out this type of study, equipment has to accelerate particles and examine the debris arising from atomic collisions. Making an entrance into scientific research was the particle accelerator or atom smasher. The atom smasher provides the mechanism to speed up particles to great kinetic energy in order to observe a high velocity, head-on crash of target atoms. The impact releases various fragments and forces that hold the atom together. The testing is ongoing. Crashing protons into protons or heavy ions into heavy ions is one of the final frontiers of modern physics, with test results shared between scientists around the world.

The world's biggest and most powerful atom smasher is the Large Hadron Collider (LHC), which sits beneath the France-Switzerland border. This particle collider, with a circumference of seventeen miles, is the most complex investigative facility ever built.[74] The underground compound includes piping, magnets, targets, detectors, computers, and manned data centers for digital reconstruction of collision events. The detector unit is a giant cylinder over sixty feet long and forty-five feet in diameter. Layered like an air or water filter, the unit tracks and captures debris from atomic collisions. Shrapnel creates signatures, giving clues of emitted matter and energy. The venture makes for enticing new physics.

Atom smashing results in the creative mapping of the Standard Model of particle physics, shown in Figure 8. The chart appears like a miniature version of the periodic table of elements from chemistry. In its entirety, the Standard Model is a collection of essential theories describing the behavior of elementary particles. Developed in stages beginning in the latter half of the twentieth century, it incorporates all that is known about subatomic particles. Some of the particles exist for only fractions of a second, while other particles combine to form more stable, composite particles. The model also contains three of the four fundamental forces found in nature.

---

74 The test facility became operational in September 2008. The collaborative effort includes participation by over 10,000 scientists worldwide. CERN *Accelerating Science*, "The Large Hadron Collider," https://home.cern/science/accelerators/large-hadron-collider (accessed Nov. 8, 2020).

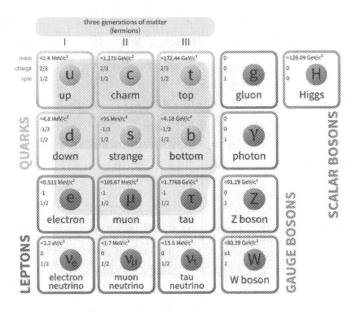

Figure 8
The Standard Model of Particle Physics[75]

The first three columns (I, II, and III) are fermions. These particles are the basic building blocks of all matter. Fermions are divided between quarks (rows one and two) and leptons (rows three and four). Quark pairs are seen in up–down, charm–strange, and top–bottom. Quarks combine to form the particles in the atomic nuclei. A proton consists of two up quarks and a down quark, while a neutron consists of two down quarks and an up quark. The leptons in row three are the negatively charged electrons, with the muon and tau being heavier versions of the electron. The leptons in row four are neutrinos. Neutrinos are neutral versions of the electron, muon, and tau.

The fourth column is set apart for gauge bosons, which are carriers of three of the four fundamental forces of

---

75 As a single concept, the Standard Model is an incredible achievement, but it lacks unity without gravity. Robert Oerter, *The Theory of Almost Everything: The Standard Model, the Unsung Triumph of Modern Physics* (New York: Pearson Educational, Inc., 2006), 204.

nature. The three fundamental forces are the strong, the electromagnetic, and the weak. The gluon represents the strong force. The strong force keeps the nucleus of positive charge protons together (++) that would normally repel one another. The photon represents the electromagnetic force. The electromagnetic force occurs because of the interaction of positive and negative charges. It is most evident in the (+) and (-) poles in magnetism. Together as gauge bosons, the Z boson and the W boson are the weak force. The weak force governs interaction and exchanges between subatomic particles and is responsible for radioactive decay.

Sitting alone in the fifth column is the only known scalar boson, which is called the Higgs boson. A scalar boson is a boson whose spin equals zero. Occupying the minds of physicists for nearly fifty years was the search for the Higgs boson. The long-sought-after particle was first theorized by Peter Higgs in 1964, but it took the construction of the LHC to uncover its existence in 2012. The Higgs boson is a massive particle that appears and then decays almost immediately. It is given credit for being the "origin of mass" for all other elementary particles that have mass.

Omitted from the model is the fourth fundamental force, which is gravity. Gravity is the force of attraction between two bodies. It holds people to the planet. Effort to combine all four fundamental forces together and create a universal model goes back to the time of Albert Einstein. A universal model is desirable because it would explain the complete interactive workings of the physical universe. In the 1960s, the electromagnetic force and the weak force were joined into the "electroweak" force. The current effort is to combine the strong force with the electroweak force. It is labeled the Grand Unified Theory (GUT). The GUT would fully assimilate the Standard Model of Figure 8.

The highest level of assimilation attempts to combine the Standard Model with the force of gravity. Together, it will achieve what is known as the Theory of Everything (ToE). In order to bring gravity into the Standard Model, a hypothetical particle must represent the force. Enter the "graviton," which is the force-carrying particle of gravity. Although not yet found, the graviton is the particle that merges gravity into the ToE effort. The graviton will help incorporate Albert Einstein's theory of general relativity, which describes gravity on a large scale. Therefore, the ToE brings together quantum physics and general relativity, which is the ultimate goal.

Extra spatial dimensions enter the realm of science when attempting to find a solution to the ToE. Ongoing research into the ToE uses the analytical approach of string theory, which later developed into superstring theory. Five superstring theories work to bring harmony between quantum mechanics and general relativity by redesigning particles in the Standard Model.[76] All particles become tiny vibrating strings, with a specific type of vibration corresponding to different particles. The broad use of vibrating strings provides symmetry. The desire is to combine the three forces (represented by the gluon, the photon, and the Z and W boson) with the fourth graviton force.

Calculations using superstring theory require the presence of not three but *nine* spatial dimensions, plus a time dimension. The higher dimensions may be on a small or large scale and hidden from view. Accepting nine spatial dimensions in these formulations is a metaphysical assertion. Experimental data cannot confirm their presence. The concept of eternity being integral in the material world via extra spatial dimensions (Table 2) uses the same metaphysics. These assertions by string theorists and theologians go

---

76 A unifying theory known as M-theory brings five separate superstring theories together. Brian Greene, *The Elegant Universe: Superstrings, Hidden Dimensions, and the Quest for the Ultimate Theory*, 2nd ed. (W. W. Norton & Company, 2010), chap. 8, Kindle.

hand-in-hand. Science and biblical theology work in tandem to draw the same ontological conclusions about higher, hidden spatial dimensions.

In the next section, the study of the hierarchy problem will add credence to the presence of at least one higher spatial dimension. The extra spatial dimension will find detection through "mass-gravity dilution."

The Hierarchy Problem

The second area of research using extra spatial dimensions attempts to solve the hierarchy problem. The hierarchy problem works to unravel concerns over both the Higgs boson and the graviton. In terms of the graviton, one dilemma is in the large difference between gravity and the three Standard Model forces. Gravity may appear like a powerful force because it holds humans firmly to the earth. But compared with the other three forces, it is quite trivial. Scientists are puzzled as to why the weak force is 10^{24} times as powerful as gravity, and why the electromagnetic force is 10^{35} times as powerful as gravity, and why the strong force is 10^{37} times as powerful as gravity.

Harvard University theorist Lisa Randall explores how particle physics can help us understand the basic nature of the universe. Working solutions to the hierarchy problem requires understanding why gravity is so insignificant compared to the weak force. In addressing the issue, she finds application for using one large extra spatial dimension.[77] The Randall-Sundrum models are a product of her research. These models describe a world containing a warped geometry with 3+1 spatial dimensions.

Randall focuses on particles with extremely low mass

---

77 Lisa Randall, *Knocking on Heaven's Door: How Physics and Scientific Thinking Illuminate the Universe and the Modern World* (New York: HarperCollins Publishers, 2012), 323.

that are situated in abnormal gravity fields. Amazingly, her findings uncover quantities of mass and gravity *migrating* into an extra (+1) dimension. The migration could be one reason why gravity is so weak compared to the other three forces. Mass and gravity moving into the extra (+1) dimension adds credence in particle physics to the presence of higher spatial dimensions. Using a theological lens, the migration of this subatomic mass adds validity to (1) supernatural events in the Bible being possible because of higher spatial dimensions and (2) eternity being an interactive part of the physical universe.

In summary, the search for a ToE using superstring theory, and the Randall study of the hierarchy problem, each find science using metaphysics in the assertion of extra spatial dimensions. The Randall-Sundrum model has some evidence for mass and gravity migration into one extra spatial dimension. It is a place where mass and gravity find a home. To the particle physicist, extra spatial dimensions have a place in this world. Legitimacy is given to eternity intertwining with the physical universe when theoretical physicists use higher spatial dimensions to unravel the mysteries of subatomic particles, which directly connect to our world.

The Discovery of Soul Substance

The cosmos is composed of ordinary matter, dark matter, and dark energy. Ordinary matter is understood as the typical matter we see and touch. It includes stars and planets, making up a small 4.9% of the cosmic structure. Dark matter comprises 26.8% and is detected by the gravity effects it has on visible matter. Dark energy contains the remaining 68.3% of the mass. Dark energy aids in the universe's expansion rate. Just like matter, energy itself has tangible mass. Dark energy, or any energy, has mass according to the principle of mass-energy equivalence ($E = mc^2$). The idea of having mass is the most fundamental aspect of being in the universe.

This section will show that physical mass is also part of the eternal realm. The study of an individual's departing soul will demonstrate the intertwining of eternity and the physical universe because the soul will have measurable weight. If a soul departs the body and enters into eternity with mass, it will continue to have linkage to the material universe. The soul will have mass in order to utilize co-presence, extra spatial dimensions, and the mass-gravity present in both realms. The idea of the third heaven, Hades, and the lake of fire being in the material universe will also relate to the idea of a soul needing to have mass.

Before delving into the test results, let's look for theological evidence as to why God may want to forever connect to the cosmos. First, one can see his unwavering willingness in the arrival of Jesus. The redemption of humankind required God to become mortal. When God was born into the world through the Son, he staked a claim in our physical world. From infant to adult, his development allowed for implanting all the social skills necessary for being human, while having to interact fully with the environmental elements of the natural world. His memories of being a child, having parents, growing up with brothers and sisters, finding a craft as a carpenter, and entering into ministry are all an indelible part of his memory on the earth.

After the resurrection, Jesus talks to, touches, and eats with the disciples, while appearing in physical form. He wants to give assurance that he is real and has not lost contact with his human origin, while also modeling the immortal spiritual body. Later in the book of Revelation, the glorified Jesus appears to John in final form. He is shiny white but unchanged in his physical structure. He is still a human being and touches John to give him the assurance of physical permanence. The entirety of his human connection sends a message. From his birth to becoming the everlasting God-man, the Lord Jesus Christ is providing proof of his eternal connection to the material universe.

A second reason is the end-time arrival of the heavenly throne to the paradisical earth, which relates to the continuation of a beautiful and inviting world. In the context of end-of-the-age theology, the event is a permanent affair. The continental land mass of Asia contains the nation of Israel and the city of Jerusalem, which will become the holy city of New Jerusalem.[78] God loves Jerusalem and intends on living in the city for all eternity. The strategy of bringing a large, glorious, and fully functioning holy place to the earth means the kingdom of God has chosen to reside in the material universe. The temple of the New Jerusalem contains the heavenly throne of God and signifies the earth is God's home—not just another planet in the universe.

The Mass of the Human Soul

In order to give support for mass being in eternity, this section will show the departing human soul has measurable weight, subject to the laws of gravity. Souls contain physical matter because mass has a purpose. The mass has use in eternity because eternity is part of the physical universe. If the ethereal was the final destination, the soul would have no reason to contain mass leaving the corpse. It would have zero mass because the ethereal realm is nothing and demands nothing of the physical world. On the other hand, the eternal realm requires mass in order for spiritual beings to gravitationally connect to other forms of mass, such as planets.

---

78 In Rev. 21:2, the New Jerusalem coming down out of heaven foreshadows the transformation of the entire earth. The planet will be made perfect in order to facilitate a proper habitation for the kingdom of God. Coogan, *New Oxford Annotated Bible*, 446 [NT].

The study begins by considering that the human soul is made up of physical matter. The matter is called "soul substance." To preserve one's natural makeup, it is reasonable to believe DNA, the carrier of the genetic code of life, replicates in soul substance. As such, soul substance will come from the body. What it is made of cannot be known. A safe guess is accepting that the basic elements of the Standard Model will form the building blocks of the soul. Soul substance can include elementary particles such as quarks, leptons, and bosons. Although the exact makeup is not clear, the soul will have quantifiable weight and occupy physical space.

The departure of the soul from the body will result in a journey to a place in the universe. If the soul has mass, it not only takes up physical space but will be bound by gravity. Ultimately, the soul requires a material destination, so it can be tied gravitationally to its surroundings. As such, soul substance having weight validates the link between eternity and the material universe. The findings will disqualify the ethereal domain as the final destination. The journey's end will either be in the third heaven or in Hades, both of which reside in the space-time continuum.

The experimental proof for soul substance centers on the early twentieth century research of Duncan MacDougall, MD, of Haverhill, Massachusetts. The premise of his report asserts the following: if the psychic functions of the mind continue after bodily death, then the content of those functions must exist in a space-occupying soul. The space-occupying soul coming from the body must include physical mass and be subject to the laws of gravity. Contained in the soul is personal identity; that is, one's personality and consciousness, the essence of which MacDougall calls soul substance.[79]

According to MacDougall, the journey for the soul into the afterlife begins at the point of death with its departure from the body. His test setup uses closely monitored and controlled conditions to detect the departure. Within the framework, he expects to perform valid investigation and data gathering on patients passing into the next world. He suspects that immediately following death, a small loss of body weight occurs. The minor weight loss is thought to represent the departure of the soul from the physical body. Ultimately, MacDougall's final test report, published in 1907, can provide scientific proof that the soul has measurable weight.[80]

In the report, MacDougall must refute the notion of soul substance consisting of aether. At the turn of the twentieth century, "aether theory" was a popular belief. It held that a medium of zero mass exists in outer space, wherein light and energy can travel. The hypothesis was later proven false by Einstein's theory of special relativity. MacDougall goes on to state that soul substance has to be organically linked to the human body and have weight under the force of Earth's gravity. If the body is subject to gravity, so is the soul, even as it leaves a deceased body. He concludes in his pretest hypothesis that detection of the soul's departure is possible with proper instrumentation.

The medical journal article allows one to envision MacDougall's test setup and procedure. Placement of dying patients is on a stable, overhead platform containing a bed, pillow, and bed sheets. Below the raised area is the test team. The critical tool is a sensitive scale that balances by sliding a

---

79 Soul substance is the mass of the soul itself. Duncan MacDougall, "Hypothesis Concerning Soul Substance Together with Experimental Evidence of the Existence of Such Substance," American Society for Physical Research, 1, No. 5 (May 1907), 237.

80 MacDougal, 237–244.

small weight. The sliding weight rides on an arm that extends into a slotted cutout at the end. The technician adjusts the sliding weight to achieve central flotation of the arm, which moves up and down inside the slot. The highly responsive "beam and poise" model allows for visual monitoring and quick adjusting of the sliding scale, which gives an accurate indication of weight gain or loss.

It is important to note the timing for the release of the weighing tool to the marketplace. The scale became commercially available for sale in 1904, and amazingly, the basic design is still in widespread use today. Because of its precision, similar-type scales find modern-day application at the doctor's office or at one's gym or fitness center. In the early twentieth century, the balancing mechanism was cutting-edge technology. Introduced by the Toledo Computing Scale Company, the floating arm scale uses the counterbalance method, where weight compensates for weight. It is a blueprint for accuracy, reliability, and repeatability.[81]

The end of a metal arm passing through a metal slot not only allows for the up and down centering of the arm but provides an audible noise when the arm suddenly moves to strike either the top or bottom of the slot. Before the test begins, scale calibration and sensitivity are known. With a centered arm, it took 0.2 oz (5.7 grams) of added weight to drop the beam to the bottom of the slot. Conversely, removing 0.2 oz (5.7 grams) would lift the arm to the top of the slot. When a slight weight change occurs, it results in a sudden metal-on-metal audible hit to the slot by the arm. Scale rebalancing quickly follows. The rebalancing centers the arm for test continuation and allows for calculation of weight loss.

---

81 Before 1900, the spring tension scale was the primary method for weighing objects. Spring tension accuracy varies with temperature and the springs tend to fatigue over time. The shortcomings made the new balance scale far superior. The company slogan for the product was "No Springs, Honest Weight."

The experiment begins after placing an individual on the overhead platform and balancing the beam. A summary of the test results for patients who die naturally during the experiment is presented in Table 3:

	Gender of the Patient	Sudden and Ensuing Losses (ounces)	Total Weight Loss (grams)	Final Notes
1	Male	0.75 oz. with no ensuing loss	21.3 g	Sudden drop of 21.3 g at death.
2	Male	0.5 oz. with 1 oz. 50 grains ensuing loss	14.2 + 31.5 = 45.7 g	Sudden drop of 14.2 g with ensuing loss of 31.5 g.
3	Male	0.5 oz. with 1 oz. ensuing loss	14.2 + 28.3 = 42.5 g	Sudden drop of 14.2 g with ensuing loss of 28.3 g.
4	Female	No data	No data	External interference with test.
5	Male	0.375 oz. with no ensuing loss	10.6 g	Sudden drop of 10.6 g at death.
6	Not reported	Test failed	Test failed	Patient died during final scale beam adjustment.

Table 3
Summary of MacDougall's Experimental Results

The results in Table 3 indicate that six patients were subjected to the test. The first column shows the number of patients and whether the patient was male or female. The last entry was not reported. The second column shows the sudden and ensuing weight losses following death and is given in ounces. The ensuing losses occur over several seconds following the initial loss. The third column mathematically summarizes the activity while converting the weight from ounces to grams. Grams provide finer granularity to the data. The final notes in the fourth column summarize the series of events, including the weight loss in grams for each patient.

The four male patients provide the core of the information. The record shows a sudden and major decrease in weight loss for all patients at the time of death. In terms of the sudden weight change numbers, patient 1 lost 21.3 grams, patient 2 lost 14.2 grams, patient 3 lost 14.2 grams, and patient 5 lost 10.6 grams. The passing away of patient 4 (female) and patient 6 (gender unknown) provides no input to the experiment. The female patient could not contribute to the test because of an unknown external test interference. Patient 6 died during the final scale beam adjustment.

Male patients 1 and 5 have a sudden loss of weight, with no ensuing weight loss. Male patients 2 and 3 have a sudden weight loss and then an ensuing weight loss. Since the ensuing weight loss is reported to have occurred over several seconds, we can attribute the added loss to a continuing life-to-death transition. The important takeaway is that patients 2 and 3 have sudden weight losses similar to patients 1 and 5. The complete range of sudden and ensuing weight loss is between 10.6 grams and 45.7 grams. The initial assessment tells us the MacDougall test is convincing about bodily weight loss occurring at the expected departure time of the soul.

With respect to the social ethics of the test, I am quite sensitive to the fact that using dying people in an experiment is a rather unsympathetic, even morbid undertaking. You may ask, "Who are these people?" The answer is that we do not know. Should not family, friends, nurses, and doctors be comforting these individuals in their final hour? Well, I think the answer is certainly yes! The only detail from the test report is that these individuals bravely volunteered and gave consent to the experiment weeks before death and that the test did not subject the patients to any additional suffering.[82]

The research by MacDougall attempts to follow the scientific method of data acquisition. To be termed scientific, the process of investigation must utilize observable and measurable data, subject to principles of human reason. The primary goal of scientific test methodology is to meticulously accumulate selective information in the form of numerical data. The statistics must not only be accurate, but repeatable. Scientific methods of investigation mandate that testing be performed under controlled conditions. Being able to reproduce the test setup in future experiments using similar equipment is part of the overall objective.

Discussing the findings requires removing any apprehension or doubt surrounding the validity of the experiment. People can be skeptical about a test conducted in the early 1900s. A research report dating back over one hundred years may seem archaic to some, casting doubt on the conclusions. Some skeptics have thought the test setup to be unstable. Others are not completely convinced the weighing system was isolated from perturbations in the human body or from the surrounding environment. Since the exact test has not been repeated, misgivings can abound over the test setup.

Important research shows there is no solid basis for rejecting the test. In 2010, the *Journal of Scientific Exploration* published an in-depth, technical report. Written by Masayoshi Ishida, it mathematically addresses the various criticisms expressed over Dr. MacDougall's experiment. Ishida uses the proper analytical and scientific approach for understanding MacDougall's test setup, capabilities, and parameters.[83] He

---

82 MacDougal, 238–239.

83 Masayoshi Ishida, "Rebuttal to Claimed Refutations of Duncan MacDougall's Experiment on Human Weight Change at the Moment of Death," *Journal of Scientific Exploration*, 24, No. 1 (Spring 2010): 5–39.

successfully addresses the following negative critiques from times past:

1. The experiment was not adequately controlled because of perspiration loss and air currents.
2. The time of death of the patients could not be accurately discerned.
3. The ability to measure weight changes was too imprecise.
4. The cessation of breathing and heartbeat after death may explain the missing weight.
5. Postmortem body swelling creates a buoyancy force that may explain the missing weight.
6. The small sample size of the experiment makes the results unimportant.

In order to properly analyze the test setup, Masayoshi Ishida employs a numerical modeling technique. He does this by creating a differential equation for inputting established constants and variables in order to assess the true validity of the test. A reviewer must put forth "real work" before making either positive or negative statements about the research of another person. Ishida's analysis is logical, thoughtful, and open for review by the public. His reporting is responsible and deliberate. He uses a meticulous scientific approach to address the issues. An evaluator must have straightforward methodology and objectivity when examining MacDougall's experiment.

The depiction of the 1907 MacDougall test has allowances. It mathematically connects some parameters to a weighing test conducted in later years. In a well-instrumented test setup in 2001, measurements were made to determine whether any weight change of sheep occurs upon death. The test arrangement for the sheep is indoors, open air, and duplicates the MacDougall experiment. The primary exception is the weighing system's use of load cells, rather than a balancing scale. A load cell is a highly sensitive tool found in modern-day weighing experiments. The load cell contains a transducer that converts weight or force into an electrical signal.

Ishida's scientific approach uses a second-order, linear differential equation for a damped vibration model to analyze the weight experiment.[84] Differential equations are a form of calculus. Calculus is the study of continuous change and differential calculus looks at the rate of change. In a weight experiment that uses living bodies, Ishida must employ differential calculus to gain a more precise understanding of the nature of motion within the system. The analysis covers the start of the test, the duration of the test, and the concluding moments of the test.

Cardiac and breathing activity in a patient creates a vibration disturbance, which could have impacted MacDougall's test. Ishida must determine the response of the weighing system to the disturbance over the time interval of the experiment. Incorporating a level of natural damping or vibration decay within the model is an inherent and necessary part of the assessment.

Understanding how the system reacts to various disturbances is important for doing error analysis. The final disturbance at death is the cessation of heartbeat and breathing by the patient. The boundaries for the system response are between the two farthest points: (a) no weight loss at death, and (b) the maximum 21-gram weight loss at

---

84 The differential equation for a damped vibration model under an externally applied force is:

$x'' + 2\sigma x' + \omega_n^2 x = F(t)/m$, where x is the small displacement in the system, σ is the vibration decay rate, ω_n (equal to $(k_{eq}/m)^{0.5}$) is the natural angular frequency, k_{eq} is the equivalent spring constant, m is the total mass and F(t) is the time-dependent external force applied to the system. Ishida, 10.

death. Using the 2001 study, Ishida accurately deduces a spring constant, a natural angular frequency, and a vibration decay rate for the MacDougall test setup.

The parametric simulation employs environmental conditions for a controlled indoor experiment. The parameters must include atmospheric pressure, temperature, and air flow. Additionally, Ishida must incorporate human body weight, heart rhythm, breathing rate, and weight loss due to perspiration. After inputting these baseline parameters, he numerically solves the linear differential equation and determines the system response levels for the duration of the test (a.k.a. noise plots).

Once the assessment is complete for the stated boundary conditions, Ishida is ready to take on MacDougall's critics. The appropriate negation to each criticism previously shown is listed in corresponding numerical order:

1. Ishida selects a robust weight loss rate due to perspiration of 28.5 grams/hour before death and 14.2 grams/hour after death. The rates turn out to have little effect on test sensitivity or conclusions. With the necessary control of bed sheets covering the patients, the maximum (worst-case) moisture loss during life-to-death transitions does not exceed 2 grams. He then addresses any added weight loss due to convection air currents. The calculations show negligible effects.

2. The sudden death of patients 1 and 5 occurs with an abrupt, audible, and clearly discernible metal-on-metal hit of the slot by the balancing scale arm. Patients 2 and 3 undergo an initial and an ensuing weight loss. It identifies as a second mode. The exact time of death is less clear in the second mode, but high weight loss is evident over the short time of expiration, making the test case valid.

3. The sensitivity of MacDougall's scale (5.7 grams) is adequate for the test. Using modern load cells would have provided twice the sensitivity. The increased sensitivity and continuous signal output of the transducer can track the weight loss due to perspiration but has no clear benefit over the balancing scale when measuring large, sudden losses of weight (10–20 grams) at death.

4. Noise plots of the system response (the graphs are available in the Ishida report) clearly refute weight loss due to dynamic effects. The high peak-to-peak vibration due to breathing and heartbeat disturbances damp out quickly at death, leaving a stable and clearly discernible system response signature. This is true for both the "no weight loss" and "21-gram weight loss" conditions.

5. In order to produce buoyancy affecting the test, the swelling of the body would have to be extraordinary (greater than 14% by volume for a 137–pound subject). Forensics by MacDougall and his colleagues did not report any such occurrence.

6. The four test cases are a small sample size, but they stand firm as pioneering research because the engineering model cannot analytically dispute the results.[85] The test methodology, measuring techniques, and observations are seen as reasonable and logically valid. Future testing under identically controlled conditions is likely to produce similar results.

Because of the painstaking system engineering analysis of Masayoshi Ishida, public confidence can increase toward the early twentieth century work of Dr. Duncan MacDougall. The test setup has been shown to be trustworthy. It is sensitive

---

85 Ishida, 23.

enough to detect small weight loss, while stable enough to be unaffected by body perturbations or environmental factors. The only relevant issue to consider is moisture loss from the body. For sudden and short life-to-death transitions, this would only account for 1 or 2 grams. The loss is minor compared to the recorded range of 10.6 to 45.7 grams. As such, MacDougall's recorded test results have been shown to be valid.

In recalling the statement made earlier in Gen. 35:18, the departure of Rachel's soul occurs *exactly* at the point of her death. The Bible supports the soul giving the physical body life and vitality. Since the soul is the incorporeal and enduring aspect of a person, the removal of the soul from the physical body is a natural consequence of physical death. The departure of the soul from the body is as soul substance. Soul substance provides the material structure through which human beings perpetuate in the afterlife. It contains the complete inner nature and memory of the person, his or her entire personality, and all that pertains to individual being.

Scientists do not expect to see any change in body weight when a person passes away. The result of physical death is the cessation of biological functions such as breathing and heartbeat. The departure of the soul from the corpse is the only remaining event. The four male test cases clearly document immediate decreases in weight from 10.6 grams to 21.3 grams following death. Since this large loss of weight is not of natural origin, one must consider MacDougall's detection of soul substance as rational. Being subject to gravity, the mass of the departing soul registers as weight loss when using a well-configured and instrumented test arrangement.

Since the departing soul has measurable weight in a field of gravity, it is safe to construe a direct mortal-to-immortal transition from our space and time continuum into the eternal realm. In having fixed weight, one can infer soul substance has a space-occupying volume containing all the mass. It is a reasonable deduction that the continuation of being, or the continuation of conscious ego, would have physical mass, be subject to gravitational effects, be contained volumetrically, and be detectable when departing a body. The test gives credible evidence for a material departure of the soul from the body, with the destination being the adjoining eternal realm.

So why is the departing soul not visible to doctors, nurses, hospital aides, or loved ones? An eternal soul may have a quantifiable amount of material weight, but it does not mandate visible observation. Examples of nonvisible matter and energy abound in our world. In the electromagnetic spectrum, most energy frequencies are invisible. You cannot visually discern the signal from the cell tower as it travels to your cell phone. The surrounding air is not visible, but its weight can be felt when the wind blows. Soul substance is in the same category. It is not visible as it moves from the physical realm into the higher dimensional space of eternity.

After soul substance moves into the domain of eternity, it experiences time as co-presence and extra-dimensional space. Extra-dimensional space will have one or more added dimensions above 3-D space. Co-presence is the time domain manifesting itself in a past-present-future makeup. Since the MacDougall test demonstrates the soul has mass, it is evident that the physical world ties closely to the eternal state because mass is necessary in order to be part of the material universe. Having taken material substance from the body, the soul is fully equipped to handle other properties of mass and the force of gravity, which exist in eternity.

The metaphysical concept of souls in eternity interconnecting with the physical realm has been given strong support because the departing soul takes mass from the body of a deceased individual. There is no need to consider the ethereal world. If soul substance under the influence of gravity has been shown to have measurable weight, then it has physical mass. The mass will stay with the soul in the eternal realm in order to connect to a material location in the physical universe, which can be a planet or even an exoplanet. The journey's end includes either the third heaven or Hades, both of which are made of a quantifiable substance and abide in the space-time continuum.

After death, the righteous soul will travel to the third heaven, while the unrighteous soul will relocate to Hades. In either case, the soul will be in the eternal state and function in the material universe. The soul's journey to the third heaven or Hades requires moving through physical space. It may also include a pathway that traverses solid objects. These functions are seen in the miraculous event of Jesus, such as when he walks through an angry crowd before his death or passes through a wall to visit the disciples after the resurrection. As will be discussed in the next chapter, soul substance will need to perform similar acts to reach its final destination.

In conclusion, a soul with mass departing into eternity will ultimately require a material destination. Like any object with physical mass, the soul occupies a volumetric space and requires a physical dwelling place. Gravitational attraction between two bodies is essential to hold the spiritual being in position at any given terminus. The final destination for both righteous and unrighteous souls will be a physical setting, such as on a planetary body. Given this understanding, locations such as the third heaven, Hades, and the lake of fire can reside in the universe.

Chapter 6

Satan and Confinement in Hades

The public notion of evil in this world does not tend to focus on a single entity. Perhaps it is more like a dark, nebulous force in the universe, rather than a devil. To most people, the idea of one spiritual being such as Satan leading a demonic army in the midst of our modern and materialistic world is at best a hoax, a myth, or a drug-induced illusion. This chapter looks to the Bible to uncover the truth about Lucifer and his minions. Satan is an unscrupulous spiritual being who despises anything good and contends with God and the holy angels. The devil's final fate remains one of doom, but his desire in the interim is to rule the earth while leading human souls to everlasting ruin.

The journey for the lost soul ends with incarceration in Hades. The facility is inside the earth. But where exactly? As shown earlier, soul substance has mass and will therefore require a physical space. With the aid of the sciences, this chapter examines the inner structure of the planet to see where voids can be found. Seismic waves from earthquakes propagate far and wide, interacting with the internal boundaries of the earth. As such, tremors provide a high-resolution, noninvasive tool for studying the planet's interior in order to determine the overall construction and composition. The review leads to the inner core being the most probable area for retaining open space.

Satan and Fallen Angels

The Bible sees Satan as a powerful archangel, existing before the creation of human beings on the planet. During the angelic period, he became prideful and then rebellious against the Creator. The most investigative readers will only find a sprinkling of information about the devil. Establishing a full understanding about Satan and his spiritual domain of darkness is not easy. Yet, in assembling the pieces together, a picture unfolds of a fallen angel with a malicious attitude who is an enemy to everything that is good. Other proper names for the devil besides Satan include Abaddon, Beelzebub, Evil One, Lucifer, and King of Babylon.

Satan's first appearance as the serpent in the garden of Eden shows the extent of his deceitful behavior, as he willingly tells lies to the woman. Working to destroy all that is good, he manages to tempt Adam and Eve into disobedience. In response to the fall, the Lord God tells the serpent in Genesis 3:15, "I will put enmity between you and the woman, and between your offspring and hers; he will strike your head, and you will strike his heel." The devil knows that a deliberate strike to the head can be a fatal blow. After the edict, he quickly turns from being our partner in crime to a hostile adversary.

Isaiah 14:12–19 explains the occasion where Satan's rebellion receives God's judgment. The first verse states, "How you are fallen from heaven, O Day Star [Lucifer], son of Dawn!" One possible interpretation of the incident has Lucifer as an archangel situated in heaven, who fell from glory due to self-centeredness. His desire was to be greater than God. Satan's longing to exalt himself led to his expulsion and relocation from heaven to the earth. The exact time of his departure is not known, but it was before the creation of Adam and Eve.

After removal from a high angelic position due to sin, the Evil One expands his reign by leading several lower-ranking angels into rebellion. Those who follow him become soldiers in his demonic army. The portrayal of Satan's militia is as unruly, vindictive beings, who despise God and contend with the holy angels. The militia contains a hierarchy of strong and weak demons who coordinate activities with one another. Some spirits will flee under the power of prayer. Other spirits are more powerful and will only release their grip through a combination of prayer and fasting.

Even though Satan is forbidden from residing in heaven, he can still leave the earth to visit heaven in order to gain an audience.[86] Entering the holiness of God's throne is a great privilege for such a shameful character. When Satan conducts business, it means slandering the Lord and disputing the faithfulness of God's people. At the conclusion of the gathering, the devil will normally depart for home, which is on Earth. The third planet from the sun is the crown jewel of the universe. It is beautifully attired with blue water and continents of green vegetation. Satan and his minions fight to control our world by infiltrating human society in order to lie, deceive, pervert, steal, and murder.

When the end of the age arrives, Satan and all his associates will become unwelcome in the gatherings of

---

86 In Job 1:6–12, Satan journeys from the earth to heaven. His role before the throne is as an accuser, who questions the motives and intent of God's people. Coogan, *New Oxford Annotated Bible*, 728 [OT]

heaven. The primary scriptural evidence barring Satan from God's presence is found in Revelation 12:7–9:

> And war broke out in heaven; Michael and his angels fought against the dragon. The dragon and his angels fought back, but they were defeated, and there was no longer any place for them in heaven. The great dragon was thrown down, that ancient serpent, who is called the Devil and Satan, the deceiver of the whole world—he was thrown down to the earth, and his angels were thrown down with him.

In the current age, Satan works to destroy the fabric of society, which begins with the family unit. He instigates dissension and disrupts social order. At the government level, demonic influence grips administrations and provokes heads of state. Leaders of various nations and terrorist-based organizations fall under the devil's persuasion. Full-blown satanic agency arises when wicked individuals mislead entire nations. The perpetrators of the Holocaust are a prime example. The racism of the Nazi regime caused suffering and death to millions of innocent people, disarray to the due order of society, and grievous loss to the world at large.

In order to harm someone's life and control the destiny of their eternal soul, Satan and his fallen angels work through multiple channels. Demonic forces manifest themselves through self-serving business organizations, the secular-humanism of educational institutions, and the ungodly attitudes fostered by society. In Hollywood productions, story lines normally overlook God in human affairs. The unspoken intent is to dissuade people from the reality of a higher being. The practice of discounting God causes people to grow distant from the Bible, spiritual matters, and the truth of Jesus

Christ. It increases the risk of dying without repentance, resulting in condemnation and eternal banishment.

The devil provides leadership to the spiritual domain of Hades. He is the operative behind a complex of evil on the earth. A spirit of lawlessness, darkness, and rebellion manifests itself through damaging words and malicious deeds. Satan wields impressive muscle and sway around the globe in his age-long, worldwide effort to bring people and their souls to ruin. Many wicked activities such as human trafficking operate under satanic influence. Lack of regard for human dignity is the trademark of the devil. Agents of Satan will end up as casualties themselves—perhaps in this life and most certainly in the next. No lasting victory can be found in allegiance to him.

While discussing Satan's evil empire, it is important to remember that demonic influence is only part of the reason why people behave immorally and commit harmful deeds. The act of sinning comes primarily from our own fallen nature, which yields to temptation. Through Adam, the inclination to sin entered the human race, and people became separated from God. In thought and attitude, we can sin minute by minute, hour by hour, and day after day for years at a time and not be fully aware of the situation. Haughtiness, stinginess, lustful desires, deceitfulness, vengeance, and a host of other ills find acceptance, becoming rooted in our souls.

Satan is a demonic being who works out of the eternal domain to affect the physical universe. His high rank as a former archangel affords him great authority, as well as superhuman power and might. Yet unlike God, Satan is not all-powerful (omnipotent), all-knowing (omniscient), or found everywhere (omnipresent). Even while residing in eternity, the devil can only be interactive with the material universe in one place at a time. His undertakings also find restriction under the authority of God. Biblical references such as "ruler of this age," "god of this world," and the "prince of the power of the air" imply a subordinate role in comparison to the Creator of the cosmos.

The Old Testament book of Job tells the story of Satan attacking a person directly. In the narrative, the Lord God lowers the hedge of protection around his faithful servant. Verse 2:6 reads, "The Lord said to Satan, 'Very well, he is in your power; only spare his life.'" After taking Job's property and children in an earlier scene, Satan goes on to afflict his body with painful boils and sores from head to toe. Humankind's vulnerability to Satan's power has not changed since Job's time. He is still out to accuse and to do violence to people throughout the planet. One perceives boundaries being set in place by God in order to protect civilization from this overpowering foe.

The Bible tells us that Satan is limited, judged, and heading for final sentencing. At the end of the age, this evil character will be permanently banished from the earth. Revelation 20:10 speaks to the torment of the devil being "day and night" in the lake of fire. As will be discussed, one possible destination with days and nights is a planet. The removal of Satan from the earth completely dethrones him. After losing influence and authority, his reaction becomes one of great anguish. The judgment of his demonic army occurs soon afterward when the content of Hades is thrown into the lake of fire. Preparation of the eternal fire is primarily for Satan and his fallen angels.

In terms of Christian demonology, the Bible considers a demon to be a fallen angel or unclean spirit. Scripture divides these invisible, malicious spirits of the eternal domain into two distinct groups. One set of demons is free to roam about the planet. A second company of demons is in underworld confinement. Satan's millennium-long quarantine will occur in the abyss or pit. Figure 9 shows a simplified breakdown:

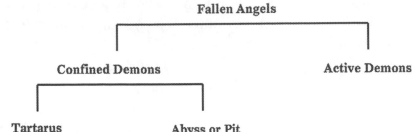

Fallen Angels

Confined Demons   **Active Demons**

Tartarus
(until the end
of the age)

Abyss or Pit
(temporary)

Figure 9
Classification of Fallen Angels[87]

The right side of the diagram shows active demons, who are continually present on the earth. These malevolent spirits work to deceive the mind, and in some cases, to enter the consciousness of people. The Gospels present clear evidence about the sinister effects of demonic possession. In Mark 1:21–28, Jesus encounters a man with a demon in the Capernaum synagogue. Later in Mark 7:24–30, a woman whose daughter has an unclean spirit asks Jesus for help. In each case, the Lord performs an exorcism to set the person free, which removes the evil spirit from the individual but leaves the departing demon to roam the planet.

The left side of the diagram shows that confined demons fall into two categories. The group on the far left is in Tartarus, remaining in chains within the darkness of the earth. When the Day of Judgment arrives, the group will receive sentencing to the lake of fire. The following scriptures portray the state of those in permanent captivity:

2 Peter 2:4—"For if God did not spare the angels when they sinned, but cast them into

---

87   Charles C. Ryrie, *A Survey of Bible Doctrine* (Chicago: Moody, 1972), 97.

hell [*tartaroo*] and committed them to chains of deepest darkness to be kept until the judgment;"

Jude 1:6—"And the angels who did not keep their own position, but left their proper dwelling, he has kept in eternal chains in deepest darkness for the judgment of the great day."

In the first passage, the Greek noun *tartaroo* translates as "Tartarus." The term appears only once in scripture and identifies a specific incarceration center in Hades where demons serve a life sentence. Rather than roaming the earth, these evil spirits are kept in chains.

The second passage in Jude cites fallen spirits who "did not keep their own position," a phrase subject to various interpretations. The expression may simply mean that a certain class of fallen angels gave up their rank, left the third heaven, and followed Satan during his rebellion. Or, for an unspecified reason, the demons were sent to chains of darkness, rather than let loose on the earth.

The second group of confined demons in Figure 9 is temporarily detained in the abyss or pit. These evil beings are scheduled for release during the tribulation period. The following scriptures support the idea of a demonic militia that has been set free to roam the earth and wreak havoc.

Luke 8:30–31—"Jesus then asked him, 'What is your name?' He said, 'Legion'; for many demons had entered him. They begged him not to order them to go back into the abyss."

Revelation 9:2–3—"he opened the shaft of the bottomless pit, and from the shaft rose smoke like the smoke of a great furnace, and the sun and the air were darkened with the smoke from the shaft. Then from the smoke came locusts on the earth, and they were given authority like the authority of scorpions of the earth."

The second passage reveals an apocalyptic event of horrific proportion in the unleashing of demonic locusts. Revelation 9:1 brings the blowing of the fifth trumpet, which signals one of God's judgments upon the earth. These demons will come out of the eternal domain of Hades, which is deep within the earth, and visibly manifest themselves on the surface of the planet.

In the ancient Near East, locusts were a symbol of destruction. Appearing in great numbers, the insects arrive like clouds darkening the sky. These pests devour everything green, leaving behind a barren wasteland. Having a ravenous appetite with few boundaries, an army of locusts will consume linens, wools, silk, leather, and even the varnish off furniture. Everything left behind by these insects reduces to shreds. It is a striking illustration of an all-consuming army. In this case, the invading locusts are not to consume anything green, but rather to go after people who have failed to repent.

Figure 10
Locust Invasion of Revelation 9:1–11

In Revelation 9:7–10, one reads a physical description of the demons, who are fully equipped to carry out the task. As Figure 10 depicts, the beasts are the size of a small horse, with a thin exoskeletal structure lightening the body weight. The face and long hair are human-like features. A light-colored circlet appears on the head. It is a "crown of gold" insignia, representing sanction from God. The long, sharp teeth resemble a lion and imply fierceness. Scales cover large portions of the extremities. An instinctive weapon, a stinging scorpion's tail, extends out the hindquarters.

To the people of Earth, it will look like an invasion of giant alien mutants coming from another world. The leader of the raiding army is Abaddon (Heb.) or Apollyon (Gk.), who is the destroyer or angel of the abyss. The countless swarming invaders arrive in packs and move quickly to cover the continents of the planet. The spreading of the wings power flight, and the bowed legs have long jump capability that add to a maneuverable body. The reverberation from hopping legs and flapping wings will be like galloping hoofs from an advancing cavalry. Their shrieking will sound like a cluster of squeaky wagons made of wood and metal that are moving quickly down a bumpy road.

The invaders are on the offensive. The army has come out to molest anyone who does not have the "seal of God" on their forehead. The term is not meant to imply a physical mark on the skin, but rather those who have an indifferent or negative attitude toward repentance. The aggressive militia marches to engage in war with the nations for five long months—not to kill, but to inflict pain and torture with a stinging tail. The creatures are insightful, callous, and persistent. Close encounters of the worst kind can only be expected because the beasts will strike at every opportunity.

Intelligence-gathering through high-resolution satellite imagery or drone surveillance aircraft may be good for assessing the extent of the invasion but will do little to slow the systematic advance of these cockroaches. The condition of the nations is dire at the time of the raid, limiting countermeasures. The previous four trumpets (Rev. 8:7–12) describe global catastrophes that have devastating consequences on the population, decisively weakening military resistance. Demons normally attack people at their most vulnerable time, and this incursion is no different. It will be difficult to rally troops, thwart attacks, or mount a resistance.

Defense using lethal force is fair game but will have limited effectiveness. The locusts appear as large targets but are nimble and move quickly. One can envision the attempted use of handguns, assault rifles, artillery, tanks, and attack helicopters. The state rule remaining after the global upheaval will unite in attempting to eradicate the infestation. A few battles may be won, but the war will be lost. By sheer numbers, the invaders will succeed in accomplishing their primary objective. Targeted individuals stung by the tail will be in relentless pain for months, wishing for death rather than life. Apparently, modern medicine will not be effective against the venom.

Confinement of Souls in Hades

To the present day, Sheol–Hades remains a physical place of confinement for lost souls in the intermediate state. As shown earlier, the underworld of Sheol in the Hebrew Scriptures has become the Hades of the New Testament. Up until the death of Christ, the destination for souls has consistently been directed toward an "under the earth" location. The faithful were originally placed in a section called Abraham's bosom. Later, the group departed with the resurrected Christ for the third heaven. With the removal of righteous souls, Sheol–Hades became a place of long-term incarceration. Captivity in Hades for lost souls will remain in effect until the Day of Judgment.

A prior section, *Sheol in the Old Testament*, conveys the idea that all departing souls prior to the resurrection were being confined under the ground. The Old Testament uses the word Sheol a total of sixty-five times in the NRSV, with a full thirty-three implying a downward direction. Biblical phrases such as "bring down to Sheol," "the depths of Sheol," "deeper than Sheol," and "dig into Sheol," as well as equating Sheol to a pit, confront the reader over and over again. In the New Testament, Jesus gave a hint to a nadir direction when saying, "Capernaum will be brought down to Hades." Consistently, the direction for the internment of souls is *downward* and into the earth.

The critical question becomes the availability of open physical spaces inside the planet. Direct access to Hades is possible with the intertwining realm of the eternal and physical operating under the earth. The soul in extra-dimensional space should have the ability to traverse the inner earth and end up in an open space deep inside the planet. The action imitates Jesus coming through locked doors to visit the apostles. The soul must travel a great distance through rock and soil. Similar to Jesus' appearance in the open area of a locked room, the ability of soul substance to pass through solid material will not lessen the need for the destination to have an open space.

Examining the Inner Earth

The ability of modern technology to examine the inner earth will come under review. Direct observation is the cornerstone of good science, but physical viewing below the earth's surface is unworkable. In order to address the matter, this section considers geology and seismic tomography. Geology is the science that speaks to the entirety of the earth's structure, addressing its history, fossil record, chemical composition, materials, and composite layering. Seismic tomography is an important investigative tool of geology. The field assesses the earth by gathering seismic waves generated from earthquakes to create 3-D images of the interior.

The geological history of our terrestrial world dates back 4.5 billion years to the formation of the solar system. Early on, the material came from a protoplanetary disc circling inside a nebula. The development of planets occurs due to the accretion process. In planetary science, accretion is the accumulation of gases and nebulous material into a large object due to gravitational attraction. The heating, cooling, and congealing into a spherical shape created the planet we live on. The four inner planets eventually formed a solid surface, consisting of compact rock and aggregates. The concentric structure has layering like the inside of an onion.

Study of the various strata of the earth is done using a cutaway to show the content. The planetary structure begins with a thin outer crust consisting of soil and rock made from volcanic processes. The sedimentation compacts as it moves into the upper and lower mantle. The layering transitions to a liquid metal outer core and finishes with a metal inner core. A radial distance of 3,960 miles extends from the surface to the center of the earth. Figure 11 from the USGS depicts the physical layout.

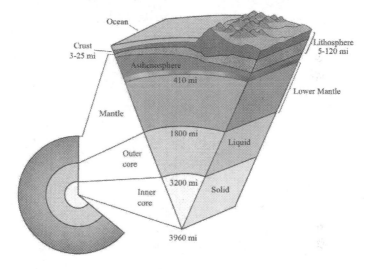

Figure 11
Interior Structure of the Earth

The crust is the outer layer of the earth. The oceans, seas, and land masses are part of the crust. The crust forms a very thin skin on the surface of our planet, covering both the dry continental ground and the ocean bottom. The crust is twenty-five miles thick under the continents, while varying between three to five miles under the ocean. Every living organism exists either inside or above the crust. It contains igneous, sedimentary, and metamorphic rocks, as well as sand, soil, fossil fuels, and various types of minerals.

Under the crust lies the lithosphere. It includes both the crust and the underlying portion of the mantle. The two-part section is dense and rigid and varies in thickness. The lithosphere extends up to a depth of 120 miles below the continents and twenty-five miles below the ocean floor. The stiff mechanical structure of the lithosphere contains divides, similar to pieces in an assembled jigsaw puzzle. The divides separate the planet into tectonic plates. There are seven or eight major plates and many minor ones. Along the plate boundaries are active shear zones where seismic events such as earthquakes and volcanic activity occur.

Directly beneath the crust/lithosphere is the upper mantle or asthenosphere. The asthenosphere has two regions that have different features. Scientists consider the upper half of the asthenosphere to be a yielding, malleable region. The plasticity gives the ability for plate tectonic processes such as earthquakes and volcanic eruptions to occur. The lower asthenosphere acts as a transition zone by getting stiffer. It is shown as a light band extending down to 410 miles of depth. The transition zone creates a boundary between the pliable asthenosphere and the rigid lower mantle.[88]

The lower mantle is made of solid, compact rock. The highly compressed aggregate extends down to the edge of the liquid outer core. Adding the entire mantle length and crust together gives a total depth of 1800 miles. The whole of the mantle itself lies beneath the thin outer crust and above the molten outer core. It is the largest section inside the earth. In totality, the upper and lower mantle contain a surprising 84% of the planet's volume.

Extending for 1400 miles beneath the mantle is the liquid outer core. It consists of molten iron and nickel. The earth's protective magnetic field originates from the motion in the

---

88 Seth Stein and Michael Wysession, *An Introduction to Seismology, Earthquakes, and Earth Structure* (Oxford, UK: Blackwell Publishing Ltd., 2003), 163.

outer core.[89] Flowing in a radial path, convection currents move hot metal up and cooler metal down. At the same time, the rotation of the planet causes the liquid metal to slowly spin. The dynamo theory describes this process by which convective flow and rotation in a conductive fluid can produce a magnetic field. Scientists generally accept the dynamo effect in the outer core as the mechanism for the creation of Earth's ongoing energy for the magnetic field.

Beneath the molten outer core lies the inner core, which extends 760 miles to the earth's center. Analysis shows the inner core consists primarily of iron-nickel alloy. As the earth formed from various elements in the nebula, these heavy metals sank and solidified in the center. Scientists do not know whether the inner core is completely solid, or contains voids, or perhaps resembles a honeycomb structure. The section is not accessible to complete seismic waves study because of the liquid outer core. The inability to analyze the inner core will be discussed in an upcoming section.

The earth's interior volume can be determined easily because it is nearly a perfect sphere. The equation for the volume of a sphere is $V_{Earth} = 4/3 \pi r^3$, with r being the radius of 3,960 miles. The total volume under our feet calculates out to 260,120,252,602 mi^3 or 260.1 billion cubic miles, which is amazingly large. The volumes for the sections are shown below for the upper mantle, lower mantle, outer core, and the inner core.

$V_{Upper\ Mantle}$	=	72,718,491,229 mi^3	or	72.7 billion mi^3
$V_{Lower\ Mantle}$	=	145,188,407,079 mi^3	or	145.2 billion mi^3
$V_{Outer\ Core}$	=	40,374,575,898 mi^3	or	40.4 billion mi^3
$V_{Inner\ Core}$	=	1,838,778,396 mi^3	or	1.8 billion mi^3

---

89 The magnetic field envelopes the earth and stretches into space. Life may not have been possible without the energy field, which deflects the solar wind from the atmosphere. James F. Luhr, ed., *Smithsonian Institute: Earth* (New York: DK Publ. Inc., 2003), 55.

Estimating the Size of Hades

If Hades exists in the material universe, it will take up volumetric space inside Earth. It may be one large space, or perhaps several hundred smaller spaces. The exact configuration cannot be known for certain. Nevertheless, we can calculate a ballpark volume of space necessary to house lost souls. The volume could then be split among multiple locations. The calculation will assume an estimate of individual jail size and the total number of occupants. In comparison to Earth's vast inner volume, the size of Hades will turn out to be extremely small.

This study will recognize Hades to be a subterranean cavern hidden deep within the earth. A random size needs to be selected for the hollow. Let's begin with 1 mi^3 of volume and then break it down. One mile is 5,280 ft. and so a cubic mile will be (5,280)^3 or 147,197,952,000 ft^3.

The volume finds use in creating a prison shape. In order to do so, we first assign a floor-to-ceiling jail cell height of ten feet. Dividing the interior volume by a ceiling height of ten feet leaves a total floor space of 14,719,795,200 ft^2. This number represents the total area for the prison, which can be used to formulate the length and width of cells.

If one assumes each prison cell will have a length of 10 ft and a width of 10 ft, then dividing the total area by 100 ft^2 will give the number of cells inside the detention center. Dividing 14,719,795,200 ft^2 by 100 ft^2 leaves 147,197,952 jail cells. If we deduct 20% for a common area, the remaining 80% reduces the number of available jail cells to just under 120,000,000. If the incarceration center holds one inmate per cell, it will allow for 120,000,000 captives. So amazingly, one extremely small 1 mi^3 cavity in Earth's interior can hold almost 120 million prisoners.

The next step is to find out how many unrighteous souls are under the earth. The number of lost souls will determine how many cavities of 1 mi^3 space are necessary to detain everyone in Hades. In order to do an estimate of those in captivity, we first have to determine the total number of individuals who have ever lived on the planet. Having that information, we can then approximate the total number in perdition.

The number of people who have ever lived is an evaluation undertaken by the Population Reference Bureau. The organization assists decision makers around the world in setting policy for issues pertaining to population, health, and the environment. The information goes to advance the well-being of current and future generations. According to a 2019 estimate, an amazing 108.7 billion people have lived on the planet.[90]

Of these billions, a certain number of deceased individuals have been found unworthy of heaven, with the soul departing for Hades. But how many? It is impossible to know. Due to a high infant and child mortality rates throughout the centuries, countless babies and young children have gone to heaven. This will reduce the number of people who are in Hades. So, by assigning a lost soul amount of 55% to the 108.7 billion, we will deliberately overestimate the inhabitants who are in Hades. The number turns out to be a population of 60 billion unrighteous individuals under the earth.

If 60 billion lost souls require incarceration and 120 million prisoners can be held in one underground penitentiary of 1 mi^3, then dividing 60 billion by 120 million will determine the number of detention centers. The calculation turns out to be 500. The 500 prisons of 1 mi^3 would occupy a total volume of 500 cubic miles. The 500 mi^3 can be in one large facility or 500 facilities spread out in separate locations within the heart of the earth. The shapes can vary with the site still

90 Population Reference Bureau, "How Many People Have Ever Lived on Earth?" http://www.prb.org/Publications/Articles/2002/HowManyPeopleHaveEverLivedonEarth.aspx (accessed Nov. 9, 2020)

maintaining an internal volume of 1 mi^3. As seen in the next section, the probability of finding any cavity under the earth is low until reaching the inner core.

Geological Detection Capabilities

The study of the history, composition, physical structure, and processes of the planet requires using fields such as geology, chemistry, oceanography, seismology, volcanism, geochronology, and geomagnetism. Of all disciplines coming into play, seismology specializes in deep-probing the earth. Seismologists analyze the vibrations generated from earthquakes and other large-scale events, such as volcanic eruptions and atomic explosions. The field requires the review of wave propagation occurring throughout the planet. Typically, seismic events generate two types of impulses: surface waves and body waves.

As the name implies, surface waves move along the ground's surface. A seismic event will create two types of surface waves: Love waves and Rayleigh waves. Love waves cause an abrupt side-to-side shift or lateral shaking of the ground. Rayleigh waves cause an "up and down" or rolling action to occur. It feels like an ocean wave passing underneath. A person can experience one, both, or a combination of each wave during an earthquake event. Love waves and Rayleigh waves can cause extensive damage to buildings and transportation networks. Due to these waves, a large seismic event on the ocean floor can trigger a tsunami.

Seismologists do study surface waves, but many find greater interest in body waves that move through the inside of the planet. The two main types of body waves generating from seismic events are primary (P) and secondary (S) waves. Spreading through the expanse of the planet, these two waves reflect and refract off internal boundaries. The waves travel at differing speeds through various densities. The propagation of the energy waves is elastic, which means the medium does not move from its original position due to the wave passing through it. The analysis of these waves is the only reliable method for researching Earth's inner structure.

The newscast of an earthquake event will normally mention the epicenter, which is situated on the planet's surface. The true origin of an earthquake is the hypocenter, which sits directly beneath the epicenter. Following an earthquake, wave detection takes place using seismographs, which locate the hypocenter. Seismographs consist of a seismometer and a digital recorder. The Global Seismographic Network uses these instruments for monitoring seismic episodes at permanent stations around the world.[91] Additionally, thousands of smaller stand-alone networks and other portable array systems are strategically situated to keep track of Earth's movements.

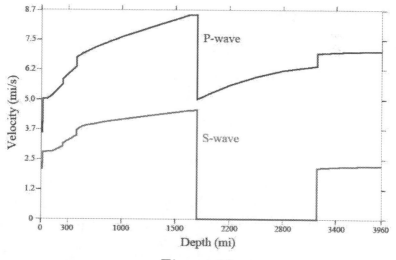

Figure 12

IASP91 Velocity Model of S- and P-Waves

---

91   Over 150 stations actively monitor and record seismic events on a global scale. Incorporated Research Institutions for Seismology (IRIS), "Global Seismographic Network," https://www.iris.edu/hq/programs/gsn (accessed March, 31, 2020).

Geologists determine Earth's structural characteristics by studying the journey of the P-waves and S-waves. The velocity–depth seismic graph in Figure 12 provides a two-dimensional glimpse of wave travel to the earth's center. The formulation of the original diagram was in the early 1940s. Technical revisions since that time have brought only minor changes to the mapping. The one shown in Figure 12 is an IASP91 velocity model developed in 1991 by the International Association of Seismology and Physics of the Earth's Interior (IASPEI).[92]

The graph plots the velocity of P-waves and S-waves against the travel depth when moving from the earth's surface to the center of the planet. The lithosphere and asthenosphere zones show jagged rises in wave velocity. At 410 miles, the waves pass the transition zone and smooth out. The velocities continue to rise in the mantle because the mantle density increases with depth. Higher density allows seismic waves to travel faster in the medium.[93] When the waves strike the liquid metal of the outer core, the velocity drops sharply, with the S-wave near zero. When the waves hit the solid inner core, a step increase of wave velocity occurs.

The upper line in the graph is the primary wave. Primary waves (P-waves) are compression waves—that is, the wave motion and wave propagation are in the same direction. In other words, as a P-wave passes, it is vibrating along the same route that it is moving. Primary waves progress readily through the earth's interior. Being highest in travel velocity, the wave will arrive first to a seismic station. P-waves

---

92 IRIS has a repository of earth models available to the research community. Incorporated Research Institutions for Seismology (IRIS), "Data Services Products: EMC-iasp91 (P & S velocity reference Earth model)," http://ds.iris.edu/ds/products/emc-iasp91/ (accessed April 15, 2020).

93 C. M. R. Fowler, *The Solid Earth: An Introduction to Global Geophysics,* 2nd ed. (Cambridge, UK: Cambridge University Press, 2005), 336.

typically travel at speeds of between 0.5 and 8.7 mi/sec. Slower speeds occur through liquid, while the fastest speeds happen when going through the lower mantle.

The lower line in the graph is the secondary wave. Secondary waves (S-waves) are shear waves—that is, the wave motion is perpendicular to wave propagation. In other words, as an S-wave passes, its vibration is being felt 90 degrees perpendicular to the path that it is moving on. S-waves traverse readily through the mantle, but the wave dies down in the liquid outer core before rising again in the inner core. S-waves typically travel at speeds between 0.5 to 5.0 mi/sec. The slower value corresponds to travel in loose sediment, while the faster number represents velocity in the lower mantle.

Tracking the velocity of S-waves and P-waves is the key to analyzing Earth's interior. The arrival time of S- and P-waves to various stations is the result of the distance and route taken. When traveling, waves will encounter various mediums and boundaries within the global structure. The waves move at speeds which are dependent on material properties, such as density and the modulus of elasticity. The waves also reflect and refract across the borders of dissimilar rock. How the waves interact with the interior structure infers the existence of features within the planet. Looking at travel times and pathways helps scientists "see" into the earth.

Unfortunately, looking at graphs of the earth in 2-D yields little information. In order to see the vast array of physical features, which includes any chance of finding open spaces, requires 3-D seismic tomography analysis. Achieving 3-D seismic tomography requires combining 2-D results from several seismic stations. Geoscientists can then better understand core, mantle, and outer-shell makeup. Images come together with the assistance of computer models, which readily assimilate the data. Looking inside the earth with

3-D may seem boring and uninspiring to some, but seismic tomography is an evolving and dynamic discipline.[94]

For medical diagnostics, doctors rely on technology known as Computer Aided Tomography, or the CAT scan. The CAT scan uses a radioactive source that directs X-ray beams through a patient, who is lying on a motorized table. The movement of the patient by the table allows for the CAT scan to create many 2-D images. Computers then reconstruct individual slices into a single 3-D image to show the patient's internal organs, bones, and soft tissue. CAT scans allow doctors to search for cancerous growths or treat various conditions. Other important types of 3-D imaging techniques include Magnetic Resonance Imaging (MRI) and ultrasound.

Seismic tomography works using the same principle as the CAT scan. When an earthquake or other seismic event occurs, seismic monitoring stations around the world pick up the signal and assimilate the wave data. The distance from the hypocenter to various stations differs considerably, so the arrival time and signature of the S- and P-waves will fluctuate. Computer processing of unique 2-D slices from each station allows for reconstruction into a 3-D image, revealing Earth's inner features.

Seismic tomography is the only credible means scientists have for peering into the planet. The field takes advantage of S- and P-wave travel times as they pass through different mediums. Unlike the steady radiation source used in medical testing, seismic tomography cannot control the intensity, length, or location of emissions. This problem is not a deterrent to geologists, however, because small tremors are a frequent global occurrence and seismic data amasses readily.

---

94   Using one of the world's fastest supercomputers, a team from Princeton University is creating a detailed 3-D picture of Earth's interior from seismic data. *Science Daily*, "A Seismic Mapping Milestone: Team Produces 3-D Map of Earth's Interior," https://www.sciencedaily.com/releases/2017/03/170328135508.htm (accessed July 22, 2020).

Additionally, clarity and precision of modeling improve with the increasing number of network locations and continual advancements in computer processing of incoming data.

Earth's Apparent Solidity

This section discusses Earth's compactness and the possibility of openings in the interior. The earth was originally formed by the congealing of an interstellar dust cloud, requiring gravity and accretion to work in tandem. The process includes radioactive heating and melting that tightly binds the material together over time. The differential layering leaves the heavier metals in the center, while other bedrock materials situate above. Earth's formation under gravity and hot solidification processes leads to the collective belief about a rock-hard, compact earth containing few cavities or open spaces.

Let's begin at the earth's surface, where there are openings such as caves. The study of caves is known as speleology. It is the science of the structure, formation, biology, and physical features of caves. A cave is a natural chamber (or series of chambers) in the earth that form through the dissolution of soluble rocks, such as limestone and dolomite. Most caves form above sea level and are found on the sides of hills or mountains. The deepest caves in the world begin at higher altitudes, descending for great distances until hitting a sump below the floor of the earth. The sump is an indication of reaching the water table.

Since groundwater migrates freely, cave systems below ground will house tributaries and small pools. Being part of the earth's hydrologic cycle, groundwater is considered a natural reservoir for fresh water. An abundant global resource, water tables can reach depths of thirty thousand feet. The water fills the pores of soil, the spaces between sand, and the fractures of bedrock. A large groundwater collection under the earth that readily transmits its water is called an aquifer. An aquifer allows for the successful digging of wells. Depletion of an aquifer does not create open spaces, but rather, it is an absence of water from permeable materials.

Another important fluid filling the voids and fissures of rock is oil. Oil and natural gas are present within the earth's crust as a result of hundreds of millions of years of decomposition of dead plants, creatures, and organic matter. The oil naturally resides in the tiny spaces and porosity of bedrock. Stored heat and pressure underground allow for the rise of natural gas and oil into a well. Drilling a well is akin to sticking a straw into a drenched sponge and watching the straw draw up fluid. The solid sponge remains after the pores empty. In the same way, oil extraction does not leave cavernous spaces. Oil and gas removal leaves a vacuum that fills with water. Realizing that oil, water, and natural gas reside in the pores of soil, sand, and bedrock helps to establish the solidity of the crust.

Sitting below the crust is the rigid lithosphere. The lithosphere is where you find plate tectonic boundaries. Plate tectonics is a theory that divides the lithosphere into a number of crustal plates. The stiff plates ride above the flexible asthenosphere. As the asthenosphere moves, the plates collide with, slide under, grind past, or move apart from adjacent plates. Geologists group these boundaries into categories, depending on how the plates move. Three types of boundaries are known to exist: convergent, divergent, and transform boundaries:[95]

---

95 Beyond the primary boundaries, some types of boundaries exist where plate interaction is not fully understood. United States Geological Survey (USGS), "Understanding Plate Motions," https://pubs.usgs.gov/gip/dynamic/understanding.html (accessed June, 13, 2020).

At *convergent boundaries*, plates push toward each other, resulting in high contact pressure and movement of the plates. Subduction can also occur, where one plate angles down under the other plate.

At *divergent boundaries*, plates move apart to allow for volcanic activity. It is where mantle plumes carry lava upward in columns that eventually mushroom and flow along the surface.

At a *transform boundary*, faces of adjoining plate material grind past each other horizontally in a side-to-side motion, which can produce cracks or openings on the surface of the planet.

The primary cause of these dynamic forces is convection processes. Convection is two-directional: up and down. At convergent boundaries, cold, dense slabs drive down toward the pliable asthenosphere. The sideways and downward action is known as subduction. At divergent boundaries, hot, dense material such as molten lava rises up. The consequence of the thermal exchanges is seen in earthquakes, volcanic activity, and mountain building. The movement of plate material at the boundaries is age-old and never-ending. Internal pressure assures that any gaps or spaces left from the spewing, shifting, or lifting of material are quickly filled.

Moving further down into the planet, we come upon the upper and lower mantle. In examining the graph in Figure 12, we see an interesting trend. There is a rising slope evident for both the S- and P-wave velocities when moving through the mantle depth. As mentioned earlier, the increasing speed of the waves is due to the increasing density of the substrate. As the wave moves down toward the outer core, it is hitting denser and denser rock. We can conclude that the rock-solid mantle is increasing in compactness and will not allow for any voids or openings.

An abrupt change from solid rock to metal happens when reaching the liquid outer core. The molten mass of iron and nickel is at superheated temperatures and under tremendous pressure. Estimates for the temperatures of the outer core are about 5,000°F at the mantle and 7,000°F near the inner core. The outer core has a similar composition to the inner core, only it is in liquid form. Analysis of the movement of the molten metal indicates it is in a low viscosity state. Low viscosity means the liquid metal is runny, rather than thick and gummy. The flowing liquid metal does not allow for the possibility of creating an empty space.

Situated in the center of the earth is the inner core. At the depth of 3,200 miles, a transition occurs from liquid to solid metal, and the inner core begins. The shroud of liquid metal circling the inner core severely limits seismology testing for features such as solidity. It is the first location where the possibility of voids, openings, and spaces begins. The IASP91 velocity model has the S- and P-waves flat-lining through the region, with the inner core S-wave velocity being less than 2.5 miles per second. A review of available seismic wave data traveling through the inner core will be made in the next section. The uncertainty of solidity will raise the possibility of openings under Earth's surface.

Proposal for Hades in the Inner Core

An earlier calculation for the size of Hades found that 500 cubic miles of space was sufficient to house up to 60 billion lost souls. One detention center would have a space of 500 mi^3, 100 centers would have 5 mi^3 of space, 250 centers would have 2 mi^3 of space, and 500 detention centers would have 1 mi^3 of space. Any of the void combinations easily fits within the inner core volume of 1.8 billion mi³. Using the motion of earthquakes, seismologists have attempted to determine the interior structure and solidity of the earth's center. The inner core provides a tough challenge, because it is hidden under a large body of moving metallic fluid in the heart of the planet.

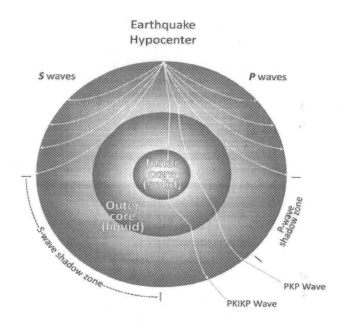

Figure 13
S- and P-Wave Propagation through the Earth

Figure 13 depicts an earthquake originating in a hypocenter near the north pole. As mentioned previously, the hypocenter is the focal point of a seismic event, where all wave activity begins. Earlier in the section, primary (P) and secondary (S) waves were shown to be the principal means for tracking seismic events. These two waves not only reflect and refract at internal boundaries but are able to travel through the bulk of the planet for detection at great distances. The ray diagram shows the dispersion of waves passing through the planet's inner layers and gives evidence for two shadow zones: one for the S-wave and one for the P-wave.[96]

As the diagram indicates, S-waves and P-waves are picked up readily in the Northern Hemisphere. The inability to pick up S-waves and P-waves in the Southern Hemisphere is due to blockage by the liquid outer core. The lack of S-wave passage is shown by the large S-wave shadow zone. S-waves cannot pass through the liquid, so the blockage covers the bulk of the Southern Hemisphere. P-waves can pass through the earth, but it requires the wave to enter the liquid at a high angle of incidence. Otherwise, the wave simply bounces off the outer core. As a result of these deflections, the P-wave shadow zone covers about half of the Southern Hemisphere.

A passing P-wave receives designations as either a P-wave, a PKP wave, or a PKIKP wave. If it passes only through the mantle, it remains a P-wave. If the P-wave traverses through the mantle (P), outer core (K), and mantle again (P), then it shows as a PKP wave. If a P-wave passes through the mantle (P), outer core (K), and inner core (I), then it must depart following the reverse route (KP) in order to exit the earth. In this case, the wave encounters detection at a seismic station as a PKIKP wave. Since the PKIKP wave is the only wave which passes through the inner core, it becomes the focal point for wave analysis by scientists studying the inner core.

The question now becomes, "Can scientists use the PKIKP wave to determine the solidity of the inner core?" As will be shown, the answer is no. PKIKP waves cannot provide data about voids or openings. What the wave can do is reveal information about material properties. One discovery is that the core is anisotropic. Anisotropy means the iron-nickel behaves differently along different axes. For instance, seismic waves traveling from pole to pole through the inner core

---

96 The S-wave and P-wave shadow zones are shown separately for clarity. *Encyclopedia Britannica*, "Primary Wave," https://www.britannica.com/science/primary-wave (accessed Aug. 1, 2020).

arrive six seconds faster than seismic waves traveling the same distance on the equatorial plane. This large variance in speed along the two major axes brings out the anisotropic nature of the nickel-iron alloy.[97]

In order to analyze the solidity of the inner core, seismologists attempt to detect another wave, the PKJKP wave. This wave can confirm the presence of voids. The PKJKP is not shown in Figure 13 because it is a derivative wave. The PKJKP wave originates from S-waves that are locally present in the inner core after a seismic event. The letter "J" denotes that it is a shear wave, sourcing in the inner core. Researchers occasionally publish reports that identify and analyze PKJKP waveforms. The summary sections of the reports often admit to the difficulty of picking up the wave, even when using high-quality test equipment.[98]

In 2011, the Scripps Institute of Oceanography in San Diego, CA, issued a report reviewing the stacks of over 90,000 long-period seismograms. The results were not encouraging for detecting PKJKP waves coming from the inner core. The publication concludes that seeing the wave is questionable due to the small amplitude. A reader finds in a close review of the article that the PKJKP wave is trivial in strength compared to noises and vibrations coming from either the test setup or upper mantle.[99] As such, data acquisition of PKJKP seismic

---

97 The reason for the anisotropy may be due to a uniform orientation of iron crystals in the inner core. The mechanism causing the positioning remains a mystery. Xiaodong Song, "Anisotropy of the Earth's Inner Core," *Reviews of Geophysics*, American Geophysical Union 35, No. 3 (Aug.1997), 297–313.

98 A. Cao and B. Romanowicz, "Constraints on Shear Wave Attenuation in the Earth's Inner Core from an Observation of PKJKP," *Geophysical Research Letters*, 36, No. 9 (May 2009): 5.

99 Peter M Shearer, Catherine A Rycher, and Qinya Liu, "On the Visibility of the Inner-core Shear Wave Phase PKJKP at Long Periods," *Geophysics Journal Intl.*, 185, No. 3 (2011): 1379–83.

waves remains tenuous. The limitation casts doubt on the ability to ever evaluate the inner core for solidity.

From the information, we can draw a safe conclusion. Given the constraints of modern technology to access Earth's center, science can neither confirm nor deny that voids are present in the inner core. That being said, it is realistic for Bible believers to accept that people who went down to Sheol in the Old Testament, or who go down to Hades in the New Testament era, are in fact going to the center of the earth. The finding of the anisotropic nature of the inner core will only speak to material properties. Valid testing is not possible to display solidity in the center. The avenue remains open for voids and spaces being present as detention centers for Hades.

Biblical Instance of an Inner Core Journey

Let's look to a biblical example of souls going from the surface of the earth to Sheol–Hades under the earth. In the Old Testament, an uprising against Moses occurs in Numbers 16. A Levite ringleader, Korah, and members of his family, seek to supplant Moses' leadership role. The act was a rebellion against the authority of God, who had given place to Moses as the head of the tribes. In verse 33, judgment falls upon the house of Korah when the ground splits apart underneath them in an earthquake. The verse reads, "So they with all that belonged to them went down alive into Sheol; the earth closed over them, and they perished from the midst of the assembly."

In the story, physical bodies disappear into a large fissure and go directly to Sheol. A key detail is the location of the Korah incident. Prior to the event in Numbers 13, the children of Israel camped at the Wilderness of Paran at Kadesh. After the incident in Numbers 20, Moses leads the Israelites to the Wilderness of Zin at Kadesh. At some point in the journey, the uprising of Korah occurs in chapter 16. So, in all likelihood, the incident took place in the Kadesh wilderness. The duration of the stay in Kadesh is thought by historians to be extensive, since it is located near the gateway to the Promised Land in the northeast corner of the Sinai Peninsula.

Today, geologists realize the Kadesh wilderness is near a fault line, which defines the boundary between the western African Plate and the eastern Arabian Plate. Amazingly, this Sinai fault line classifies as a transform boundary. Transform boundaries have plates grinding and slipping past each other. It is the type of boundary that allows for earthquakes to produce fissures. Fissures are large cracks or openings on the earth's surface. Known as the Dead Sea transform boundary, it could have sat directly under the Israelite campsite. The large camp would only have to situate centrally in the northeast corner of the peninsula in order to be near the fault line.

So, what happened to the house of Korah? The Israelites fell into a fissure and died. Their souls left their bodies as soul substance and went into the afterlife. In order to get to Sheol–Hades, the souls would have to pass through solid matter before emerging in a void in the inner core. Obstacles would include the crust, mantle, and liquid outer core. The soul would have to traverse great distances of the lower earth using the higher spatial dimensions of eternity. In a show of consistency, the travel of living souls from the Korah household to Sheol was using the same capability as the resurrected Christ did to walk through walls, only it covered a much greater distance.

Lost souls in the intermediate state are residing in the eternal realm of Hades. These souls require the same open area to physically appear as Moses and Elijah did during the transfiguration of Jesus. The inner core of the earth appears to meet the open space criteria for spiritual beings.

In terms of the environment, there is no real way to measure temperature and pressure in the earth's center. It is thought that the heat of the inner core is as high as 9,800°F, with a pressure ranging from about 3.3 to 3.6 million atmospheres. The direct spiritual effects of extremely high temperature and pressure on souls and demonic beings residing in Hades cannot be known.

In terms of additional evidence for the location of Hades, we turn to another Christian text. Corroboration for perdition being situated in the inner core is made reference to in the book, *23 Minutes in Hell*, written by Bill Weiss.[100] In the account, he discusses his afterlife experience, reporting the position of Hades to be 3,700 miles below the surface of the planet. The number fits in well with known depths. The radial distance from sea level to the border of the outer/inner core is 3,200 miles. Earth's center is at 3,959 miles. The difference leaves Hades' depth sitting between 3,200 and 3,959 miles with his 3,700-mile distance being reasonable.

Conclusion on Sheol–Hades Under the Earth

Death occurs frequently in the Hebrew scriptures, so attention is often given to the final resting place of departed souls. Over half of the sixty-five scriptures discussing Sheol indicate a nadir direction (downward) into the heart of the planet. In the New Testament, Jesus affirms the direction when discussing the fate of Capernaum. In Luke 10:15, he states that the city would be "brought down to Hades," reaffirming the common notion of Sheol–Hades situating inside the earth. Before the death of Jesus, the direction of *all souls* going into the afterlife was descending. After his

---

100 Because of his exclusive use of the KJV Bible, Weiss mistakenly uses "hell" instead of "Hades." In Christian writing, one should reference a number of Bible translations. Bill Wiese, *23 Minutes in Hell* (Lake Mary, FL: Charisma House, 2006), 1-193.

resurrection, the direction of *unrighteous souls* going into the afterlife remains descending.

In being deep inside of Earth, and having the ability to retain open space, the metallic core qualifies as a place for the captivity of lost souls. Spatially, the 500 cubic miles of open space for Hades fits easily within the large 1.8 billion mi^3 spherical volume of the inner core. The centrality of the core adds to its credibility as well. Heading in a nadir direction from every spot on the earth's surface leads directly to the center. A thorough review finds that seismologists can verify the solidity of the earth, except for the inner core. As such, the metaphysics for Sheol–Hades being in the heart of the planet receives both biblical and technical sanction.

According to the MacDougall study, soul substance departs and causes bodily weight loss once a human being passes away. Souls will then enter the intertwining world of eternity and the physical universe. The righteous soul will depart for heaven. The unrighteous soul will depart for Hades and begin to traverse the inner earth. Like Jesus passing through an angry crowd, or negotiating a solid wall to visit the disciples, the soul will supernaturally pass through the crust, mantle, and liquid outer core until reaching the netherworld of the inner core. Able to manifest its weight and volume in a hollow space, soul substance will then take up residency.

Arriving in Hades, an impenitent person would quickly learn that the grace and goodness of God is absent. Detention in the inner parts of the planet lacks any pleasure. The chamber would be completely dark and exist under high temperature and pressure. Removing God from any habitation creates a bad situation. The confines are empty of his influence and attributes. The only thing remaining would be despair, torment, misery, and dread. How can there be love or affection, tranquility or rest, joy or contentment without God? In a real sense, Hades is a hot, isolated, pitch-black, and unpleasant holding tank for unrighteous souls waiting for final judgment.

The devil wants little to do with the underworld, though he has aided many in going there. Satan's punishment of one thousand years in the pit speaks to his distaste for Hades. His desire is to roam the earth, to practice evil, and to deceive people. Hollywood sometimes depicts the devil in human form wearing a tight red outfit. He has two horns and an arrowed tail and brandishes a pitchfork while sitting on his throne. Fire blows from his fingertips as he points in defiance. While masterminding mayhem, he seems to enjoy his residence in the inner earth. All of that is nonsense. In truth, credence cannot be given to Satan making Hades his home or finding any pleasure there.

The parable of the rich man and Lazarus gives a representative scene in Hades, where a conversation takes place between departed souls. Does this mean dialogue is possible? Can souls leave a private cell and gain access to a common area, where they can see and speak to one another? The passage in Isaiah 14:9–17 discusses bringing Satan down to Sheol. The last two verses state, "Those who see you will stare at you, and ponder over you: 'Is this the man who made the earth tremble, who shook kingdoms, who made the world like a desert and over threw its cities, who would not let his prisoners go home?'" The passage lends credibility to being able to interact with others in Hades.

Is it possible to derive any good news about the underground prison? Not really. The residents are simply waiting for the Day of Judgment. Every human being, both small and great, will stand before the throne of the Holy One. Souls emptying out of the netherworld of Hades will be equipped with immortal spiritual bodies for a final appearance on the earth's surface. Every person will stand on his or her own accord before the great white throne. Life reviews will contain acts of sin, and individuals will be held responsible for those actions. Excuses are not acceptable and no advocacy will be available. A finding of guilty is the expected verdict in this court setting.

After final judgment on the earth's surface, transport to the lake of fire is the next step. Departing into the atmosphere means seeing the renewed planet Earth for one last time. Feelings of loss and sorrow will come to those being permanently barred from a restored, beautiful world. Lost people have forfeited the privilege of a paradisical abode and will be heading to the surface of a dismal world. What follows is the boredom and discomfort of living on a hot, dry, desolate, and extremely undesirable planet or exoplanet filled with volcanic spew. Being above ground, planet surfaces such as Venus are an improved venue over Hades. Still, it provides little satisfaction for the long term.

Chapter 7

Unveiling Venus as a Place of Perdition

In the mid-twentieth century, elective college courses in astronomy were scarce. There was simply not enough information known about space. Through advances in telescope technology, knowledge has evolved to the point where students can access plenty of material about the universe, galaxies, stars, and planets. Planetary science can examine the formation, composition, and orbital dynamics of distant worlds. Being multidisciplinary, planetary science utilizes fields such as geology, volcanology, atmospheric science, chemistry, and space physics. In giving an overview of our neighboring planet, the chapter will draw upon these disciplines.

Information about Venus unfolds slowly over human history. Our review begins with stargazing thousands of years ago by ancient civilizations and ends with present-day spacecraft exploration. Venus is a luminous planet and can be seen during the day. By outshining all stars and planets, the celestial body has attracted great attention over the centuries. After the sun and the moon, Venus is the brightest object in the sky. It has the unique ability to cast shadows at night. The brightness is due to its size, proximity, and albedo. Albedo, or reflective power, comes from its cloud cover, where an extraordinary 76% of incident sunlight reflects off the cloud tops.

Venus is known as our sister or twin planet because of two factors. First, she retains an atmosphere and is about the same size, mass, and composition as our planet. Second, her orbit is in close proximity to the earth's orbit. The use of "sister" or "twin," however, is tongue-in-cheek. Even upon simple inspection, parallels between the two worlds diminish. For example, Venus has no moon and is continually cloaked by cloud cover. The clouds mask many secrets. The reader will discover that breakthrough knowledge about the second planet from the sun did not come about until the early 1960s.

Success in being able to unveil Venus came through (1) reliable rocketry, which was a milestone of the space race, and (2) the maturity of communication hardware aboard spacecraft. The electrical bus of a spacecraft provides the infrastructure necessary for mounting payload equipment such as antennas, radiometers, magnetometers, spectrometers, synthetic aperture radar (SAR), and visual imaging systems. Once in space, keeping the communication link going between the spacecraft and ground control becomes essential. Together, the two technological advances of the Space Age were able to bring new insights about the inner planet.

When information about Venus unfolds, biblical comparisons to perdition develop. The reader becomes aware that this place could become the future abode of the unrepentant. Each section will relate planetary findings to scriptural references of hell and the lake of fire. The gathering of the facts will culminate in a tabular summary at the end of the chapter. The recap brings focus to perdition being located in our solar system. Similar to heaven being on Earth, our neighboring planet acting as perdition brings the physical universe and the eternal realm into one accord. New urgency will arise about avoiding banishment to Venus, or any similar-type exoplanet in the cosmos.

Venus through the Naked Eye

The word "planet" is derived from the Greek word *planetes*, which means "wanderer." Beyond a doubt, Venus is a wanderer. The planet switches back and forth in the night sky between the morning star in the east and the evening star in the west. As the evening star, Venus drops into the dark, starry horizon of the night as it slowly follows the sun after sundown. As the morning star, the planet rises up out of the predawn, leading the sun in the final hours before daybreak. The term "star" derives from the amazing brightness of Venus. Far more luminous than any real star in the sky, Venus does not fade or appear to twinkle, but rather glows with a steady light.

The ancient Egyptian and Greek cultures made the mistake of classifying the morning star and evening star as two separate objects in the night sky. During the Hellenistic period, the Greeks came to realize the two objects were the same planet. Other cultures were more astute in studying the heavens. By judicious stellar surveillance, the ancient Babylonians were able to understand Venus as a single celestial body. The Babylonian record of nightly observation was kept intact. The clay tablets of Ammisaduqa, compiled in mid-seventeenth-century BC, document Venus setting in the evening, and at later times, rising in the morning.

Venus' name comes from Roman mythology, which parallels Greek mythology. To the Greeks, Aphrodite was the goddess of sexual love, beauty, and fertility. Being the daughter of Zeus, Aphrodite led a life of beguiling gods and men alike. She laughs sweetly or mockingly at those overcome by her charm and deceit. The Romans gave her the name Venus, the goddess of love and beauty. Venus is the only planet in the solar system named after a female. It may be due to the captivating glow of the celestial body. Images of the goddess Venus situate in many places around the world. She comes across as an alluring woman in sculptures, paintings, and mosaics.

In the Americas, the Maya, Aztec, and Inca civilizations paid close attention to Venus. The Mayan people were faithful observers of the sky who built shrines dedicated to nighttime observation and mapped out phases of the moon. One structure, the El Caracol, in the ancient archaeological site of Chichen Itza, Mexico, is a domed building resembling an observatory. Slots cut out in the rock of the dome look out toward points on the celestial sphere, where Mayan astronomer-priests charted heavenly bodies such as Venus. The role of the planets in the culture went beyond casual observation to being objects of worship and markers of times and seasons.

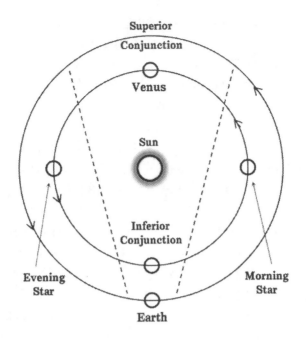

Figure 14
Viewing Venus from Earth

In looking down at the sun's north pole, Figure 14 shows Earth and Venus in their respective paths. Venus is sixty-seven million miles from the sun, while Earth is ninety-three million miles. While Earth orbits the sun in the outer circle, Venus is orbiting faster on the inner circle. Being closer to the sun, Venus has a stronger gravitational lock, meaning she is higher in angular velocity about her orbital path. Earth revolves around the sun in 365.24 days, while Venus takes 224.7 (Earth) days for the same voyage. On successive views as an evening star, Venus sprints to catch up with us. Later, when she appears as a morning star, Venus moves away, leaving us trailing behind.

As a sphere of hot plasma, the sun rotates on its axis in an asymmetrical manner. At the equator it takes twenty-four days to fully rotate, while at the poles it takes closer to thirty days. In continuing to look down at the sun's north pole, one will reference the sun spins in the counterclockwise (CCW) direction. In like manner, the paths of Earth, Venus, and all planets follow the CCW direction. With both planets orbiting counterclockwise, Venus' closest approach to Earth occurs once every 584 days, when the planets catch up to one another. The two dotted lines cut through the orbit of Venus, dividing up the 584-day cycle.

The out-of-view period for the planet is inside the dotted lines. It is a time when Venus cannot be seen from Earth. The out-of-view period contains inferior and superior conjunction. A conjunction occurs when two celestial objects, such as the sun and Venus, appear in close proximity in the sky. Inferior conjunction is where Venus is in front of the sun and closest to Earth. Superior junction is where Venus is farthest from Earth and behind the sun. The out-of-view period is much longer at superior conjunction than it is at inferior conjunction.

The in-view period for the planet is outside the dotted lines. The diagram shows Venus as the evening star on the left and the morning star on the right when it is in view. As the evening star, it sets nightly in the western sky over the course of several months. Then, following inferior conjunction, it begins its pre-dawn rise in the east. The placement of the two circles for the evening and morning star in Figure 14 is at the point of maximum elongation. At maximum elongation, you can see the inner planet at its highest elevation in the night sky, which is 47.5° above the horizon.

How many evenings per year can a person see Venus? To begin with, Venus will either be following the setting sun or leading the rising sun. As the sun rises and sets, it will move north and south with the seasons. The inner planet follows the sun's repositioning. The main factor for determining in-view time is location on the earth. In the mid-latitudes, you can expect total observing times in the east and west to go beyond 200 days a year. A smaller variable affecting viewing is the pattern Venus happens to be making in the night sky. Over an 8-year period, the planet will display five different patterns, with some patterns hovering closer to the horizon than others.[101]

The ability to see Venus from Earth will not change at any point in the future. And the future includes the second coming of Christ. When the saints return to the third planet from the sun with Jesus, the second planet from the sun will still be observable in the night sky. The evening star will still set in the west, and the morning star will still rise in the east. The question then becomes, "Does any scripture in the Bible suggest that righteous individuals will have the ability to see the unrighteous in perdition?" Intuitively, the idea of heaven on Earth as a perfect place of happiness and contentment would tend not to back up such a notion.

The first passage supporting a viewing of the unrighteous is from Isaiah 66:22–24, which was shown in chapter 2. Verses 23 and 24 tell of all flesh worshipping the Lord from new moon to new moon, while being able to "look at the dead bodies of the people who have rebelled against me." All people loving God is indicative of being in a heavenly place, such as the paradisical Earth. In verse 24, the people are able to look upon the suffering of the dead, which includes an unquenchable fire and their worm never dying. Jesus uses these same terms to describe perdition. So, Isaiah 66:24 seems to imply the righteous have visibility into the state of affairs of the lost.

A second enlightening passage is in Revelation 14:10, which reads, "they will also drink the wine of God's wrath, poured unmixed into the cup of his anger, and they will be tormented with fire and sulfur in the presence of the holy

---

101 Over successive eight-year periods, the five patterns repeat nearly identically. David H. Grinspoon, *Venus Revealed: A New Look Below the Clouds of Our Mysterious Twin Planet* (Reading, MA: Addison-Wesley, 1997), 10.

angels and in the presence of the Lamb."[102] The prophecy speaks about God's anger, then tells of the fate of the sinful, and concludes with a viewing of the situation by spiritual beings. The word for "presence" (Gk. *enopios*) can mean "in the sight of." Those living in the company of angels and Jesus Christ can witness the retribution of fire and sulfur toward the guilty.

A final passage backing up righteous people seeing those in distress is in the parable of Luke 16:19–31, discussed in chapter 2. In the account, Abraham and Lazarus can see the sufferings of the rich man firsthand while in Hades. Situated in Abraham's bosom, the righteous can see the suffering of the unrighteous in an adjacent habitation. Though taking place in Hades before the final judgment, the scene can foreshadow a time after final judgment when those who have been saved will see the plight of those who have been banished.

Assimilating the idea behind the three passages of Isaiah 66:22–24, Revelation 14:10, and Luke 16:19–31 can suggest that those living on Earth will be able to look into the night sky at the dismal abode of perdition. The Bible does not reveal any pious planning to keep God's people blind to the fate of the lost. In the afterlife, the righteous can observe the fate of the unrighteous in a designated place of distress, whether it be on Venus, or perhaps a star with an undesirable exoplanet. The night sky is clearly visible when outdoors in this present age. In the age to come, the same night sky will be visible to those who are outdoors on the restored and paradisical Earth.

---

102 John the Baptist uses the term "Lamb of God" for Jesus in John 1:29. The imagery of the Lamb is drawn from the Passover lamb in Exodus. Jesus was the sacrificial lamb led to slaughter at the crucifixion. Coogan, *New Oxford Annotated Bible*, 149 [NT].

Venus through the Telescope

A telescope is an optical instrument designed to make distant objects appear near, aiding greatly in their study. The arrangement of lenses and mirrors collects and focuses light, thereby allowing magnification of the resulting image. By using a telescope, you would think astronomers could gain significant knowledge about Venus. After all, enlargement of Mars can distinguish polar ice caps and determine the planet's rotation rate and axial tilt. In the outer solar system, telescopes help pick out several moons of Jupiter as well as its Great Red Spot. Pointed further out toward Saturn, the telescope is able to discern the planet's amazing rings as well as many of its natural satellites.

The surface of our neighboring inner planet, however, is not agreeable to telescopic observation. The perfect cloaking device against optical instruments is dense, perpetual cloud cover. Seen through the telescope, Venus' thick atmosphere completely blocks the surface of the planet. Finding features on the celestial body is nearly impossible with an obfuscating view that never changes. The clouds present a yellow-white tinge of color but are otherwise bare and lacking in detail. Not known by early observers, the yellow tinge is due to sulfuric acid, a clear-yellow chemical in the cloud cover.

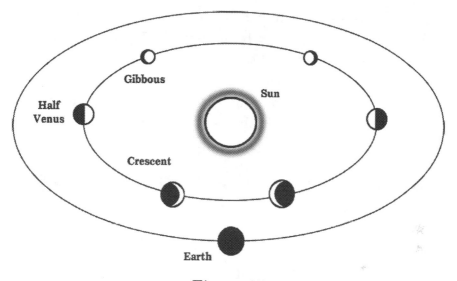

Figure 15
Orbital Phases of Venus

The first observation of the night sky using an optical telescope took place in 1610 by the Italian astronomer Galileo Galilei. The 20x magnification of his new tool showed Venus as a disc rather than a bright pinpoint in the sky. In being the first person to look at the actual shape, Galileo made meaningful discoveries. As depicted in Figure 15, the disc appears in phases, like a waxing and waning moon. Seeing phases in a nearby celestial body was groundbreaking. The revelation allowed for accepting Venus, and all the other planets, as orbiting the sun. As a result, Galileo disputed the (Ptolemaic) geocentric model and fully accepted the heliocentric model of Copernicus.

Additionally, Galileo took note of the image size of the inner planet. As the evening star, the first sighting is in the gibbous phase, when the planet is farthest from Earth and displays the smallest image size. The planet moves to become a half Venus with increasing girth. It finishes in the crescent phase, showing its greatest span while being closest to our world. Following inferior conjunction, she appears as the morning star and reveals the large crescent image in reverse. The planet then moves to become a half Venus. It finishes farthest away in the gibbous phase before disappearing behind the sun at superior conjunction.

As noted in Figure 14, Venus goes through two out-of-view periods due to the sun's obstruction—that being superior conjunction and inferior conjunction. At superior conjunction, a full Venus occurs between the gibbous phases. It is not shown in Figure 15 because it is behind the sun and not visible from Earth. At inferior conjunction, a new Venus occurs between the crescent phases. Again, it is not shown because it lacks visibility from Earth. Venus will normally cross either above or below the sun, with the sun's brightness blocking observation. On very rare occasion, a new Venus will transit in front of the sun and become visible.

The book's cover depicts the last transit for this century, captured by NASA's Solar Dynamic Observatory in 2012. Venus is seen as a small, dark disc moving across a fiery solar surface. Venus is at inferior conjunction every 584 days, but the time between transit pairs ends up being over 100 years.[103] This means the planet finds itself crossing above or below the sun most of the time. Routinely missing the disc of the sun is due to Venus' orbital plane inclining 3.4° relative to Earth's orbital plane. The tilt results in very long waiting periods between transits. Since the average lifespan of a human is about eighty years, not everyone can live to experience the event.

Finding Venus in the night sky is not the exclusive privilege of people living in dark, rural areas or poorly lit

---

103 Transits of Venus occur in pairs, separated by eight years, after which no transit occurs for over a century. The last transit pair was in 2004 and 2012. Future transits pairs are 2117 and 2125, and 2247 and 2255. *Sky and Telescope*, "Transits of Venus Explained," https://www.skyandtelescope.com/astronomy-news/observing-news/transits-of-venus-explained/ (accessed Nov. 2, 2020).

small towns. The brilliance of the inner planet makes it an urban attraction. Normally, celestial bodies are not visible in a metropolis due to bright streetlights. Stars fade badly under high-wattage illumination. Venus resists the candlepower of the electric grid and shows up near the horizon. She will shine through car windows, sliding glass doors, across parking lots, and inside stadiums. The inner planet will watch you pick up a Starbucks coffee at 6:30 a.m. or drink your favorite beverage at an outdoor café at 9 p.m.

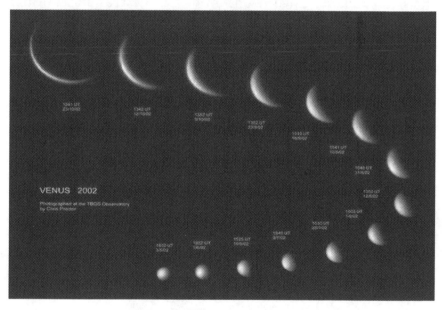

Figure 16
Apparent Size of Venus in the Sky

The photo in Figure 16 shows Venus increasing in size to a crescent as it approaches the earth as the evening star. Angular diameter will measure the planet's size in degrees. In angular terms, one degree breaks down into arc minutes (1/60th of one degree) and then into arc seconds (1/3600th of one degree). Stars and planets range from 0.005 to 66.0 arc seconds. Venus' appearance in the small gibbous phase measures 9.5 arc seconds, and when it grows to the crescent phase it becomes 66 arc seconds. The crescent is the largest and brightest object in the sky, excluding the sun and the moon. The sun and the moon are 1800 arc seconds or 0.5 degrees in diameter.

Following the success of Galileo, telescopes became the primary method for observing the night sky, with the inner planet being one focus of attention. In the transit of Venus in 1639, Jeremiah Horrocks and William Crabtree of England became the first astronomers to make record of the event (no public documents have been found for the transit in 1631). Horrocks made use of a Galilean-type refracting telescope to project the sun's image onto a fixed screen behind the eyepiece. His data log reveals an apparent diameter of 65 arc seconds, which correlates closely to modern measurements.[104]

Giovanni Battista Riccioli, an Italian astronomer and Catholic priest of the Jesuit order, was the first to notice a subtle blush emanating from the dark side of Venus' disc. Documented in 1643, the event became known as "ashen light." Since his discovery, many astronomers have observed the same phenomenon. The radiance appears as a transient, low-level shine. In the twentieth century, viewing the planet in the infrared wavelength (which lies on the edge of the visible spectrum) attributed the radiance to intense thermal heat emanating from the planet's surface.

Cloud cover smothering the world in perpetual secrecy was not known to observers until the transit of Venus in 1761. At the time, Russian scientist Mikhail Lomonosov was using leading-edge optics. The new lensing led to seeing a hazy perimeter around Venus during the sun's crossing. The blurring of the rim is due to refraction of sunlight through the clouds. Secondary evidence for a prominent atmosphere came from the planet's fuzzy edge rising up slightly during ingress (entering) and egress (exiting) of the sun's border.

---

104 Patrick Moore, *Venus* (Great Britain: Octopus Publishing, 2002), 94.

The astronomer's observation of global cloud cover was the last new discovery about the planet for hundreds of years.

Imaginations of Venus

Over the next two centuries, scientific facts about Venus were never realized. Wishful thinking took its place. A span of this length without new information about a nearby celestial object is extremely long. During the period, many advances were made. Electric light bulbs took the place of candlelight. Hand manufacturing gave way to specialized machinery and tools. Inventions such as the automobile, airplane, television, and computer were brought forth. Yet, Venus' blurry disc remained an enigma. Telescopic records on file show carefully drawn surface features such as continents, polar ice caps, and canals, all of which amount to little more than fantasy.

Naturally, two centuries without any news about our neighbor led to generations of people speculating about life on the planet. Basic questions arose, such as "Does Venus have an oxygen atmosphere?" and "Is there water on the surface?" After all, Venus is a terrestrial world that is about the same size as Earth. Being in a nearby orbit means the planet is in our habitable zone, which supports life. Perhaps the cloud cover compensates for Venus being closer to the sun and helps to retain necessary moisture. Lying beneath the canopy could be a high-humidity planet, experiencing constant rainfall. The steady rain must create marshlands, lakes, rivers, and even large oceans.

Emerging from the mind's eye was a sister world filled with jungles and lush, tropical rain forests, teeming with dense, impenetrable vegetation and succulent plants. By extension, a marshy globe where water and plants exist in such abundance could support marine and animal life. So naturally, fish, birds, amphibians, reptiles, and mammals could exist on the surface.

In 1903, a Swedish physicist and chemist, Svante Arrhenius, received the Nobel Prize in Chemistry for his discovery of electrolytic dissociation. He later became interested in planetary atmospheres and their role in climate. Being a Nobel laureate, his writings garnered lots of attention. In 1918, he authored a book titled *The Destinies of the Stars*. It gave a dramatic and alluring view of our neighboring planet.

Arrhenius describes Venus as an extremely humid place covered with swamplands, where everything is dripping wet. He calculates an average temperature of 115°F in the equatorial latitudes. It is a world where expanses of lush vegetation are accelerated in growth by dampness. He compares Venus' evolutionary phase to the earth's Carboniferous Period. The Carboniferous Period was a geologic era 360 to 300 million years ago when amphibians, swamplands, and plant life covered our planet. His assessment was the best science could offer at the time.

Science fiction was a genre containing a vibrant picture of Venus. Scholars classify the late 1930s through early 1950s as the "golden age" of science fiction writing.[105] In *Perelandra* (1943), the second book of *The Space Trilogy*, C. S. Lewis describes Venus as an oceanic paradise where animals live on free-floating rafts of vegetation. Influential author John W. Campbell, who helped shape the science fiction age, republished *The Black Star Passes* (1953). It contains an account of Venus as the home of an advanced civilization. In Ray Bradbury's short story collection, *A Medicine for Melancholy* (1959), we find the provocative narrative, "All

---

105 University of Hamburg English Department, "A Virtual Introduction to Science Fiction: Online Toolkit for Teaching SF," http://virtual-sf. com/?page_id=239 (accessed March 24, 2021).

Summer in a Day," in which a colony living on rainy Venus sees the sun for only one hour every seven years.

Also manifesting belief in Venus as a nurturing and populated planet were television and film. The traditional Hollywood gender assigned to the Venusian is female, as the planet's feminine name seems to dictate the sex of the inhabitants. Law enforcement adventures by *Space Patrol*, an admired 1950s television and radio science fiction series, has an Earth-based interplanetary police force frequently encountering alien outlaws. On swampy Venus, the crew of patrolling astronauts finds a world teeming with dinosaurs and tribes of Amazon women.

The 1957 sci-fi movie, *20 Million Miles to Earth*, opens with the end of a round trip to Venus by a United States spacecraft. The title of the film is an estimate of the distance between the two planets. Starring William Hopper, Joan Taylor, and Frank Puglia, the movie presumes crewmen return safely from the inner world. The ship carries a sealed metal box containing a gelatinous mass that hatches into a small Venusian creature. Eating sulfur along the way, it grows rapidly into a hideous, gargantuan monster that wreaks havoc. After a chase scene, the beast falls to its death from the top of the Colosseum in Rome, Italy.

The popular 1958 movie, *Queen of Outer Space*, is the story of Venus under the rule of a colony of women. It stars Zsa Zsa Gábor, Eric Fleming, and Laurie Mitchell. In the film, an exploratory space crew from Earth crash-lands on the twin planet. The team of men wander around the lush, habitable surface until captured by a multitude of eye-catching females. The space travelers learn the planet is under the dictatorship of cruel Queen Yllana. She is a masked woman who has either killed off or banished the males of the planet. The incarceration is short-lived, as the women rebel against the queen's rule and seek after the love of the men.

Uncovering the Truth About
Our Neighboring World

In the 1930s, scientists began researching the idea of gathering data from space by going outside the visible band. A wider breadth of the electromagnetic spectrum allows for using microwave and infrared frequencies. Hardware advances were to bring the advent of the radio telescope, which is a large dish antenna. Staring into the night sky in the 1950s was a 50-foot receiver mounted at the US Naval Research Laboratory (NRL) in Washington, DC. Pointed toward Venus in a passive collection mode, the antenna undertook a "listening ear" operation. In 1956, the NRL gave a report about the signal collection coming through Earth's atmosphere from the sister world.

The microwaves arriving from Venus were in the wavelength range of 3 to 10 cm, which calculates to a temperature source exceeding 500°F. The results were given to the technical community. At first, scientists were skeptical, viewing the data as questionable. Over the many months, ideas began to emerge about a hot inner planet that could not support life. It became a top priority for the first spaceflight to precisely determine the location of the radiation. It could come from either a thick ionosphere in the cloud cover or emanate from the planet's surface. The vision of a tropical, moist Venus, teeming with vegetation and animal life, was a bubble on the verge of bursting.

The desire for Venus to be a lush planet is a stark reminder about the paradox of the night sky. The romantic allure of a full moon, the luster of the Milky Way galaxy, and the dazzle of Venus attach to our emotions. Unless proven otherwise, you should consider celestial locations to be harsh and unpleasant. Consider the high esteem given to colonizing Mars. The red planet is an uninviting and dangerous place. A reality check brings into focus a cold, dry, dusty, and barren world with no oxygen or water supply. Even the soil is toxic and cannot grow food because of perchlorates. When compared to our warm, safe, and beautiful home planet, other worlds lack quite a bit.

Does the Bible address a celestial afterlife in a negative way? Consider some illuminating statements made by the Lord when warning against perdition. In three passages of the Gospel of Matthew (8:12, 22:13, and 25:30), Jesus cautions people about not being "thrown into the outer darkness, where there will be weeping and gnashing of teeth." For centuries, perplexed Bible readers have been asking, "What is the meaning of outer darkness?" One possible answer is evident. Being "thrown into outer darkness" is depicting a journey from the earth's surface into the blackness of the night sky, with the final destination being an unpleasant location.

One mainstream Bible commentary tries to explain "outer darkness" in Matthew 22:13 as being outside a building. In the parable, a certain man ends up in outer darkness for not being properly attired for a wedding banquet. The wedding banquet is symbolic of the kingdom of heaven. Supposedly, the banquet is being held indoors in a well-lit ballroom at night. So, exclusion from the festivity represents being sent outside the facility and into outer darkness. The problem is Matthew 8:12 and 25:30 also warn against going into outer darkness with no mention of a wedding celebration. So, the commentary cannot satisfy the three uses of the term "outer darkness."

A better explanation is to consider "thrown into the outer darkness" to mean the darkness of the night sky; that is, the blackness of the celestial realm. Darkness is a naturally occurring condition of outer space when looking up into the sky after the sun has gone down. In the first-century travels by Jesus and the apostles, the night firmament was exceedingly dark, with stars filling the night sky due to the lack of outdoor lighting. Gazing up into the expanse of a pitch-black, star-lit sky of a late evening campsite, the Lord could intuitively have warned his apostles about the danger of lost people being transported into the outer darkness overhead.

Given the first-century mindset, one can see how mysterious and confusing the term "outer darkness" would have been to individuals. The collective consciousness of Jewish society had souls going downward toward Sheol, not upward. The writings of the first century occur in a time of general societal ignorance about outer space. Grasping the idea of Earth revolving around the sun and being part of a solar system of planets, which was then part of a larger Milky Way galaxy was incomprehensible. To most people, the multitude of stars were simply distant suns circling in allegiance to Earth. Like the oceans, the vastness of outer space was beyond understanding.

On a clear, sunny day, the blue skies of Earth are brightly lit. Light from the sun absorbs and reflects off our atmosphere, which consists of gas molecules and particulate matter. Blue light scatters readily because of its shorter wavelength, making it the visible color. Beyond our planet, outer space is black because of the absence of an atmosphere. Sunlight cannot be absorbed or reflected in the vacuum of space, so the surroundings lack color and brightness. A voyage exiting Earth on the way to Venus (or an exoplanet) will go from light blue skies to dark surroundings. The sensation of going from light into an outer darkness would be the result.

By the early 1960s, radio telescopes were making new contributions to space science by using active radar. A radar system can be active, rather than passive, when it generates an outbound signal on one antenna and then picks up the return signal on a second antenna. The outbound and return antennas are set up in different locations. High-frequency radio waves bounce off nearby celestial objects and then return to the earth. It allows for mapping of solid bodies by gathering data about surfaces and shapes. Success with ground-based radar was first reported after World War II, when waves echoing off the moon could measure surface roughness.

Active radio telescope work was done on Venus in 1961–62 by the Goldstone Observatory, located in the Mojave Desert near Barstow, California. Two eighty-foot dish antennas, one transmitting and the other receiving, were set up six miles apart at the facility. Pointing toward the inner planet, the antennas detected faint topographic features on the planet's surface. When features were isolated, the scientists could conduct a timing study. The timing study would uncover information about axial rotation.

The observatory made two surprising discoveries. The first concerns the directional rotation of the inner planet, which is backward or retrograde. In contrast to Earth and other planets in the solar system, Venus spins on its axis in the opposite direction. The one difference is Uranus, which rotates on its side in reference to the plane of the planets. So, depending on your view, Venus is either (1) spinning upside down, or (2) spinning right-side-up in the reverse direction. In either case, a person standing on Venus' surface would see daybreak on the western horizon and nightfall on the eastern horizon.

The second finding at Goldstone was the spin rate of Venus, which is extremely slow. The planet rotates on its axis at a snail's pace. It has a sidereal day lasting 243 Earth days. A sidereal day measures one complete spin of a planet relative to a fixed reference frame, such as distant stars. On Earth, a sidereal day lasts 23 hours, 56 minutes, and 4 seconds, while a solar day lasts 24 hours. The daily difference of 3 minutes and 56 seconds between sidereal and solar time eventually necessitates a leap year. The leap year adds the 29th day to February every four years, keeping the Gregorian calendar year synchronized with the solar year.

The question then becomes, "With such a lengthy sidereal day, how long does a solar day last on Venus?" A solar day provides a better understanding of what is happening on the surface. It measures the time it takes for a person on the planet to see the sun travel around once, returning to the same position in the sky. It gives a complete "day and night" cycle to the residents of the planet. Calculating a solar day on Venus requires a special formula. The computation considers the backward spin direction, the sidereal day (243 Earth days), and the orbital period around the sun (225 Earth days).[106] The calculated time for the event comes out to about 117 Earth days.

Knowing a full "day and night" period on Venus lasts 117 Earth days brings up an interesting thought. The length of the Venusian day will divide evenly between the daylight and nighttime. From the perspective of an earthling, living on the planet Venus would mean having 58.5 days of consecutive daylight (overcast skies) between sunrise and sunset, followed by 58.5 days of consecutive darkness between sunset and sunrise. The day and the night are extremely long periods of time on Venus.

With this in mind, we can again consider Jesus' warning about being "thrown into the outer darkness." First, his depiction can be seen as a dimly lit journey through the outer darkness of outer space. Second, it may now include the final destination as well. People are normally used to about twelve hours of daylight, followed by twelve hours of darkness. Relatively speaking, the 58.5 days of cloudiness followed by 58.5 days of nightfall would seem drab and

---

106 The formula to calculate the duration of a solar day is as follows: Length of Solar Day = Length of Sidereal Day / 1 + (Length of Sidereal Day / Orbital Period of Planet). In a practical sense, the exceedingly slow movement of the sun across the Venusian sky occurs because of two virtually equivalent impulses: the spin of the planet and the coursing of the planet around the sun.

gloomy to someone from Earth. The long, dark nights on Venus could easily bear a resemblance to living in a place of outer darkness, as one endures a two-month absence of daylight.

One final ground-based discovery about the inner planet was made by the Anglo-Australian Telescope, located in New South Wales, Australia, in June 1983. The twelve-foot-diameter Cassegrain reflector was specially equipped with an infrared (IR) imaging spectrometer, which was attached to the body of the telescope. Using the arrangement, a spectrometer can separate out frequencies of electromagnetic radiation when observing a celestial body. The astronomers could then focus directly on the IR portion of the spectrum, which can pick up invisible sources of thermal radiation or heat.

Operating a few wavelengths longer than visible light in the near-IR, Venus' dark side displays amazingly bright, gaseous swirls. It turns out the intense 865°F heat emanating from the surface of the planet could be picked up in the IR range using the spectrometer. The temperature is hot enough to create a visible radiance in the infrared, which readily penetrates through the cloud cover. The result is seeing glowing swirls that ebb and flow on the dark side of the planetary disc. The findings provided technical validation for the first telescopic sighting of ashen light by Italian astronomer and Catholic priest, Giovanni Battista Riccioli in 1643.

The Spacecraft Revelation of Venus

A spacecraft is a vehicle capable of operating beyond Earth's atmosphere, with or without a crew onboard. Spacecraft are used for a variety of purposes, with planetary exploration being one application. The combined efforts of the United States, the former Soviet Union, Japan, and the European

Space Agency (ESA) have contributed to the spacecraft exploration of Venus. History reveals over forty attempts to launch spacecraft carrying sensors to the inner planet. The desire to explore strange new worlds requires pushing scientific know-how to its limits, and then pushing further. This section will review some of the successful spacecraft endeavors and their discoveries.

Initially, space exploration by the United States and Soviet Union began in the late 1950s as a space race between the two nations. Space missions divide into two categories: manned and unmanned programs. Manned flights going to the moon are feasible for humans because of proximity. Depending on the mission, the time for the round trip is one to two weeks. The period pales in comparison to one-way voyages to places such as Venus and Mars, which end up taking many months. The primary goal for these missions is the successful remote control of electronics and robotics over tens to hundreds of millions of miles in the hopes of sending back data.

By the early 1960s, aerospace technology or "rocket science" reached the point of producing accurate and repeatable launches, giving a place for spacecraft in Earth's orbit and beyond. Vehicles traveling past the moon and into deep space require dependable communication systems and directional antennas. The key capability is to reliably transmit ground commands, have the spacecraft receive the signal, and then conduct a task, maneuver, or return of data. On the earth, proper geographic location for control stations, as well as suitable antenna size and signal strength, are essential for continuous contact and data exchange.

Understanding how to deal with the environment of outer space is critical for interplanetary travel. As noted earlier, outer space is not an empty vacuum. The intergalactic, interstellar, and interplanetary mediums contain energized particulate matter. For example, the sun brings heat to our planet by way of the solar wind, which generates from nuclear fusion in the sun. The energy source is seen in the steady stream of charged particles entering the atmosphere at the poles, creating an aurora effect. The solar wind occupies a vast, spherical region of space that surrounds the sun. It moves unimpeded through the solar system, extending far beyond Pluto and the Kuiper Belt.

The increasing intensity of solar radiation moving toward the sun must be taken into consideration for spacecraft heading toward Mercury and Venus. The plasma of the solar wind will vary in intensity over time. Solar activity such as sunspots and solar flares exacerbate the amount of emitted radiation going into the heliosphere. The heliosphere is the name given to the bubble-like expanse of space surrounding the sun that contains the energy of the solar wind. The journeys of Voyager 1 and Voyager 2 spacecraft reveal the strength and expansiveness of the heliosphere, with the furthest edge stretching out to eleven billion miles.[107]

Two other concerns of interplanetary space exploration are cosmic rays and micrometeoroids. Cosmic rays are high-energy, atomic-size elements from outside the solar system, which travel close to the speed of light. Usually in the form of a proton, the particle can damage electronics, causing mission-altering events. A micrometeoroid is a particle about the size of a piece of dust that travels at high velocity. Even though the projectile is small, it has penetrating power. It can physically enter and damage areas of a spaceship. With or without a crew onboard, cosmic rays, micrometeoroids, and the solar wind pose a continual threat to vehicles in outer space.

---

107 On Sept. 12, 2013, NASA announced Voyager 1 had left the heliosphere and was moving into interstellar space. Subsequently, Voyager 2 left the solar system on Nov. 5, 2018. NASA, "How Do We Know When Voyager Reaches Interstellar Space?" http://www.jpl.nasa.gov/news/news.php?release=2013-278 (accessed Dec. 15, 2020).

With the target being Venus, the United States was the first country to achieve a successful mission to another planet. On August 27, 1962, an Atlas LV-3 rocket with an Agena-B second stage lifted off from Cape Canaveral, carrying the Mariner 2 spacecraft. Minor attitude control and solar array issues occurred along the way before reaching Venus on December 14, 1962. NASA's Mariner 2 flew by the inner planet at a distance of 21,600 miles and scanned the atmosphere for forty-two minutes. Radiometers were onboard to measure for temperature, while a magnetometer and Geiger-Müller particle tube sought to detect the magnetic field and any radiation belts.

Mariner 2 was able to clearly discern the source of the high temperature microwave radiation found by the U. S. Naval Research Laboratory radio telescope in 1956. It was coming from the surface of the planet, not the ionosphere or cloud cover. The high atmospheric cloud cover was relatively cool in temperature, but scans made on both the light and dark side of the planet showed temperatures at several hundred degrees Fahrenheit. The bad news permanently changed attitudes about the planet. Today, we know the average surface temperature to be near 865°F. The scorching heat at Venus' surface will liquefy tin at 450°F, lead at 620°F, and zinc at 787°F.

The dreadful temperature of 865°F makes Venus the hottest planet in the solar system.[108] The global cloud cover creates a greenhouse effect, locking in heat from the sun and creating sizzling temperatures. The inferno guarantees that "life as we know it" is impossible on the planet. Disappointed by the Mariner 2 findings, scientists and multitudes of space

---

108 The planet Mercury is an airless terrestrial world that both bakes and freezes while orbiting the sun. The sun side reaches 800°F, but temperatures on the dark side approach minus 290°F. Space.com, "How Hot is Mercury?" https://www.space.com/18645-mercury-temperature.html (accessed Nov. 1, 2020).

enthusiasts said goodbye to the idea of a nurturing inner world. Soon forgotten was a terrain of tropical rain forests, vast oceans, islands of vegetation, sea creatures, and any form of organic life.

The futility of inhabiting Venus' surface in this life does not preclude its occupancy in the afterlife. With the domain of eternity in the physical universe, Venus' hellish conditions will remain in the hereafter. It will be impossible for resurrected spiritual bodies to escape the scorching heat when the world becomes their home. The gravity of the planet will hold fast to the physical weight of the spiritual body. Immortality brings durability to a spiritual being who, like the rich man, can endure hot conditions. The global expanse of uniform heat on Venus produces a biblically based, everlasting lake of fire, which maintains a steady temperature both day and night.

The Mariner 2 magnetometer did not detect a magnetic field in the space envelope around Venus. Later readings would determine Venus' magnetic field strength to be less than 1% of that on Earth. The weak magnetic flux removes the ability of the planet to deflect charged particles coming from the sun. The Geiger counter did not detect the presence of ionized radiation, giving further evidence of no magnetosphere. As a consequence, a punishing stream of solar wind continuously strikes the planet's atmosphere, stripping away natural safeguards and disassociating molecules. Over the eons, Venus' environment was depleted of life-giving elements.

Compare the deleterious condition of Venus' atmosphere to that of Earth. The protective magnetosphere of our planet originates from the flow of liquid metal in the outer core. The strength of the magnetic field is so great that it extends into outer space. The energy field protects the earth from the solar wind and high-energy cosmic rays. The electrons and protons from the sun hit the magnetosphere and form boundary layers. These are belts of ionized radiation, which surround the earth. So essentially, the magnetic field acts as a deflector shield, safeguarding the planet's atmosphere. It allows for a flourishing biosphere, where oxygen and water are in abundance.

Examining Venus' Atmosphere

After a five-year hiatus, spaceflight would achieve a second successful encounter with Venus. While not a planned concurrent arrival, Mariner 5 (USA) and Venera 4 (USSR) reached the inner planet just three days apart in October 1967. Mariner 5 flew close to Venus, at a distance of around 2500 miles, while Venera 4 attempted a payload drop to the planet's surface. The signals from both spacecraft showed atmospheric temperature and pressure to be high, with atmospheric content consisting primarily of carbon dioxide (CO_2).

Venera is the Russian name for Venus, with the Venera 4 spacecraft being one in a series of Soviet-made vehicles. The descending bus carried an atmospheric probe. The parachuting capsule provided data for over ninety minutes before ending transmission somewhere above ground. Sensors found the air consisting mainly of carbon dioxide, with atmospheric pressure at high levels. Future missions determined Venus surface pressure to be ninety-two times more than on Earth, which is astonishingly high. It is equivalent to a depth of six-tenths of a mile under the ocean.

The discovery of high carbon dioxide content and high pressure in Venus' atmosphere requires a closer look. On the earth, CO_2 is present in a gaseous state because it is under normal temperature and pressure (NTP). In chemistry, NTP is 68°F and 14.7 psia (which is equal to 1 atmosphere). The surface of Venus, however, is not a normal place. Pressure and temperature are so extreme that carbon dioxide is no longer a gas. It is in the form of a supercritical fluid, which has the properties of both a gas and a liquid. In material science, a supercritical fluid will appear on a phase diagram, which is an x- and y-axis plot of pressure vs. temperature.

For the substance of carbon dioxide, the phase diagram will show either in a solid, liquid, or gaseous state. Venus' high pressure and temperature will place its CO_2 above the liquid and gas boundaries, meaning it simultaneously acts like a gas and a liquid. The gas–liquid mix covers the surface globally. The supercritical expanse will retain heat very efficiently, meaning there is no day-to-night heat loss. This results in the searing air temperatures of the gas–liquid CO_2 remaining the same overnight. In drawing upon a biblical phrase, the planet can be likened to a "lake of fire" that never cools down. Winds will not help either, since speeds average less than 3 mph.

The harshness of Venus' air quality will not affect the health of an immortal being. The hot, heavy, supercritical CO_2 air will feel far worse than a muggy summer day while lacking the water content. To the unrighteous person banished to the planet, the surface air will be a thick, eerie, and uncomfortably hot mix. In the dense, gas–liquid CO_2 bath, any ground motion will look strangely slow. Normally, the air will be still for long periods and not able to provide a breeze. When a gust does occur, the sand will look like pebbles under shallow water being pushed by small waves.

Venera 7 and 8 visited Venus in 1972 and 1974, respectively. The design of each probe was modified to be able to handle the high temperature and atmospheric pressure. Although data acquisition was limited on Venera 7, it made history by being the first spacecraft to transmit information from the surface of another world. Engineers believed the vehicle tipped over after landing, misdirecting the antenna signal. Venera 8 was more successful in returning data. The sensors made an estimate of ground visibility, which is about a half mile. The amount of sunlight is similar to a heavily overcast day on Earth, making the surface suitable for photography.

Mariner 10 was the last spacecraft in the Mariner program. Launched in late 1973, the mission objective was an encounter with two planets. There was one flyby of Venus, followed by a flyby of Mercury three times. The vehicle was the first to use a gravitational slingshot maneuver, where Venus' gravity goes into accelerating the vehicle toward Mercury. An imaging system with twin telescopic cameras and a digital recorder were onboard. At a distance of 3,600 miles from the Venusian world, Mariner 10 sent back photographs of a cloud-shrouded planet.

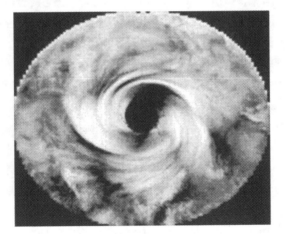

Figure 17
South Polar Cloud Vortex

The camera system on Mariner 10 was able to create photographs detailing the clouds of Venus. Figure 17 is a mosaic of images gathered from the south pole. Use of the camera's ultraviolet filter brings out dark portions in the cloud cover. The material is considered an "ultraviolet absorber" because the darkened color is due to the substance soaking up ultraviolet rays. The dispersion of the substance flows smoothly within the cloud structure. Scientists believe the material to be sulfur-based, possibly containing large amounts of gaseous sulfur dioxide.

An enormous vortex over the south pole is evident from the image. A similar-type vortex occurs over the north pole. The vortices are a constant presence in the upper atmosphere at the poles. The dynamics behind the strange occurrence are driven by convection. Beginning at the equator, the clouds heat up from the sun's rays and then move toward the poles. As the clouds move to the higher latitudes, the altitude of the clouds increases, while the wind speed slows. Low air pressure at the poles then contributes to the formation of a vortex, which collapses the air mass.

Let's review the results of the Venus Express program, which happened forty years after the Mariner 10 expedition. It will help to better explain some of the details behind the vortex. Venus Express was Venus' first weather satellite. Operating in an elliptical orbit, it could study circulation patterns and the mechanism behind the super rotation in the upper atmosphere. The diagram in Figure 18 shows the wind flows depend on altitude.

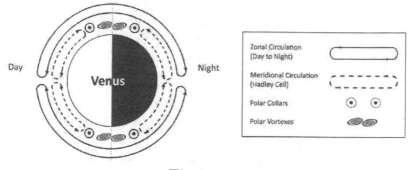

Figure 18
Zonal and Meridional Circulation

The airflow in the Venusian atmosphere divides into two distinct levels, which are the zonal and meridional circulation.[109] In Figure 18, the zonal layer is in the upper altitudes, which is shown by solid lines of stretched ellipses. The zonal layer is a thermally induced, *lateral flow* with day-to-night circulation. Situating at high altitude, the airstream can average speeds of 220 mph. Known as superrotation, the airstream is sixty times faster than the rotation rate of the planet. The greatest wind speeds occur near the equator and extend north and south to 45° latitudes. Once above the midway point of 45°, the zonal wind velocity decreases to under 100 mph.

The second layer below the zonal layer is the meridional winds, which are known as Hadley cells. It is shown by the dotted lines of stretched ellipses. The earth has similar-type Hadley cells, which cause the trade winds to blow in the tropics.[110] The meridional wind speeds are much slower than the zonal flow. The currents begin at the equator and moves toward the poles during the day in a *longitudinal flow* (and from the poles to the equator at night). The dayside Hadley cells will move toward the poles until hitting the polar collars at around 65° latitude. The polar collars appear as circles with a dot in the middle. The collars are barriers, which prevent the airstream from getting to the poles.

The polar collars contain a dense, relatively cool air mass. The cold collars wrap 360° around the north and south poles. The meteorological cause for the existence of the polar collars is not known. When the meridional flow hits them, these lower-altitude winds turn back and move toward the equator.

---

109 Hakan Svedhem, Dmitry V. Titov, Fredric W. Taylor, and Olivier Witasse, "Venus as a More Earth-like Planet," *Nature*, 450, No. 7170 (2007): 629–32.

110 The Hadley Principle uncovers atmospheric circulation pattern above the earth's tropical regions. The eighteenth-century research by George Hadley found the cell moves north-south in a closed-loop pattern to create the trade winds. Anders Persson, "Hadley's Principle: Understanding and Misunderstanding the Trade Winds," in *History of Meteorology* (Swedish Meteorological Institute, 2006) 3:17–42.

The same is not true for the higher zonal winds. As shown in the Figure 17 image, the swirling zonal clouds can hurdle over the polar collar obstruction. When these zonal flows near the top of the poles, a sudden and distinct descent of the clouds creates an enormous vortex.

The Venus Express mission helps to better explain the underlying reason for the vortex effect. The breadth of a polar vortex is much larger than a hurricane on the earth. When the mass of air draws down into the low-pressure polar center, it creates a plughole effect; that is, it looks like the swirl seen in a drain after the plug is removed. The vortex penetration is up to thirty miles deep, extending to the bottom of the cloud layer. Recurring observation of the phenomenon reveals that the vortices never expire, but undergo a continual change of configuration, sometimes transforming into a double vortex at a single pole.

What is the chemical composition of the swirling clouds? The makeup is of interest both scientifically and in drawing analogies to biblical passages on perdition. Essentially, the clouds consist of sulfur dioxide (SO_2) and droplets of sulfuric acid (H_2SO_4). From a chemical property standpoint, these are dangerous substances. Exposure to sulfur dioxide impairs the human respiratory system, damages the foliage on trees and vegetation, and is a leading cause of acid rain. Sulfuric acid is a strong, corrosive chemical that produces severe burns and tissue damage when contacting the skin. An overhead atmosphere of these toxic chemicals will bring uneasiness to residents below.

Venus' escalating atmospheric vortex is unique. In Revelation 14:11, the Bible states: "The smoke of their torment goes up forever and ever. There is no rest day or night for those who worship the beast and its image and for anyone who receives the mark of its name." The idea of "no rest day or night" is a reference to an afterlife on a rotating planet orbiting about the sun. The state of affairs of having the smoke of their torment go up forever and ever links to the clouds of sulfur dioxide and sulfuric acid, which rise in the zonal circulation prior to vortex entry. The noxious mix of cloud cover is a representative reminder of the distress of spiritual beings down below.

Examining Venus' Surface

Returning to the timetable of Venus' exploration, we look to the twin missions of Venera 9 and Venera 10. The June 1975 launches were the beginning of the next generation of Soviet spaceflights with the design being a two-part orbiter and lander. This study focuses primarily on Venera 9 since both vehicles achieved the same goals. The Venera 9 flight is historic in that the orbiter was the first to circle Venus, while the landing probe was the first to transmit an image from the surface of another world. Acting as the communications link, the orbiter was the relay back to Earth. The lander hit the surface on October 22, 1975, and promptly sent up data.

The black and white photograph in Figure 19 is the first from another world. With the camera lens of the lander sitting three feet off the ground, Venera 9 transmitted a clear 180° panoramic image of Venus' surroundings. The slide is shown three times over and gives amazing detail of a sand and rock basalt terrain. The Venera 10 landing site was 1,364 miles away and would supply similar photographs of a basalt surface, but without the slabs. Basalt is a fine-grained, igneous material, forming from the solidification of molten lava. Basalt is quite drab compared to other types of rock, such as granite, obsidian, or pumice. It covers 90% of the Venusian surface.

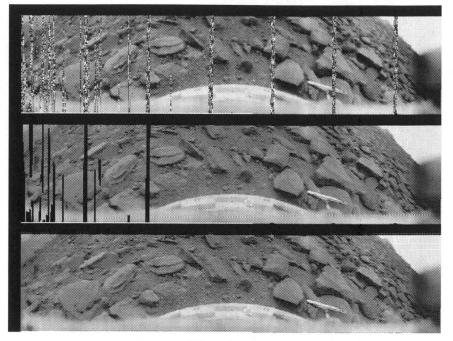

Figure 19
Surface of Venus from Venera 9 Lander

The original photograph is at the top. It includes vertical lines of interference, caused by communication lags between the Venera 9 lander and orbiter. Post-data processing in the two lower photographs removes the lines, making for a clearer image. The picture shows an assortment of flat basalt rocks strewn around the landing site. The optical system utilizes a fisheye lens, which captures a wide-angle 180-degree view. The fisheye curvature near the edge of the frame creates some distortion. The foot of the lander is visible on the center-right of the picture. In the upper right-hand corner, a hazy horizon can be seen in the distance.

It is hard to believe that modern technology can bring visibility to a possible place for hell, except for one important fact. It is God's desire for no one to go there. What could be a better deterrent than spacecraft photography of a planet that is nothing more than a hot, empty wasteland? Not one tree, not one plant, not one shrub, not even one blade of grass could conceivably exist in this inhospitable world. No animals, birds, or reptiles could ever be seen in the environment. The relentless, scorching surface temperature makes Venus an inferno. Covered in gloomy and desolate lava fields, the planet lacks in attractiveness and is void of any form of life.

Newberry National Volcanic Monument lies near Bend, Oregon. It is suitable for tourism and scientific research in volcanism. The Newberry preserve imitates conditions on a volcanic, desert landscape. It contains vast stretches of erupted basaltic lava and obsidian flow. The dry, sprawling fields of solidified magma are suggestive of the moon's surface. Even when visiting on a sunny day, the vast expanse of volcanic basalt is dreary and oppressive to your senses. The only area of curiosity is the section of black, glassy obsidian rock. If you can suffer monotony with lava fields here on Earth, imagine the difficulty of Venus.

In December 1978, both Venera 11 and Venera 12 came to Venus. Each vehicle consisted of a flyby and a lander. The flyby unit replaced the orbiter in order to improve ground contact time. Sadly, the color imaging system failed on each lander when two sets of lens caps did not deploy. All attempts at soil sampling failed because the devices did not function correctly. Despite the letdowns, the spacecraft did record indications of lightning and found evidence of an orange-yellow sky. The thick clouds filter out blue light, leaving an orange and yellow mingling. Known as Rayleigh scattering, the effect occurs on Earth at sunrise and sunset, bringing out the reds and yellows.

December 1978 was also the time when two spacecraft from the United States reached the inner planet. One was the Pioneer Venus Orbiter (Pioneer 12), and the other was Pioneer Venus Multiprobe (Pioneer 13). Placed in a highly elliptical orbit, Pioneer 12 carried seventeen experiments. The technique of spinning the vehicle body 360° every 12 seconds was used for dynamic attitude control. The orbiter was able to detect lightning, measure the temperature and composition of the atmosphere, and study the interaction of the solar wind with the ionosphere. The artificial satellite had an especially long life, transmitting data until October 1992.

The other vehicle, Pioneer Venus Multiprobe, was designed to deploy four cone-shaped probes to the planet's surface. One large probe and three smaller probes collected data during the plunge. Two probes had a dayside descent while the other two were on the nightside. The probes found the cloud cover to have a high level of sulfuric acid. The lack of water in the atmosphere was acute. The scarcity of water lessens the notion about Venus harboring life in airborne particles. At low altitude, the two nightside probes saw glowing or flashes of light. Since the observation was near the ground, the idea emerged that the light came from hot bursts during a volcanic eruption.

The next journey to the planet was in 1981–82 by the USSR. The Venera 13 and 14 missions were an effort to reproduce the Venera 11 and 12 missions by obtaining color pictures and analyzing soil samples. One can gather from the repetition of the undertaking that the Russians were relentless in exploring Venus. Venera 13 was able to transmit panoramic color photographs, revealing a reddish-brown desert. Venera 14 collected similar-type photographs 620 miles away. The soil collection device worked well on both landers. Reports on the basalt surface were made using an X-ray fluorescent spectrometer. The soil analysis was the first-ever on the planet.

Figure 20
Venus Horizon from Venera 13 Lander

The black-and-white photo in Figure 20 shows the landscape outside Venera 13. The wide-angle view is shown in a natural perspective, which means the image has undergone rectilinear conversion to remove the distortion of the fisheye lens. Telling details show manmade items such as the tooth edges of the lander, a ladder-like testing arm, and the semi-circle lens cover. The surrounding area appears to consist primarily of flat rocks and compact, barren basalt. The photograph extends out to the visible horizon, which is perhaps a half mile away. A cutout or passageway appears in the distance, along with some indistinguishable small hills.

The Venera 13 image endorses the idea that little or nothing on Venus' surface can hold a person's interest for very long. The lava spew may find initial appeal to a geologist or planetary scientist, but the fascination will wane. Venera 14 took pictures hundreds of miles away, showing the same gloomy surface. It is apparent that the parched and depleted landscape covers the entire globe. Venus is a world gone awry by an acute greenhouse effect, which has completely baked the terrain. Arriving spiritual beings will face extreme heat and complete monotony. In looking at the hot volcanic surface, the adjective "hellish" comes to mind.

The next venture to Venus was the Vega program. In cooperation with other European nations, the Soviet Union led a mission consisting of two sister ships: Vega 1 and Vega 2. The objective was to investigate Venus first and then to do a flyby of Halley's Comet, which was traveling through the inner solar system. In June 1985, each Vega spacecraft jettisoned a descent module toward Venus before moving on to watch the comet. The modules consisted of a balloon probe and a lander. The spherical balloons were carried for a great distance by the clouds, collecting valuable meteorological data. One of the two landers was able to successfully collect soil samples.

Assessing the Planet's Data

After the mission of the two Vega spacecraft, there was a four-year lull in the exploration of Venus. The pause became a time for technical dissemination about the harsh and uninviting world. Students and researchers found publications such as the 1985 text *The Venus International Reference Atmosphere* (by Kliore, Moroz, and Keating) to be an invaluable tool for study. The book is helpful for modeling planets with atmospheric cycles driven by the sun. By examining planets similar to our own, scientists learn about the history of Earth and predict future environmental trends.

On our planet, the biosphere includes the hydrologic cycle. Clean water is critical to the survival of humans, with sourcing being an important topic in every society. Life-giving water ties the land, oceans, and atmosphere together to form an integrated hydrologic cycle. The sun's energy affects the system because water circulates as rain on to the land and eventually flows out to the ocean, while evaporating back up to the clouds. The water is redistributed from one reservoir to another through natural processes such as precipitation, condensation, evaporation, and runoff. By providing fresh drinking water, the cycle has a direct effect on the quality of human life.

The carbon cycle also plays a critical role in the biosphere and provides further capability to sustain life. Carbon is prominent in the earth's atmosphere as carbon dioxide. Exchanges between the air and land, and between the air and the ocean, facilitate the cycling of CO_2. Carbon dioxide leaves the air by plant photosynthesis and enters the ground. The gas also dissolves directly into bodies of water. In effect, the ground and ocean act as reservoirs. Going in the opposite direction, the burning of fossil fuels raises the amount of CO_2 in the atmosphere. In recent decades, the increasing levels have brought concern about the health of the planet.

On Venus, sulfur stands out as the main element circulating within the environment. The sulfur cycle has a dominant presence. The inner world teems with hot sulfur because it combines to form various sulfur compounds. Many of the mixes are foul-smelling and poisonous to humans. Sulfur actively moves throughout the atmosphere. It uses the ground, atmosphere, and clouds as reservoirs. It bubbles up from the gaseous eruptions of volcanoes as hot sulfur dioxide. The gas moves from low to higher altitude, where it cools down. It then interacts to produce liquid sulfuric acid. The acid situates in the clouds, which extend up to forty miles in elevation.

Sulfur happens to be one of the few chemical elements mentioned in the Bible. Revelation 19:20, 20:10, and 21:8 mention sulfur burning in the lake of fire. Drawing a parallel to this sulfur is the huge presence of sulfur and active sulfur compounds on Venus. Some English translations of the scriptures refer to sulfur by the name brimstone, which means "burning stone." Brimstone is lemon-yellow in color. In ancient Near East times, the mineral was found in rocks and stones along the shore of the Dead Sea. When thrown into a fire, the element reaches an ignition temperature and begins to burn. The hot, blue flame emits sulfur dioxide, which has a suffocating odor.

In the biblical narratives, the mention of sulfur attaches to divine retribution, resulting in the ruin or death of disobedient people. In Genesis 19:24, the Lord rained down fire and sulfur out of heaven on Sodom and Gomorrah, likely resulting in burns and death by asphyxiation. Psalm 11:6 tells of the wicked receiving coals of fire and sulfur as their portion. In the Apocalypse, sulfur connects to punishment. The sixth trumpet in Revelation 9:17–18 sends four angels, releasing the three plagues of fire, smoke, and sulfur that kill great multitudes of people on the earth. In Revelation 14:9–10, people worshipping the beast and receiving a mark will be tormented with fire and sulfur.

Sulfuric acid is a sulfur compound. It is a pungent, clear-yellow liquid that is highly corrosive. The substance is not found in nature due to its great affinity for water. A manufacturer will create several grades of H_2SO_4 for application in industry. Commercial uses find sulfuric acid in the cells of lead-acid batteries and as an active ingredient in drain cleaners. The chemical is good at dissolving tissue paper, the protein in hair, and various greases that can clog pipes. Sulfuric acid is quite hazardous, burning the skin to the touch because of its hygroscopic nature. It is alarming to consider that such a dangerous substance resides naturally in Venus' clouds.

The atmosphere of Venus can be broken down into four distinct regions. Each region handles sulfur, or substances containing sulfur, in a different way. The four zones from highest to lowest altitude are: (1) the photochemical zone, (2) the evaporation and thermal dissociation zone, (3) the thermochemistry zone, and (4) the mineral buffering zone, which includes the volcanic surface.[111] The following discussion pertains to each zone and its relationship to sulfur.

- **The Photochemical Zone**

  The upper atmosphere of Venus is the photochemical zone. The layer's top is forty miles overhead. Through chemical reactions, the zone uses the energy of the sun, along with sulfur dioxide, carbon dioxide, and small amounts of water vapor, to produce sulfuric acid. The cloud covering is made of gaseous SO_2 and liquid H_2SO_4 with day side estimates indicating a cloud thickness stretching down for twelve miles. After making concentrated H_2SO_4, the saturated clouds will rain down copious amounts of the hazardous liquid.

  A planet's protective cloud cover showering down a toxic and dangerous chemical is a paradox. It will be a bad omen for banished immortal spirits to pass through banks of sulfuric acid clouds. On Earth, human beings live under pleasant and tranquil skies, experiencing weather changes brought on by seasonal climate patterns. On Venus, the forecast will never change. Awaiting residents of the lake of fire are caustic clouds and scorching temperatures.

- **The Evaporation and Thermal Dissociation Zone**

  The sulfuric acid raining down from higher elevations will experience an air temperature rise that cooks the chemical. After dropping to twenty-five miles above ground, the caustic drizzle reaches the evaporation and thermal dissociation zone. In this region, the

---

111 Grinspoon, *Venus Revealed*, 95–97.

rain becomes a virga, meaning the acid droplets reach a boiling point and evaporate. The precipitation breaks down into a gas that rises again into the upper atmosphere. The gas will be used to create more precipitation, continuing the cycle.

Further examination of this zone requires data from the Venus Express mission. An important verification for lightning came in 2007 with the detection of whistler waves. A whistler wave is a very low frequency radio wave generated by lightning. The Venus Express whistler waves add credibility to earlier detections of lightning by the Pioneer Venus Orbiter and Venera missions. The lightning lacks verification and remains an unsolved mystery, but it could involve sulfur and sulfur-based compounds.

• **The Thermochemistry Zone**
The thermochemistry zone is the next region of the atmosphere. The zone begins just below the sulfuric acid evaporation region and finishes around five miles above ground. The air temperature ranges from 200°F to 380°F, making the zone thermally active. High heat is normally a catalyst for chemical reactions. The temperature of the zone will increase the molecular motion and mixing of gases. During the process, sulfur atoms can move around quickly to combine, break down, and then recombine into various mixes.

• **The Mineral Buffering Zone**
The mineral buffering zone is located from five miles overhead to the ground and is the hottest region. Air temperatures at the surface are around 865°F. One can assume the touch temperature of the rocks and soil to be the same. Russian scientists' analysis of

soil samples from the Venera and Vega missions were provided to the international technical community in the book *Venus Geology, Geochemistry and Geophysics: Research Results from the USSR* (by V. N. Zharkov). Using X-ray analysis, the scientists were able to quantify eight different types of mineral oxides, including the presence of pure sulfur and chlorine in the soil.

The mineral buffering zone is home to a world of volcanism, with countless volcanoes sitting within expansive fields of basalt. The 1990 Magellan mission allowed for mapping the planet's surface and distinguishing various types of topographical formations. The mapping shows the surface is studded with raised blemishes, which have been identified as small and large volcanoes. The total quantity of volcanoes on the planet remains unknown, with estimates to date numbering over one hundred thousand.[112] In contrast, the entire surface of the earth has fewer than two thousand volcanoes.

The large number of volcanoes leads to the belief of ongoing volcanic activity. Early on, researchers gave credit to the Pioneer Multiprobe mission for detecting volcanic-type flashes.[113] The later Venus Express mission reported

---

112 Mosaic-like images of Venus' surface are speckled with countless volcanoes, whose diameter ranges from five to twenty-five miles. Fredric W. Taylor, *The Scientific Exploration of Venus* (New York: Cambridge University Press, 2014), 58.

113 The flashes obtained from the probe data may involve "chemical fires" near the surface of the planet. Eric Burgess, Venus: An Errant Twin (New York: Columbia University Press, 1985), 95.

seeing three red-hot surface swells.[114] Volcanic emission will produce detectable light from the bursts of hot lava and ash. In July 2020, the University of Maryland and the Institute of Geophysics at ETH Zurich, Switzerland, published their results in the journal *Nature Geoscience.* The report identifies thirty-seven active volcanic structures on Venus.[115] In June 2021, the National Academy of Science released a report of a mobile lithosphere on Venus.[116] These recent investigations provide some of the best evidence yet that the planet is still geologically active.

If the scientific evidence points toward ongoing volcanic activity, then clouds of sulfur dioxide, hydrogen sulfide (H_2S), and carbonyl sulfide (COS) would be rising in the air, along with hot ash and lava flow. The rising gases from this activity can correlate to Revelation 14:11a in the Bible, where "the smoke of their torment goes up forever and ever." Spiritual beings on the surface of Venus will be able to hear volcanic activity, see emissions rising, and then smell the sulfur compounds. With the exceedingly large number of volcanoes on the Venusian surface, eruptions will be a common affair.

In summary, all four thermal regions are active in the sulfur cycle. Zone 1 creates sulfuric acid, which rains into zone 2 and becomes a virga. Lightning flashes are possible in zone 2. At these high altitudes, the lightning would be cloud-to-cloud, rather than cloud-to-ground strikes. The lightning origin is unknown but could involve sulfur substances. The

---

114 The detection of hot ground swell was done using an Infrared Thermal Imaging Spectrometer. New York Times, "Spacecraft Spots Active Volcanoes on Venus," https://www.nytimes.com/2010/04/10/science/space/10venus.html?searchResultPosition=1 (accessed June 22, 2020).

115 Phys.org, "Scientists Discover Volcanoes on Venus are Still Active," https://phys.org/news/2020-07-scientists-volcanoes-venus.html (accessed May. 18, 2021).

116 PNAS.org, "A Globally Fragmented and Mobile Lithosphere on Venus," https://www.pnas.org/content/118/26/e2025919118 (accessed June 28, 2021).

zone 3 high temperature acts as a catalyst for chemical reactions that use sulfur substances. In zone 4, sensors from Pioneer Venus and Venus Express record red-hot flashes from objects thought to be live volcanoes, which generate large amounts of sulfur dioxide and sulfur-based compounds.

In reviewing biblical passages, Revelation 19:20 tells of the beast and the false prophet being thrown into "the lake of fire that burns with sulfur." In Revelation 21:8, we read about "the lake that burns with fire and sulfur, which is the second death." Burning sulfur is part of the backdrop for people banished to the lake of fire. The biblical imagery fits with Venus because of the hot chemical reaction of sulfur compounds in the air and the eruption of lava from volcanoes on the ground. The bright flashes from overhead lightning events, or red-hot lava bursts from nearby volcanoes, are audible and visual reminders to residents of Venus that it is a place burning with fire and sulfur.

On Earth, a lightning flash normally precedes thunder. A sudden, loud burst of thunder is very distracting to hearers. Witnesses to volcanic eruptions recall the sound of thunder as well. These types of noises generating on Venus will be far worse. The supercritical carbon-dioxide atmosphere is in a dense, compact state. As such, it will dramatically amplify and propagate sound waves. The gas–liquid CO_2 medium assures that any thundering or eruption is heard over great distances. As a result, individuals banished to Venus will have to live with routine audible bursts of burning sulfur compounds coming from the surroundings.

To unrighteous people residing on Venus, the flashes of lightning and sounds of thunder will bring back memories of storms on Earth. The difference is that the disturbance will never bring forth rain. Below the cloud tops, life-giving water measures in parts per million. Like the rich man in the story of Lazarus, the desire for immortal spirits to quench a thirst will continue in the hot and desolate world. Sipping a drop of water will not be possible, but the sights and sounds associating to rain will continue, as sulfur compounds burn throughout the atmosphere.

Volcanic eruptions give off foul odors. An odor comes from volatile substances found in low concentrations in the air that humans can perceive with their sense of smell. The inner planet's atmosphere is primarily composed of carbon dioxide at 96.5%, followed by nitrogen at 3.5%. The trace amounts of other gases in the Venusian atmosphere will measure in parts per million (ppm). These include sulfur dioxide at 150 ppm, argon at 70 ppm, water vapor at 20 ppm, carbon monoxide at 17 ppm, helium at 12 ppm, and neon at 7 ppm. Additionally, hydrogen sulfide and carbonyl sulfide are present as byproducts of volcanic emission.

The human nose is sensitive and can detect certain gases to a level of only a few parts per million. Chief among them is sulfur dioxide, which is an ongoing byproduct of volcanism. At 150 ppm, the gas would produce a distinct odor. The smell of SO_2 aligns closely with the smoke trail from a freshly lit match. As a result, the atmosphere on Venus will not only be hot and dense but heavy with a sulfur stench. After rising from the dead, Jesus could fully enjoy eating food with his disciples because his resurrected body had a functioning sense of smell. Seeing and smelling the volcanic environment is part of the displeasure for spiritual beings banished to Venus.

Viewing Venus' Topography

Space exploration to the inner planet resumed four years after the completion of the Vega 1 and 2 missions. The goal of NASA's Magellan program was to bring a complete unveiling of the planet's surface. Magellan was the first interplanetary probe deployed from the Space Shuttle. The release of the Magellan spacecraft from the cargo bay of Atlantis occurred in May 1989. The vehicle was attached to an inertial upper stage (IUS) booster. The assembly jetted off to reach Venus, with operations beginning in August 1990. Magellan is named for the sixteenth century Portuguese explorer Ferdinand Magellan. His maritime mapping expedition was the first to circumnavigate the earth.

Magellan would serve as an imaging satellite, surveying Venus' topography. From a highly elliptical polar orbit, the vehicle circled the planet every 3 hours and 15 minutes. Data collection began by activating a SAR recording system.[117] With every near pass, Magellan would collect a 16-mile swath of Venus. In its orbital path, the vehicle remains fixed in inertial space, while the planet rotates slowly beneath. In order to get complete coverage, Magellan performed three consecutive 243-day (one sidereal day) imaging runs. By September 1992, high-resolution imaging of Venus' surface reached a level of 98% coverage.

The outstanding data collection brought a comprehensive overview of the surface, which contains a plethora of volcanic features. Extensive study of the satellite imagery was made by geologists. The team went on to identify three major zones, each containing a different topography. Since Venus has no oceans, scientists must assign a reference point to sea level in order to categorize elevation differences. The sea level reference is known as the "zero-datum line."

The first zone is the highland terrain, which makes up 10% of the surface. The mountainous highlands compare to the high-altitude portion

---

117 Synthetic aperture radar is a remote sensing and mapping technology. High-energy radio waves emitted from a dish antenna reflect off the ground and return to the spacecraft. During the brief interval, the relative change in satellite location causes a phase shift in the returning radar signal. Onboard computers process the affected signal and produce a high-resolution image. Angelo, *Encyclopedia of Space and Astronomy*, 599.

of Earth's continents and situate well above the zero-datum line.

The second zone is the volcanic plains, which makes up 70% of the surface. The various landforms of the extremely vast region situate near the zero-datum line and compare to the land masses at sea level in our world.

The third zone is the lowland plains, which makes up 20% of the surface. The lowland plains compare to the ocean basins of the earth and situate well below the zero-datum line.

The first geographic zone contains two high continents: Ishtar Terra and Aphrodite Terra. Of special interest is Ishtar Terra in the northern latitudes. The continent stands out with four mountain ranges that surround a high plateau. It is akin to the Tibetan Plateau of the Himalayas in Asia. Ishtar Terra contains the highest peak on the planet, Maxwell Montes, named after the Scottish physicist James Maxwell. It reaches an elevation of 6.8 miles, exceeding Mount Everest by over one mile. Maxwell Montes is a standout in this lowland world, with its high altitude bringing a slight reduction in both atmospheric temperature and pressure.

The second geographic zone, the volcanic plains, contains over one hundred large volcanoes, which are at least sixty miles in diameter. It is a massive region that hosts many types of unique landforms that result from volcanism. The shapes of some landforms were new to geologists. Mountains having numerous radial legs extending out were labeled "ticks" because of an insect look. Oval shapes containing an internal network of large cracks were like a spider's web. These features were called "arachnoids." Finally, mysterious mounds and depressions that were surrounded by concentric rings or fractures were named "corona."

Within the second zone lies Alpha Regio and Beta Regio. The two areas are distinct landmasses containing interesting features. The Alpha Regio terrain sits a mile above the zero-datum line and looks like a tile floor. Beta Regio has many shield volcanoes, which contain radial fissures or large cracks emanating from the flanks. The fissures allow lava to flow for long distances from the summit. On the earth, a good example of an active shield volcano is Kīlauea on the island of Hawai'i. Beyond Alpha and Beta Regio, the remaining volcanic plains stretch to enormous distances.

The third geographic zone, the lowland plains, compares to the ocean floors on the earth because it sits well below the zero-datum line. The basin comprises one-fifth of the area of Venus. The region is relatively smooth, lacking in large volcanic shapes. Features include bowl-like depressions and extended lava channels.

Resulting from meteorite strikes is the formation of impact craters, which are randomly distributed over the three zones. Totaling nearly a thousand in number, these craters range from 2 to 174 miles in diameter. The edges of many craters are amazingly sharp. To a geologist, sharpness suggests freshness due to minimal surface erosion. The young-looking craters indicate that a cataclysmic, global resurfacing of Venus may have occurred "recently." A recent resurfacing in planetary geology means in the last 300-600 million years. Such a resurfacing would have wiped out all previous indications of craters.

Venus Express and Future Missions

Following Magellan, the next voyage to the inner planet did not happen until the twenty-first century. The mission was called Venus Express. It lifted off in November 2005 and was operational until January 2015. The Venus Express program was successful in attaining many of its goals. As the first ESA mission to Venus, it carried a powerful array of spectral and imaging instruments. The spacecraft was placed in a highly elliptical orbit with perigee at the south pole. As shown from Figure 18, the spacecraft provides atmospheric convection details. The clarity of the airflow was a significant achievement for the program.

Acting as a weather satellite, the vehicle not only examined the dynamics of the atmosphere but was able to produce the first temperature map of the Southern Hemisphere. Small temperature changes do occur with increasing elevation, even in the blistering heat. A dip to around 790°F was found at the higher points of the terrain. As noted earlier, the mission verified the presence of lightning on Venus, with scientists believing the event to be common. After more than nine years of near perfect operation, Venus Express was deorbited by making a controlled plunge into the atmosphere.

Japan has been exploring the inner planet using the Akatsuki Venus Orbiter (AVO). Also known as the Venus Climate Orbiter, the spacecraft operates under the administration of the Japan Aerospace Exploration Agency (JAXA). The Akatsuki, whose name means "dawn" in Japanese, arrived in December 2010, but a failure in the bipropellant engine occurred during orbit insertion. After working through a difficult safe-hold condition, the team reactivated the onboard systems, only to find the spacecraft leaving the Venusian world and heading toward the sun.

After remaining in solar orbit for a few years, JAXA managed to transfer the AVO to an elliptical orbit around Venus in late 2015. It made its final trajectory adjustments in March 2016, and the climate orbiter began regular science operations the next month. Akatsuki dedicates itself to studying atmospheric stratification and dynamics, as well as cloud physics. Maps in 3-D were released in 2017. In

April 2018, the AVO finished its planned mission and went into extended operations. As of 2022, minimum levels of fuel are available on Akatsuki. In the current orbit, mission operations could be closed out or extended, depending on the funding.

The recent discovery of a biosignature of phosphine in the upper atmosphere is prompting new mission interest to the planet. After using the James Clerk Maxwell Telescope in Hawaii and the ALMA telescope in Chile, an international team of astronomers went on to publish compelling evidence in September 2020. Driven by the phosphine discovery, a new analysis of data from the 1978 Pioneer Venus mission was undertaken by researchers at Cal Poly. Evidence was seen not only for phosphine, but for chemical disequilibrium in Venus' atmosphere, which is an encouraging sign of biological activity.[118] These findings have led to renewed interest toward the inner planet.

The Indian Space Research Organization (ISRO) has plans to launch the Shukrayaan-1 in the 2024–26 timeframe. The mission will reveal more information about the planetary environment. Three program goals are the study of (1) surface and subsurface features, (2) the atmospheric chemistry, dynamics, and variations in composition, and (3) the interaction of solar wind with the atmosphere. The program has shortlisted instrumentation and has available payload space. ISRO is inviting the international community to participate in the venture and has two candidate Russian payloads under consideration.

To learn more about the evolution of Venus, NASA chose the VERITAS and DAVINCI+ missions for its Discovery

---

118 EarthSky, "Possible Life Signs in the Clouds of Venus," https://earthsky.org/space/phosphine-disequilibrium-venus-atmosphere-pioneer-venus-1978 (accessed April 16, 2021)

Program.[119] Lockheed Martin will design, build, and operate both spacecraft, which will launch in the 2028 to 2030 timeframe. The twin missions to Venus aim to challenge the possibility that the planet was once habitable. The VERITAS orbiter will examine geological processes by performing high-resolution topography, exceeding the Magellan focus by greater than 10X. The DAVINCI+ probe will descend into Venus' atmosphere to determine chemical composition and whether oceans ever covered the surface. The instruments will analyze a host of gases and hope to verify the presence of phosphine.

The next ESA mission to Venus will be the EnVision low-altitude polar orbiter.[120] EnVision will provide an all-inclusive view of the planet from its inner core to upper atmosphere in order to determine why and how Venus and Earth evolved so differently. As part of the effort, the spacecraft will perform high-resolution radar mapping of regional and targeted surfaces. The spectroscopy suite will provide compositional data on rock types, perform extremely high-resolution atmospheric measurements, and monitor trace gases in the atmosphere, including the mysterious ultraviolet absorber in the Venusian upper clouds. The target launch date is 2031.

Venera-D is a program proposed by the Russian Federal Space Agency.[121] The mission includes an orbiter and lander.

---

119 VERITAS is an acronym for Venus Emissivity, Radio Science, InSAR, Topography, and Spectroscopy, while DAVINCI+ is short for Deep Atmosphere of Venus Investigations of Noble Gases, Chemistry, and Imaging. NASA, "NASA Selects 2 Missions to Study 'Lost Habitable' World of Venus," https://www.nasa.gov/press-release/nasa-selects-2-missions-to-study-lost-habitable-world-of-venus (accessed June 3, 2021)

120 European Space Agency, "ESA Selects Revolutionary Venus Mission EnVision," https://www.esa.int/Science_Exploration/Space_Science/ESA_selects_revolutionary_Venus_mission_EnVision (accessed Aug. 5, 2021)

121 Russian Space, "New Promise for the Venera-D Project," http://www.russianspaceweb.com/venera-d-2021.html (accessed July 16, 2021)

The orbiter will study the structure and dynamics of the atmosphere and the nature of the greenhouse effect. On the scorching surface, the primary goal for the lander is to go beyond the previous operating time of 90 minutes. The letter D in the name stands for *dolgozhivushaya*, which means "long-lasting." A cooling generator will operate along with the lander's electronics in order to extend survival on the ground. The lander will study the composition of the surface and perform chemical analysis. The current launch date target is no earlier than 2029.

Findings Relating to the Bible

The summary of findings relating to the Bible begin with the Magellan mission. How do Venus's vast volcanic features contribute to being a place for biblical perdition? The answer requires looking at lava flow and what the flow can produce. Geological study unveils a myriad of channels and conduits on the surface. Lava flow creates an unlimited number of lava tubes, lava caves, vertical rift caves, and subterranean fractures on the sides of volcanoes.[122] The interior of many of the features is hollow. If one reasonably assumes that sheltering for resurrected spiritual beings takes place, then open spaces inside lava forms a natural enclosure for residency.

Lava tubes are the most common type of dwelling. The formation of a lava tube begins when molten lava erupts and creates a flowing channel. As the hot lava flows over long distances, it tends to harden around the outside because the surrounding air is cooler than the lava. The process creates an insulating barrier for the molten lava to advance

---

122 The volcanism of Venus is teeming with cavernous places such as lava tubes and lava caves. Ronald Greeley, *Lava Tubes in the Solar System* (6th International Symposium on Vulcanospeleology, Tempe, AZ: Arizona State University Planetary Geology Group, 1992), 228.

in the center. The progression of the lava creates an open space because the interior lava continues to flow after the exterior has solidified. The final form is a cylindrical cavity surrounded by solid walls of basalt. The shape finds use as a habitation.

Before exile to the land of volcanism, spirits in Hades will face a Day of Judgment. At the final judgment, resurrected humans and demonic beings alike will be made visible to the eye as higher spatial dimensions come into view at the great white throne. The domain of eternity will reveal itself in the physical universe, resulting in seeing immortal spirits in the material world. Ordinary time will move into time as co-presence, which has a past-present-future makeup. Angels, demons, and people will have material substance, which retains the property of mass. Having mass means being subject to gravity, which will hold all entities firmly to the surface of a planet.

Spiritual beings sent to the lake of fire will reside in some form of encrusted lava dwelling. After arrival, any of the three geographic regions can facilitate incarceration for large numbers of demons and resurrected people. The following table gives highly speculative locations for spiritual beings cast into the lake of fire. In keeping with the sequence of passages in Revelation, occupation begins with the beast, false prophet, and Satan. These spirits will select a place to reside, favoring the higher altitude locations. The arrival of resurrected human beings will be last, leaving lost people to situate in the remaining space.

Reference	Immortal Entity	Planet Location
Rev. 19:20	The Beast and False Prophet	Ishtar Terra
Rev. 20:10	Satan	Maxwell Montes
Rev. 20:14	Second Death	All of Venus
Rev. 20:14	Hades (demons)	Ishtar Terra Aphrodite Terra Alpha Regio Beta Regio
Rev. 20:15	Anyone not found written in the book of life.	Volcanic Plains Lowland Plains

Table 4
Hypothetical Dispersion of Beings
Cast into the Lake of Fire

It would not be out of character for Satan to occupy the peak elevation in order to have the best location on the worst terrestrial planet. His pride led to his fall, and now it works to secure the highest mountain. In this desolate world, the soaring terrain of Maxwell Montes serves as the extraordinary spot for the self-serving devil. The high ground brings seclusion and a sense of superiority, while offering slightly cooler temperatures and lower pressures. The better piece of real estate does not mean Satan escapes the emotional distress of his deportation.

Satan's suffering primarily relates to his expulsion from the earth and loss of authority. The devil has no need to direct his demonic army because spiritual warfare with God, the holy angels, and all of humanity has drawn to a close. With the spiritual domain of Hades being exiled to Venus, the devil finds his demonic army still within his grasp but serving no useful purpose. Two of his accomplices in deception, the beast and false prophet, are given domicile nearby in Ishtar Terra. At the end of the age, minions of Satan suffer banishment while taking many resurrected humans with them.

The fallen angels working within the spiritual domain of Hades will be vanquished at the final judgment. These malevolent beings have tempted, attacked, oppressed, hindered, and deceived countless people throughout human history. Sent to Venus, these evil spirits are likely to occupy the higher ground below Satan. Once Ishtar Terra and Aphrodite Terra fill, the demons will inhabit the areas of Alpha Regio and Beta Regio. The second death is also thrown into the lake of fire. The first death was a biological cessation of life functions for human beings on the earth. The second death is a spiritual state of ruin, which spreads upon all who live on the planet.

Unrighteous human beings in Hades will undergo a resurrection of condemnation. After the white throne judgment, immortal spiritual beings will be banished from the paradisical Earth in order to face eternal ruin on Venus. Placement will be in the remaining open areas below Alpha Regio and Beta Regio, which are vast. The expansive volcanic plains around the zero-datum line can host large multitudes of lost humanity. Revelation 21:8 warns about the faithless, the polluted, the murderers, the fornicators, and all liars having a place in the lake of fire and sulfur, which is the second death.

Unsaved individuals will be transported to Venus by an angelic workforce under orders to place individuals in a specific lava cave. Untold numbers of angelic beings, who serve as messengers of God and protectors of God's people, will be employed in the relocation effort. Jesus addresses the final judgment in Matthew 13:49–50, telling the audience, "So it will be at the end of the age. The angels will come out and separate the evil from the righteous and throw them into the furnace of fire, where there will be weeping and gnashing of teeth." It is not hard to accept that angels and unsaved immortal spirits can easily travel through outer space to reach another planet.

Once outside the exosphere of Earth, lost people will be able to look back and see the "blue marble." The Blue Marble is the name of the famous photograph taken by astronauts during the Apollo 17 mission in 1972. In space, the crystalline sphere of Earth contains blue ocean waters, bright white clouds, and sandy-colored continents, forming a large, stunning blue marble. For the lost, the spectacle is a last look at what could have been home. The stars of the Milky Way galaxy will be numerous and bright during the interplanetary voyage. As the journey reaches Venus' clouds, individuals get one final view of the surrounding galaxy.

After dropping through the caustic cloud cover of the inner planet, unsaved people will arrive at a repulsive environment shaped by volcanism. Due to the material substance of the resurrected body, all spirits in the afterlife will be subject to gravity, just as with the human body. He or she will be trapped in the despair of the Venusian world. Gravity acts upon the mass of all inhabitants, so it will be impossible to break free from the grip of the planet. The angels will deliver each individual to an encrusted lava dwelling on the Venusian surface, which will serve as a residence.

Each person will appear as an independent, self-sufficient, and responsible adult who will coexist in a shared space. The members in a cave dwelling are likely to have similar cultural backgrounds. One fissure may have individuals from North America, while another cave has inhabitants from Europe, while still another has occupants from Asia or Africa. People living on the earth during a certain period of history will likely be grouped with people who lived during or near the same time. Conversation will flow freely between members of the group. Individuals are able to relate his or her life stories and circumstances to one another.

Lava tubes provide a place to reside for small clusters of lost people. Caves that house other groups are not necessarily nearby. Cavernous locations can exist miles apart because of the vastness of the planet's surface. The Venusian landscape does not facilitate venturing out on long field trips to find others. Getting your bearings straight on this vast, unchanging wasteland is impossible at night. During the day, the heavy cloud cover will obscure the sun. Perhaps a hazy, circular outline will be evident from time to time. Using the shape could provide brief periods to follow a directional course, as the sun's position changes slowly over 58.5 days.

In the first column of the following table is *personal effect*. Being in perdition manifests itself in either a visible or physical way to those who are banished. The second column gives the *impact* that the feature will have on immortal beings held on Venus. The third column connects the description in the second column to *biblical passages*, which describe hell and the lake of fire. These Bible verses have been cited throughout the chapters of the book.

Personal Effect	Description / Impact	Biblical Reference
Visible	In a future age, the righteous living on Earth will know the fate of the unrighteous when looking at Venus. On the planet, the unrighteous will see the dreariness of their volcanic world of fire and sulfur.	Rev. 14:10 Isa 66:24a
Physical	A temperature of 865°F is the hottest planetary environment in the solar system. Felt by the inhabitants, the unchanging heat from day to night is indicative of the unquenchable fire of hell.	Matt. 3:12 Mark 9:43
Visible	Travel to the inner planet begins by going into the outer darkness of outer space. Living on Venus, the 58.5 days of continuous night brings a sense of outer darkness to spiritual beings from Earth.	Matt. 8:12 Matt. 25:30
Visible	Flashes from volcanic eruptions give evidence of red-hot ash/lava and sulfur dioxide emission, creating a lake that burns with fire and sulfur.	Rev. 19:20 Rev. 21:8
Visible	The cold polar collars cause a lifting of caustic clouds at the north and south poles. Ongoing volcanic activity emits sulfur compounds. These events produce a rising smoke of torment going up forever and ever.	Rev. 14:11a
Physical	Having no rest day or night, as well as being in torment day and night, occurs on a dreadful rotating planet that is orbiting the sun.	Rev. 14:11b Rev. 20:10
Physical	The vignette in the next section addresses personal emotional issues resulting from being sequestered to Venus.	Mark 9:48

Table 5
Features of Venus Relating to Biblical Passages

As shown by the descriptions and biblical references, the summary points in Table 5 associate Venus to a place of perdition. The technical evidence amasses by using the unaided eye, telescopic surveillance in the visible and nonvisible spectrums, and space vehicle exploration. The complete assessment covers atmospheric conditions, rotation, orbit, chemical makeup, and meteorology. *The integration of two fields of study allows for the metaphysical assertion of planet Venus becoming the eternal place of banishment for unsaved human beings and demonic spirits.* It has support from the sciences and correlates directly to the Bible, which describes hell and the lake of fire.

The information in this chapter works along with previous findings where the soul and resurrected body have weight, occupy space, and are subject to gravity. After final judgment, resurrected human beings will require separation from God in the material universe. The terminus for such an exile will likely be an undesirable planet. A celestial body can apply a retaining gravitational force to the immortal spiritual body. As a member of the solar system, Venus fully qualifies as a journey's end to exile. Since the renewed Earth becomes the paradisical state of heaven, it requires perdition to be in a separate location in the physical universe.

A Drama of Six Men in a Lava Tube

At the end of the millennium—the thousand-year period during which Christ rules on Earth after his return and during which Satan is bound—Hades empties out and the unrighteous come before the throne of God. It includes the small and great of the human race, dating back to Adam and Eve. During the review, various books will be retrieved that contain a summary of every person's life. An appraisal of thoughts, words, and deeds will be weighed against existing moral code. At the end of the proceeding, the book of life opens to determine a person's eternal status. If someone's name is not found in the book, the individual will face the final sentence of banishment to the lake of fire.

The Day of Judgment did not go well for six men in the following vignette. As foretold by the scriptures, sentencing results in condemnation and departure from the presence of the Lord. Removal from the earth and relocation to the lake of fire is the final phase of the plan. Living on a dismal world such as Venus is a terrible fate for these male residents. The following speculative scene depicts a conversation between them, which reflects the struggle of being on the planet.

The end of the age brought the second coming of Christ in 2145, resulting in his reign of one thousand years on the earth, until 3145. After the final rebellion by Satan and his casting into the lake of fire, the great white throne judgment occurred in 3146. Twenty years have passed since the sentencing of humanity, and it is now 3166. Banished from the earth permanently, six men from the United States have been sitting in a lava tube in the Venusian lowlands the entire time. The cave situates about two hundred miles south of the Venera 14 landing site.

Three of the men were part of the baby boom generation. The group was born between 1946 and 1964. It was a time in history that was blessed with good job opportunities, as well as political and economic stability. These people had ample material goods, general worldwide peace, and the benefits of retirement.

Three other Americans lived between 2050 and 2145. Being born a century later, the three men entered into a host of chaotic events recorded in the book of Revelation. The tribulation period between 2138 and 2145 led to their deaths. In recalling the many sufferings, one plague was the arrival of the demonic locust invasion, which appears in the Figure 10 illustration.

Larry, Eric, Bob, Steve, Jeff, and Roy live together in a lava cave. The following is some personal history on each individual:

- Larry was a regional sales manager from Fort Wayne, Indiana, who died in 2033 at age 81.
- Eric was a high school English teacher from Chicago, Illinois, who died in 2036 at age 88.
- Bob, a physical therapist from Bridgeport, Connecticut passed away in 2037 at age 84.
- Steve was a lawyer from Houston, Texas, whose life on the earth ended in 2143 at age 83.
- Jeff, who departed this life in 2143 at age 94, was a security guard from Baltimore, Maryland.
- Roy expired in 2144 at age 79 and had been a construction worker from Sacramento, California.

The moral character of these resurrected beings has not changed from the corporeal state. The men did not allow the Holy Spirit to convict them of their need for repentance in order to receive salvation during their lifetime. Unwillingness to acknowledge a need for God resulted in the six men retaining a sinful nature at death. Soul substance carries the traits of the individual into the afterlife, violating the divine intention. Prior to final judgment, the soul is resurrected from Hades to an immortal spiritual body, which carries the same corrupt disposition. Estranged from God in the spiritual state, the men are banished from Earth and placed together on Venus.

Our story opens as the group considers making a run from the lava tube. After arriving on the planet two decades earlier, the men endure the doldrums day after day. The quarters are tight inside the abode, and there is little to do outside on the barren terrain of the lava fields. The boredom of a cave, extreme heat of the barren surroundings, and unending overcast skies offer little pleasure to an immortal being capable of enjoying so much more. Feelings of emptiness and unfulfillment are prevalent.

Generally, the men get along very well, but the monotony of the lava tube leads to restlessness and a longing to leave. Edginess creeps in because of the unceasing hot temperature and the ongoing sounds of volcanic eruptions. The vast and barren terrain is an issue because the topography looks nearly identical in all directions. Rather than venturing out alone, they are compelled to exit in a group. But the members of the cave dwelling cannot agree on when it is best to go. One difficulty lies in the limited ability to navigate by day and the complete inability to navigate by night. In reality, the most serious problem is the hopelessness of escape from the planet.

Before banishment from the earth to the lake of fire, the men were able to see and identify righteous individuals being admitted to the kingdom of God. Being aware of those admitted to heaven is found in Luke 13:28. As a result of missing out, Jesus warns several times that perdition will cause the "weeping and gnashing of teeth."[123] Sadness can result in weeping, which is an expression of grief and sorrow. Other people gnash their teeth, which is an emotional reaction to being angry or even furious. A third group of people is in the middle, having a calm and composed response to the situation.

Bob and Larry have been distressed since arriving on Venus. In one corner of the hollow, the men can be found vacillating between shedding dry tears and having no expression at all. Venus' hellish landscape is not a good place, so both men are against the idea of trying to move from the

---

123 The passages warning against the weeping and gnashing of teeth are in Matthew 8:12, 13:42, 13:50, 22:13, 24:51, and 25:30. Coogan, *New Oxford Annotated Bible*, 18, 28, 42, 47, 48 [NT].

location. Feelings of hopelessness keep Bob and Larry "safe" in the cave.

Expressing a counter temperament, Steve and Roy are outraged about having been cast into the lake of fire, occasionally gritting their teeth in anger. Both men have anxiously scouted the terrain during the extended daylight. At the next opportunity, they are ready to leave the cave.

Eric and Jeff have not shown a lot of emotion over the years. Clearly, the surface of Venus is not a good place, but in a relative sense, it seems better than the underground confinement of Hades. Maintaining an even temperament and trying to be supportive, they spend time with Bob and Larry, hoping to encourage them. Eric and Jeff entertain the idea of leaving but have not made up their minds.

Halfway through the 58.5 days of the Venusian night finds the small group sitting around a large, natural basalt rock near the entry of the lava cave. The stone has become the centerpiece of the communal setting. Steve, who is annoyed and on his soapbox about leaving the lava tube, comments flippantly,

"Okay, sports fans, are we ready to blow this pop stand? We've been hanging around this lousy cave for twenty years and it's getting pretty mind-numbing."

Eric responds, "And where, may I ask, do you think we should go? The horizon is blurred by clouds and that disgusting lava field looks the same in every direction."

"Well, we can start traveling due east at dawn with the light at our back," Steve offered. "I'm sure we'll hit upon something—maybe another cave with people we can talk to."

Bob joins the conversation but can only muster sadness, "But the angel who dropped me off here said not to leave the cave. I'm sure you were told the same thing."

Roy is incensed. "And what do you think your reward is going to be for following those instructions? Besides, since when are you into obeying God? We need to stop this idle chatter and leave this place."

"But wait a minute, Roy," Jeff countered. "Those grotesque demon locusts could be out there—the same ones that tormented us on Earth. What if we run across those creatures?"

Roy picks up a flat basalt rock. "Then it's payback time! I was stung by one of those beasts and suffered for months. I'm ready to deal with them now." He breaks the rock in two to emphasize his determination.

"Payback?" Jeff scoffs at Roy. "Using what? Your bare hands? Those creepy things are big and fast. We need weapons and we can't make any, at least not here."

With remorse in his voice, Larry adds his piece, "We should have repented in our lifetime, trusting Jesus Christ as our Lord and Savior. None of us would be here if we had made the right decision."

Steve is irritated. "Are you going to bring up that same old stuff again? It's over with now. We made up our minds back on Earth. Let's deal with reality and stop feeling sorry about the past."

Eric responds, "The reality is that it is extremely hot here and we are bored out of our minds. I now understand what was meant by 'where their worm never dies.'"[124] He surrounds his words with air quotes. "We just sit here day in and day out with absolutely nothing to do, except continually lament our situation."

Steve is angry. "That's precisely why I'm trying to get us out of here! We can keep ourselves busy by scouring the planet for other people and places. We don't sleep; we never get tired. What's to stop us from succeeding?"

---

124 Isa. 66:24 gives warning to rebellious people saying "their worm shall not die." In Mark 9:48, Jesus follows up with a similar warning about lost people in hell. Coogan, *New Oxford Annotated Bible*, 1072 [OT], 76 [NT].

What's your idea of success, Steve?" Eric asks curiously. "Finding other people on Venus who are suffering in this heat like us? So what? We will listen to their stories and undergo monotony again in a few months."

Larry asks the others, "Do you remember seeing the beautifully restored Earth on Judgment Day? Who wants to spend time walking through these volcanic fields feeling heartbroken?"

"Well, it sure is better on the surface of this planet than in Hades," Jeff retorted. "I still remember the fear, the total darkness, and the lack of human contact while in confinement."

Roy concurs that this is a better place, relatively speaking. "It was hard for me to breathe down there. At least the stench is not as bad in this place—well, except for when the nearby volcano erupts."

Bob agrees. "The flashes of light and thundering sounds from volcanic eruptions are really intimidating. I don't want to be near any of those flare-ups."

Eric sums up the conversation. "Sounds like we're lacking a consensus on leaving, Steve. If you and Roy really want to go, you could make a run for another cave in the morning."

Steve concedes, "I can't see Roy and me leaving just yet. It's just too risky to go out there with only two guys. We'll just have to wait here and talk about it another time."

"Steve, if I decide to join you and Roy in the future," Jeff offers, "the group would be evenly divided. A team of three men should be safe enough. We can always come back."

Eric is dubious. "I'm not sure if or when you guys would ever get back. The landscape is too confusing."

"Hey Jeff, maybe you can pray about it," Roy says sarcastically. "In the meantime, I'll be leaving when Steve decides to go."

This brief scene depicts the frustration of being separated from God for eternity. Perdition is a coherent, rational, and unpleasant place in the material universe where spiritual beings will reside. It is not a black hole in the space-time fabric, or an unimaginable place in the ethereal realm, as some would perceive it to be. Although a dramatization of futuristic events, this vignette could play out in the afterlife.

The resurrected spiritual body is durable enough to endure the harsh Venusian environment. The question becomes, "Where will this group end up that will improve the situation?" The entire world is scorching hot. What benefit is there to having eternally enduring features and ground mobility on a planet with the same weather everywhere? True escape is impossible. You cannot break away. Gravity has your resurrected body held to a mind-numbing lava field. By ignoring the call to salvation, some people today risk a perpetual state of loss with banishment to another planet. It is a road to death and destruction that this book is trying to help people avoid.

The antithetical state is everlasting life, which our heavenly Father originally intended for these men. 2 Peter 3:9 tells the reader that God is "not wanting any to perish, but all to come to repentance." In the intermediate state, the beauty of the third heaven will be completely counter to Hades, a cavity inside the earth. And after final judgment, heaven on Earth will be far more glorious than Venus' volcanic nothingness. Heaven is not only God's home but is a place of supreme beauty and harmonious living. Blessed by the presence of God and surrounded by friends, family, and angels, paradise completely lacks pain, evil, or monotony.

The lava tube scene provides a possible view of conditions for lost people. The communal cave addresses the afterlife of the unbeliever: those without belief in God, those who have heard and rejected the gospel, and those who think the Bible is fiction. The vignette is helpful for refuting annihilationism and universalism, where eternal places of separation are deemed irrational. When Christians buy into universal salvation, they believe God will act differently toward unrepentant people than what Scripture teaches. As a familiar celestial object, places such as Venus present a scientific, scripturally-based, and physical location for perdition.

Chapter 8

Exoplanets as Perdition Candidates

Therefore, the wicked will not stand in the judgment,
nor sinners in the congregation of the righteous;
for the Lord watches over the way of the righteous,
but the way of the wicked will perish.

Psalm 1:5–6

The success of the *Star Wars* and *Star Trek* movie series provides clear evidence of the public's appetite for adventure beyond the solar system. Hollywood does a great job creating storylines of travel into deep space, where alien crew members and extraterrestrial encounters are the norm. To bridge the vast distances, starships travel at warp speed, which is many times faster than the speed of light. High tech weapons and defense shields are onboard to combat threatening forces. A big part of the exploration involves trips to exoplanets. Circling the planets of distant stars in the Milky Way, these storybook worlds contain both friendly and hostile inhabitants.

The real-world ability to travel into space lies with agencies such as NASA, ESA, JAXA, ISRO, and Roscosmos, as well as commercial enterprises such as SpaceX and Blue Origin. These groups place humans in the International Space Station and launch spacecraft to explore the moon, planets, and even exoplanets using uniquely crafted space telescopes. As noted earlier, the existence of distant planets was not confirmed until the mid-1990s. Today, experts consider most stars in the galaxy to have at least one orbiting body. A conservative report by the California Institute of Technology (Caltech) suggests a minimum of one hundred billion exoplanets are in the Milky Way galaxy.[125]

With the number of confirmed findings growing by the week, we can say science is entering the golden age of exoplanets. Several programs are in process to search out the worlds. The orbiting Transiting Exoplanet Survey Satellite (TESS) is expected to confirm up to fifteen thousand exoplanets during its mission.[126] The James Webb Space Telescope (JWST) was launched on Christmas day 2021. The Planetary Transits and Oscillations of Stars (PLATO) is an ESA spacecraft planned for 2026. On the ground, the Extremely Large Telescope (ELT), the Giant Magellan Telescope (GMT), and the Thirty Meter Telescope (TMT) will emphasize extrasolar planet observation.

Exoplanet Discoveries

Astronomical study by scientists in the twentieth century led to the initial belief that our solar system was the blueprint for other solar systems. The ordering within our planetary system appears logical, so other stars with orbiting planets must follow a similar pattern. Planets forming closest to the

---

125 California Institute of Technology (Caltech), "Planets Abound," http://www.caltech.edu/news/planets-abound-37829 (accessed Sept. 9, 2020).
126 The Astrophysical Journal, "A Revised Exoplanet Yield from the Transiting Exoplanet Survey Satellite," https://iopscience.iop.org/article/10.3847/1538-4365/aae3e9 (accessed July 2, 2020).

sun will be small, compact, and rocky. Further out, planets do not coalesce as well and become gas giants. Finally, the outermost planets are coldest and become gas giants, containing more ice.

It did not take long for the cosmos to dispel the blueprint rationale. Chaos reigns in the Milky Way galaxy. As an example, many stars have gas giants orbiting at wildly fast rates close to the parent star. The startling discovery led to new theories about nebular disc formation and planetary migration. Many astronomers began seeing the beauty, comfort, and advantage of living in our orderly planetary system.

The discovery of worlds orbiting distant stars is on the rise. Outside the galaxy, extragalactic planets are hard to detect, so the focus is on the Milky Way. Inside our galaxy are thought to be 100 to 400 billion stars. NASA began the search by employing the Kepler spacecraft to be a stalwart exoplanet hunter. Until retirement in October 2018, its mission was to survey planetary systems and uncover near-Earth-size exoplanets (exo-Earths) circling in a star's habitable zone. The Kepler Space Telescope is responsible for discovering over twenty-five hundred exoplanets. As exoplanet detections climb, knowledge continues to grow.

Special detection methods uncover telescopically faint bodies that circle distant stars. One technique used by Kepler is called transit photometry. Photometry evaluates light. When a distant planet orbits in front of its parent star, it blocks the emission of light by the star. The visual brightness then drops by a measurable amount, which can vary depending on the size of the planet. Even though exoplanets are small relative to a larger star, photometry is able to detect the varying drops in light intensity, confirming the existence of different size planetary bodies.

Beyond confirming distant worlds, astronomers can ascertain orbital and physical characteristics. Retired in

January 2020, the Spitzer Space Telescope used spectroscopy in the infrared (IR) to uncover features. Spectroscopy employs a spectroscope to perform spectrum analysis. In the infrared, the light of the star will dim while the planet itself brightens, revealing hidden features. Spectroscope results read like a bar code. The gaps between the lines represent gases absorbed by the exoplanet. The cumulative data can reveal the brightness, temperature, and chemical composition of the atmosphere, as well as the bulk density of the body.

Finding planets that can support life is the ultimate goal, but challenges remain. Even if a planet has the right atmosphere and retains water, concerns remain about high carbon content in the soil. Planetary carbon comes from the carbon–oxygen balance of the host star. One chemical study of star formation found the carbon–oxygen balance to be the critical factor in making planets similar to Earth. If too much carbon exists in a star, the planetary disc produces carbon-rich exoplanets. The soil would consist of high amounts of graphite and perhaps even diamonds. The study states many stars have a high carbon–oxygen balance, which is not a good omen.[127]

The scientific community has come to realize the stability of our solar system, the distinctiveness of our home planet, and the disappointment of exoplanets. The sampling to date has found the majority to be dismal worlds. A bitter taste results when dipping our finger into the Milky Way batter of exoplanets. One leading NASA scientist working in the field states, "We have been searching for heaven and finding

---

127 On the earth, the weathering of non-carbon silica produces nutrient-rich soil, allowing for life-sustaining crops to grow. *Scientific American,* "Earth-Like [Exo]planets May Be Made of Carbon," https://www. scientificamerican.com/article/a-large-lump-of-coal/ (accessed Sept. 29, 2020).

hell."[128] The pattern is likely to continue. The well spring of information reveals nightmarish worlds with terrible surface conditions. Examples are as follows:

- **Pulsar Planets**
  In 1992, the discovery of the first orbiting exoplanet was in pulsar PSR B1257+12. A pulsar is a magnetized and rapidly spinning neutron star. This pulsar locates in the constellation Virgo. With every spin, it emits a sweeping beam of light containing powerful X-ray radiation. Orbiting under constant radiation bombardment are three rocky planets. These sterile worlds are cooking to death, like shriveled, blackened chestnuts sitting in a microwave oven.

- **Hot Jupiters**
  Gas giants begin by taking shape far from a star. Hot Jupiters migrate from great distances to orbits close to the star. One finding is WASP–12b, a body 40% larger than Jupiter. The exoplanet situates only two million miles from its sun and has a high-speed orbit lasting one Earth day. Distorted into an egg-shape, the atmosphere is slowly being eaten by the parent star. The temperature of the tidally locked world is 3,500°F and wind speeds are close to 5,000 mph. The planet is a superheated convection oven.

- **Rogue Planets**
  The process of a hot Jupiter migrating inward toward the parent star creates orphan planets. During the

---

128 The quote is from the assistant director for Science Communication, Michelle Thaller, at the NASA Goddard Space Flight Center. Science Channel, *How the Universe Works*, "Planets from Hell," https://www.sciencechannel.com/tv-shows/how-the-universe-works/full-episodes/planets-from-hell (accessed Feb. 13, 2020).

journey, gravitational waves from the gas giant disrupt inner worlds, ejecting them from orbit. The expulsion results in the exoplanet becoming rogue, drifting aimlessly between stars. An observer on the surface would see a sky festooned with stars, but they would also freeze to death. Without a sun, temperatures get to 375°F below zero. The perpetual night on these roving bodies epitomizes them as a place of outer darkness.

- **Super-Earths**
  A super-earth can have a mass that is two times the size of our earth. The planet will have a solid surface and large circumference, but it may or may not be in the habitable zone. Physical features vary widely. One example is CoRoT–7b, a tidally locked exoplanet extremely close to its parent star. On the sun side, the terrestrial body contains a sea of red-hot magma. The lava spews high into the air and condenses as falling rock. It is a literal lake of fire. On the dark side, frozen lava fields cover a bitterly cold landscape.

Like Venus, exoplanets are capable of containing individuals banished from the paradisical earth. Some exoplanets will not qualify because spiritual beings cannot exercise cognitive thinking there. Parables such as the rich man and Lazarus imply a place where unsaved people can have time for rational thought. Perdition is a state where one thinks clearly and logically. The acceptable sites must allow for one to consider choices and outcomes made in life. The Bible implies Hades is a coherent and orderly place. By extension, the lake of fire should be the same way. The six men in a lava tube converse well on Venus. The environment on an exoplanet should be comparable.

A complete list of exoplanetary types is lengthy, and the

list breaks down into classes by size, orbital regime, and composition. The category of exoplanets that includes pulsar planets and super-Earths is under "rocky planets." One type of exoplanet quite different from a rocky planet is an ocean world. When an ice giant similar to Uranus and Neptune migrates close to the parent star, the body will basically thaw and become a global sea of liquid. The depth of the fluid will reach tens of miles. Would such a place make biblical sense for spiritual beings? A liquid surface is unstable due to wave agitation and does not correlate well with the idea of an unquenchable fire.

Pulsar planets are few in number. Except for the vast amount of radiation exposure, scientists know little about them. A planet orbiting a pulsar would be a scorched world. Scientists debate whether Mercury or Mars are dead planets because their surfaces reveal little or no volcanic activity. The same question goes for pulsar planets. The surface is probably case-hardened by eons of radioactive dosing. Without volcanic activity or lava flow, there is no hot sulfur in the environment. It lessens the likelihood that the planet qualifies biblically as a place of perdition.

Finding large numbers of hot Jupiters or "roaster planets" was a big surprise to astronomers. These beasts normally circle at ferocious speeds close to the parent star and are tidally locked.[129] This mayhem is far different from our solar system, which is one of order. Unable to rotate, roaster planets dissipate heat from the sun side to the dark side by spinning the atmosphere, creating fast-moving jet streams and scalding whirlwinds. Situating a spiritual body in such a place would be difficult because it lacks a solid surface. Even

---

129 Finding tidally locked worlds is an ordinary event. *UWNews*, "Tidally Locked Exoplanets May Be More Common than Previously Thought," http://www.washington.edu/news/2017/08/14/tidally-locked-exoplanets-may-be-more-common-than-previously-thought/ (accessed Oct. 9, 2020).

if it were possible, the question arises, "How can one think clearly in the hurricane wind speeds of a hot inferno?"

Countless rogue planets are displaced from their sun. Traveling through interstellar space, these orbs once had a happy home inside a solar system. Having experienced expulsion from the parent star, the bodies move aimlessly through the darkness of space. Surfaces are bitter cold and covered with icy-rock. While the planet continues in its eons-long journey as an orphan, the geological layers cool to the point of not having an internal heat source that can create volcanic activity. This results in the planet's surface not being able to produce hot conditions.

Some dark worlds in isolation are actually brown dwarf stars. These stellar misfits once sustained nuclear reactions in the core before fizzling out. The bodies are not cold like rogue planets; they stay indefinitely warm by retaining fusion heat. Being failed stars, brown dwarfs will produce hot temperatures from residual fusion reactions rather than from volcanic activity. Being an unsuccessful star, the surface would be more like a plasma, instead of solid or rocky. Consequently, the ability to host clear thinking spiritual beings would not be good.

A tidally locked super-Earth in close orbital proximity to the parent star will produce a nightmarish world. One example is CoRoT–7b. The sun side of the planet will have boiling magma seas (analogous to a lake of fire), while the dark side will have expansive fields of frozen lava (analogous to outer darkness). Rising smoke and sulfur compounds would be present in the atmosphere. Having a sun side and a dark side means that spiritual bodies could experience both a lake of fire and outer darkness. This can be accomplished if they are living in lava caves along the terminator. The terminator is the dividing line between the light and dark side of a planet.

Table 6 presents a summary of undesirable exoplanets.

Each body is compared to a list of eight descriptions of perdition from the Bible. The first item derives from Hades, where the rich man and Lazarus are able to think and reason. It is a condition that continues in perdition. The remaining seven come from descriptions of hell and the lake of fire. When a passage is thought to be suitable for an exoplanet, an X is placed in the box. In assessing elements 1–8, metaphysics gives the nod to a super-Earth becoming the biblical lake of fire. It will best substitute for Venus.

	Element	Pulsar Planets	Hot Jupiters[a]	Rogue Planets	Super Earths[a]	Brown Dwarfs	Ocean Worlds
1	Ability to Think and Reason	X		X	X		
2	Star Visible from Earth	X	X		X		X
3	Unquenchable Fire	X	X		X	X	
4	Outer Darkness	X	X	X	X	X	X
5	Sulfur Compounds				X		
6	Rising Smoke of Torment		X		X	X	
7	No Rest Day or Night	X	X		X		X
8	Emotional Distress	X	X	X	X	X	X

(a) Assumes planet is tidally locked and close to parent star
References: (1) Luke 16:24, (2) Rev. 14:10, (3) Mark 9:43, (4) Matt. 8:12, (5) Rev. 21:8, (6) Rev. 14:11a, (7) Rev. 20:10, (8) Mark 9:48

Table 6
Exoplanets as Places for Perdition

The table has super-Earth checking the box in all eight categories. A tidally locked version of the world orbiting near a star would be blistering hot on the sun side and continuously cold on the dark side. Resurrected spiritual bodies located along the terminator could reside between the day and night flank. Housing in lava tubes would be available from the volcanism. The existence of boiling lava fields would create smoke and sulfur rising into the air. The large size creates oppressive gravity, with the effect being similar to the high atmospheric pressure of Venus. Finally, the parent star of the super-Earth could be visible in the night sky.

After final judgment, angels will guide the unrighteous to the proper exoplanet. Immortal spiritual bodies have rest mass. Objects with rest mass travel through space well below the speed of light. Many super-Earths are light-years away from our planet. So, undertaking a rapid interstellar trip to perdition may require using the higher dimensions of eternity present in the universe. In theoretical science, physicists cite a wormhole for possible faster-than-light time travel. Stemming from general relativity, a wormhole is a tunnel linking two points in space-time. Wormholes can exist as a special solution to Einstein's field equations.

Summary of the Sections

The Bible, theology, and science, as well as input from metaphysical space, time, and being, blend together to form a unifying search for the truth. It presents Christians with fresh ideas about personal eschatology and perdition. The originality of the account is a result of working with the creative model of Fruitful Integration. In light of the new concepts presented in the book, it is in the reader's best interest to conduct a chapter-by-chapter summary. A review and encapsulation of the material will aid in remembering a majority of the ideas. The following section gives a synopsis of the critical points.

Introduction (Concluding Remarks)

The introduction provides an overview of four ways to approach the Bible and science. The methods include the Sovereign, Conflict, Complementary, and Fruitful Integration models. The "give and take" of the Fruitful Integration model shows that God's written account of creation in Genesis and the visible handiwork of creation can be consistent. The following biblical–theological positions, summary views of science, and metaphysical propositions about space, time, and being were made by the author in an attempt to create a complete vision.

The Bible

1. Consider Old Earth creationism, while questioning the doctrine of Young Earth creationism. Valid scientific evidence shows the earth and universe are billions of years old.
2. Understand the geological time scale of eons does not open the door to the natural evolution process (humans evolving from primates).
3. Do not align with theistic evolution as an alternate creation science. It contains biblical capitulation regarding Adam and Eve being the biological parents of all humanity, while fully agreeing with the unproven claims of natural evolution.
4. View annihilationism and universalism as incorrect Christian teaching.
5. Accept end-of-the-age theology, rather than end-of-the-world.

Science

1. Realize the Big Bang concept of "something out of nothing" (which contains the omission of God) has no basis in reality. On its own, it is a physical impossibility for the observable universe to come out of nothing.

2. Accept the lack of proof and hopelessness of abiogenesis. As the foundation to natural evolution, abiogenesis attempts to fashion simple, non-living organic compounds into basic life (without the inclusion of God).

Metaphysical

- The domain of eternity (spiritual world) is not separate from the physical universe but is an integral part of it. Beyond the edge of the universe lies the ethereal or the nothing.
- The higher dimensions of space find support in particle physics, facilitate the miracles of Jesus, and allow for the movement of departing souls to the third heaven or Hades.
- The higher dimensions of time (co-presence) allow God to hear all prayers and facilitate outcomes he chooses to control by his providence.
- The departing human soul and spirits in eternity have physical mass, take up space, and are subject to the law of gravity.
- Sheol–Hades situates in the heart (inner core) of our planet and can be a place of temporary confinement for the souls of the unrighteous.
- Because mass and gravity are present in eternity, celestial bodies such as Earth and Venus (or an exoplanet) can provide dwelling places for spiritual beings.
- When the paradisical Earth comes to fulfillment, Venus can become the eternal place of banishment for unsaved human beings and demonic spirits.

Chapter One

The first chapter provides a contextual setting for the writing, while learning basic information about the solar system and the history of space exploration. The reader gets an introduction to special revelation, general revelation, and natural theology. A biblical analysis shows the destination of "hell" or the "lake of fire" to be one and the same. A preview is given for Venus as a possible place of perdition. The final section describes spacecraft design and operation, which gives the reader a snapshot of the author's background and experience in the field of aerospace.

Chapter Two

The second chapter gives evidence for the truth of perdition in the Bible. From the Old to the New Testament, human sin separates people from God. The reader recognizes that Jesus himself introduces the penalty of hell when using the term *gehenna*, a local dumping site outside of Jerusalem. The section includes a study on the parable in Luke 16:19–31 concerning the rich man and Lazarus. The place of Sheol in the Old Testament equates to Hades in the New Testament, with Sheol–Hades being under the earth. A refutation of annihilationism and universalism addresses incorrect Christian theology. As a result, one sees final judgment and eternal banishment as credible.

Chapter Three

The third chapter gives a historical account of the division between faith and science. It examines scientism, positivism, materialism, and claims of today's astrophysicists that, without a Creator, the universe can come out of nothing. Historically, Catholicism and Protestant reformers were dubious and resistant toward heliocentricity. In modern times, the problem continues with church leaders disregarding verified scientific evidence that the earth is billions of years old. It is important to realize that God ordains faith, science, and reason to work together.

In order to interpret Scripture properly, you need to examine God's creation. This is done using special revelation and the worldview of natural theology (Figure 1). The Holy Spirit reliably guides us in a proper reading of the Bible, which is special revelation. Natural theology uses observation of God's natural world, which works alongside experience, reason, and innate conscience. Together, a correct theological construct emerges, which can blend the Genesis creation account with scientific findings. The Bible reader who relies on special revelation and natural theology will uncover the truth about the age of the universe and the world around them.

The divergent views of science and the creation sciences in Table 1 drive a study as to which one is correct. Science willingly embraces abiogenesis and the natural evolution process, which poses a problem of credibility. The dominant creation science is OEC, which uses progressive creation. OEC honors both the Genesis creation and the observable universe. Other candidates show reason for concern. YEC works against proven science, causing a faith–science schism. TE aligns itself with the uncertainty of natural evolution, while eliminating any direct acts by God in the creation. One such act is when God made Adam and Eve. Scripture clearly presents them as the biological parents of the human race.

Chapter Four

When we use the Figure 2 timeline, the Bible and science are shown to be in harmony. At t = 0, the Big Bang expansion begins to move forward. By using OEC and physical cosmology, we can create a multi-billion-year timeline covering the age of the universe. A look into the future reveals long-term health for the universe. With the return of Christ comes an unfolding of the "end of the age." God's heavenly kingdom descends to form a renewed Earth, which will be a familiar and permanent environment. Our planetary abode will become a place of joy and contentment, while planets such as Venus can become a place of loss and sorrow.

The timeline, beginning at t = 0, has scientific and biblical backing. Astrophysics verifies the truth about an absolute beginning to time within the framework of general relativity. The uniform distribution of CMBR particulate in the universe makes possible the Figure 3 convergence of the past light to t = 0. The Bible's introductory phrase, "In the beginning," serves as the t = 0 point. Biblical passages mention the period "before the ages began," which evokes activity by God before the start of time. Physical cosmology and OEC then guide the Christian in affirming the universe's age of 13.8 billion years, with a consequent 4.5 billion-year-old age for the sun and earth.

The right side of Figure 2 continues the timeline far into the future. Strong prospects unfold for a healthy planet orbiting a supportive solar system, galaxy, and universe. Although various threats may occur (global warming, nuclear war, galactic collisions, asteroid strikes, solar evolution, and the universe's final fate), these scenarios end with planetary and human species survival beyond a billion years. With the return of Christ, one sees an "end of the age," rather than an "end of the world." Biblical passages speak of a permanent Earth, with Jesus affirming in the Beatitudes that "the meek will inherit the earth." The righteous can expect to live with God in a familiar place; that is, a renewed third planet from the sun.

Chapter Five

Chapter five discusses the human soul, which contains the mind, will, and emotions. God infuses an immortal soul into a person and creates a living, breathing being. An individual is a unity of body, soul, and spirit. The soul is defined by your thoughts, character, will, and feelings. The spirit contains the conscience, which guides in ethical functions and decision-making. Following bodily death, the soul of the righteous moves on to the third heaven, while the unrighteous soul departs for Hades (Figure 6). The righteous will receive rewards at the judgment seat of Christ and will return with Jesus to a renewed heaven on Earth. The unrighteous face the great white throne judgment and an irrevocable sequestering to the lake of fire.

Existing before the creation of the universe is God's eternal realm. As shown in Figure 7, the domain enters the physical universe with the Big Bang expansion. The three domains of the *physical universe, eternity,* and the *ethereal* are then compared in Table 2. Time and space in the physical world connect to eternity via co-presence and extra spatial dimensions. Eternity also contains the properties of mass and gravity. In having material substance, the human soul and its resurrected body are inside the cosmos. The connecting properties of eternity to the physical universe facilitate the miracles of Jesus. Beyond the edge of the universe is the ethereal realm of nothing. It contains no space, time, matter, or energy and has no direct link to the physical universe.

An early twentieth century experiment by Dr. Duncan MacDougall demonstrates that human souls have material substance. Table 3 shows the bodily weight decrease of four patients upon death. A sudden weight loss coinciding with the departure of a soul means the mass must transfer to the eternal realm. An important twenty-first century system engineering study by Masayoshi Ishida validates the MacDougall test setup, shielding it from uninformed, nonscientific criticism. Being subject to gravity, the human body registers weight loss on a balancing scale after death. The handover of weight gives the departing soul physical mass in eternity.

Chapter Six

Chapter six presents a discussion of Satan, who is the great adversary of humanity. Having society under his sway, the devil roams about freely within the spiritual domain of Hades, which covers the four corners of the planet. The devil's plan is to divert people from the truth of the gospel, deceive the human mind, and negatively influence the behavior of people. His ultimate goal is for the human soul to suffer separation from God. The lost soul's confinement is in Hades, which is inside the earth. In the end times, demons in detention will physically invade the planet and intimidate the populace (Figure 10). Ultimately, Satan and his followers will be cast into the lake of fire.

The biblical notion of Sheol–Hades under the earth needs to be reconciled with the planet's structural interior shown in Figure 11. Primary and secondary waves from earthquakes allow geologists to use seismic tomography to map the inner earth. In studying the earth's solidity, the inner core emerges as the only possible place for voids that could facilitate Hades. The 1.8 billion mi^3 volume of the inner core can easily house the lost in as many as five hundred detention centers of $1 \ mi^3$ size. The rebellion of Korah in Numbers 16 is an example of souls going directly to Hades. Movement of souls through the crust, mantle, and outer core to a void in the inner core is possible using the higher spatial dimensions of eternity.

Chapter Seven

Chapter seven unveils neighboring Venus as a possible place for perdition. The earliest human records give attention to the planet due to its brightness. Being an inner planet, it leads or follows the sun closely. As the morning star, it leads the sun before sunrise. As the evening star, it follows the sun after sunset. Total viewing time is over 200 days a year. Looking through a telescope reveals the phases of the planet, which appears like a waning moon in the west and a waxing moon in the east. Up until the early 1960s, Venus captured the imagination of multitudes and was the subject of books, articles, television shows, and movies.

Enchantment ends with the sister planet in late 1962 when Mariner 2 verifies scorching surface temperatures. The discovery dampens American interest, while the USSR forges ahead with a host of space missions. Over time, data collection reveals a hot, toxic world of volcanism. Thick clouds rain down sulfuric acid, while hovering over a high pressure, gas–liquid carbon dioxide atmosphere. Lander photography exposes a hellish environment on the surface. Countless volcanoes add to a milieu of unpleasant sights, sounds, and smells. Ongoing eruptions spew hot lava, ash, and sulfur dioxide, making the planet a lake of fire burning with sulfur.

Table 5's summary of the chapter serves to relate Venus to hell and the lake of fire. The inner planet's visible and physical effects on afterlife inhabitants match biblical passages relating to perdition. The listing includes correlation to descriptors such as unquenchable fire, outer darkness, the lake burning with fire and sulfur, rising smoke of torment, and no rest day or night. The table brings warnings about the fate of the unrighteous together with findings from planetary science. As such, it becomes understandable that Venus, or a similar-type exoplanet, can correlate to biblical perdition and become the final place of banishment for the lost.

The vignette of *Six Men in a Lava Tube* is a creative drama taking place in the confines of the lake of fire. Perdition is a setting where individuals can think clearly and have memory recall. The men are aware of their surroundings—feeling sadness from boredom and distress from the heat. The situation is grave because there is no escape. The planet has a gravity lock on the resurrected spiritual body. A discussion occurs about leaving the lava tube as a group and undertaking an expedition to another destination. Success in locating people in caves will only provide short-term reprieve from boredom. No possibility exists of altering a person's destiny when they are exiled to perdition.

Chapter Eight

The discovery of exoplanets continues at a rapid pace. Articles detailing new findings circulate regularly on science websites and in periodicals. For the most part, Hot Jupiters and super-Earths reveal hostile, uninviting worlds. The matrix in Table 6 summarizes the different types of exoplanets, comparing them with biblical descriptions of perdition. Exoplanets achieve high marks for being hellish places. Being similar to Venus, super-Earths best qualify as possible places for perdition. One can conclude from the outline that in addition to our neighboring planet, other locations in the galaxy can serve as places of banishment for unrighteous humanity.

Final Thoughts

A book using the Bible would not be complete without a testimony from the author. Raised in the Roman Catholic faith, I grew up receiving the sacraments of the church. Religious practice came by attending mass. The well-organized, liturgical services help to build faith in God.

Though I did not question the sincerity of regular church attendees, the practice seemed more about quieting life's personal struggles, rather than adhering to tenets of the faith, or living by the Ten Commandments. Eventually, I stopped going to church after college. Falling away from the faith happens with disenchantment and exposure to broad-minded ideas.

Over time, suspicion grows toward the divine. It can occur after a tragic loss or when individuals around you are suffering. A person has a degree of faith from childhood and then bad things happen. Tough situations can drag out for years, causing frustration, disappointment, and sadness. A family member or friend can get seriously hurt or become gravely ill. Death is not a respecter of persons and can take a loved one away at any time. We can be overwhelmed by a world filled with sorrow, heartache, and suffering. One avenue for thinking is to question God's existence. A supreme being in complete control moves to become an imaginary thought.

A cynical attitude about faith, religion, and the spiritual world becomes dominant over the years, closing off the divine. I took a pessimistic, even sarcastic approach toward a higher power, the supernatural, the afterlife, and anything beyond the material world. If you were a negative person about religious faith and churchgoing, you would have enjoyed keeping my company. Wanting little to do with places of worship, I considered attendees to be emotionally weak and misled, or at best, lacking something better to do on a Sunday morning. A Christian stepping forward to give witness was not only wasting his or her time, but was exposing a character flaw.

The ability to achieve a complete reversal in my belief system remains a bit of a mystery. It was in my early forties when I ran across a former friend, who went to church and read the Bible daily. She was able to coax me into evaluating my spiritual health, which was quite anemic. Her pastor went on to recommend a church to attend that was within close driving distance of my home. After a few weeks of listening to good sermons, watching uninhibited expressions of worship, and hearing people speak in tongues, I became convinced of the reality of God. A firsthand witness of spiritual gifts is strong evidence for a supreme being.

What kept me growing in my faith was far deeper than spiritual gifts. It was the pardoning of all past transgressions. How could God forgive me for all the years of irreverence, profanity, unbelief, and sexual immorality? Beyond repentance, wasn't there a price to pay for all that I had done? The answer is no. A big part of the gospel message is that Jesus Christ sacrificially paid the price for the sins of the world through his own death on a cross. The willingness to submit to the leading of the Holy Spirit, the ability to live by grace, and the realization of a future eternal life in paradise keeps me in service to the Lord, who is forever merciful toward me.

An important purpose of this book is to show the love God has for every individual. His desire is to bring people home to heaven. The oppressive planet Venus, or the nightmare world of CoRoT–7b, is not for immortal human spirits in the afterlife. It is for Satan and his demonic army. To make a way for salvation, God sent his Son, Jesus Christ, into the world to be our Lord and Savior. His life of service and sacrifice was exemplified by love, compassion, and forgiveness toward others. Romans 5:6–8 reads:

> For while we were still weak, at the right time Christ died for the ungodly. Indeed, rarely will anyone die for a righteous person—though perhaps for a good person someone might actually dare to die. But God proves his love

for us in that while we still were sinners Christ
died for us.

The passage begins by revealing the helpless state of
humanity. We are weak and vulnerable to sinful habits,
resulting in alienation from God. It is not easy to always
make just and ethical choices. People selfishly seek after the
pleasures of life. Proven unable to resist sin and keep the
righteous requirements of the law, we need help in order to
be reconciled to God. An intercessor, a go-between, someone
who could live a sinless life on our behalf, is necessary to
remove our alienation from God. Having a moral and upright
character, Jesus was sinless throughout the course of his life
and ministry. His death on the cross substitutes for us and
serves as our necessary ransom.

The substitutionary nature of his sacrifice is seen in the
worship of the Old Testament. In the Jewish faith, presenting
an annual offering of bulls, rams, goats, and other animals
to the temple priest was necessary for establishing right
standing. Presenting a blameless creature before God for
sacrifice shows the need of vicarious atonement. In the New
Testament, Jesus, who was completely innocent, willingly
accepts responsibility and steps forward to make the
sacrificial atonement on behalf of all humanity. His death
compensates for every person's wrongdoing. Continuing on
in Romans 5:9–11, the scripture reads:

> Much more surely then, now that we have been
> justified by his blood, will we be saved through
> him from the wrath of God. For if while we were
> enemies, we were reconciled to God through the
> death of his Son, much more surely, having
> been reconciled, will we be saved by his life. But
> more than that, we even boast in God through

our Lord Jesus Christ, through whom we have
now received reconciliation.

Justification is the right standing of a person, who is seen
as blameless before God. The Holy Spirit comes to indwell
their spirit, helping to instill proper judgment of matters and
moral decision-making. The age, dress, physical features,
finances, or social standing of the person are of no concern
to God. The atonement of Christ brings deliverance to all
who give him their allegiance. God and the believer come to
a final resolution concerning their salvation. The rescue of
our soul means staying out of Hades. A person who trusts
in Christ moves from a position of being condemned to being
made righteous. It removes the penalty for sin and eliminates
any chance of facing eternal banishment.

Do you consider anyone an adversary or a nemesis? Do
you have negative feelings about a person you see regularly
or someone from your past? Maybe it is an annoying coworker
or neighbor. On a larger scale, what acts of wrongdoing by
people around the world have upset you? Perhaps it is the
radical factions of Al-Qaeda or the Islamic State (ISIS). These
internationally-based terrorist organizations are responsible
for the deaths of thousands of innocent people. Would you die
for one of these extremists? Would you say, "No, don't put that
terrorist to death for what he did. Take my life instead and
let him go?" The very thought is ridiculous.

Yet, the idea fully illustrates what Jesus Christ did for
us. His sacrificial death on the cross at Calvary took place
while we were still God's enemies, willfully opposing him
and his moral law. Not only does Christ's single atoning act
erase sin, but it also takes away the punishment. Accepting
the atonement through faith comes with the joy and daily
fellowship of the Holy Spirit. A renewed mind and a changed
life, as well as faith, trust, and peacefulness of heart, are all
part of the gift of salvation. Divine grace pours into our lives

daily in order to sanctify us. And in the end, the Lord gives us eternal life and the ability to dwell in his presence. This is the incalculable and unconditional love of God toward those who trust in his Son.

The real authority of the gospel became clear when Jesus rose from the dead. His grave site in Jerusalem is empty. The legitimacy of Christianity is demonstrated by the power of his resurrection. According to Paul in 1 Corinthians 15:14, if Christ is not raised, our faith is in vain. Without the resurrection, Christian belief and teaching have no meaning. Several passages in the New Testament center on this critical historical fact. The empty tomb after rising from the dead, his appearance to the apostles and hundreds of people, the testimony of many disciples and the martyrdom of some, lend support to the reality of Christ's resurrection.

The final message of the book is one of love. Scripture contains hundreds of references to love. In the Greek, four nouns for love are *eros, philia, storge,* and *agape. Eros* is romantic love, which relates to amorous feelings. The word *philia* is friendship love. It is strong loyalty to friends and family. *Storge* is the loving, natural affection of parents toward their children. At the highest level is *agape* love. *Agape* love expresses care and concern for every person in the world. In 1 John 4:8, we find the declaration that "God is love *(agape)*." It is the supreme expression of Christian faith in action, God's essential nature, and what he wants us to express.

Agape love is directed toward the unfamiliar person, the new arrival, the outsider, the foreigner, the individual in front of us at the checkout line. It is a selfless and unconditional love that cares for the welfare of humanity. This love illustrates the essence of God's nature. *Agape* love is different from other types of love because it does more than simply express an emotion. Rather, it is an act of the will based upon doing what is right. When teaching the two great commandments,

Jesus reminds the listener to first love the Lord your God with all your heart, soul, mind, and strength, and second, to love your neighbor as yourself.

A sincere expression of *agape* love comes from me to you in writing this book. I remain committed to the well-being of people—not just in attending to temporal needs, but in praying for their eternal destiny. Giving an example of perdition in the material universe points to the reality of a hell, which is not imaginary. It is a real place that everyone needs to avoid. Damnation to a planet such as Venus is a dreadful consequence, but God is rich in mercy. He made a way for people to avoid eternal separation. By trusting in the atoning work of Jesus Christ, your future is secure. Enjoying paradise on the renewed planet Earth will be your certain destiny.

APPENDIX—USAGE OF "MORNING STAR"

The text makes reference to Venus as the *morning star* and the evening star. Morning star is the common name given to the planet when it appears in the east before sunrise. Evening star is used when the planet appears in the west after sunset. Venus cannot be a star because it does not create its own light, but rather, reflects the light of the sun. In modern English usage, Venus being either the morning or evening star is simply a figure of speech for a "bright planet."

In the biblical scriptures, using *morning star* or "day star" has four different meanings, depending on its application in the verse. It can refer to Satan, singing spirits in the heavenly realm, the light of Christ, or to Jesus Christ himself.

> **Isaiah 14:12**—"How you are fallen from heaven,
> O *Day Star*, son of Dawn! How you are cut down
> to the ground, you who laid the nations low!"

The passages in the KJV and NKJV use "Lucifer, son of the morning" in place of "Day Star, son of Dawn." It is a common reference to Satan after his fall. This verse has the closest connection to the planet. In the evening, the movement of Venus (which was the morning star during its previous appearance) is of dropping into the horizon, imitating the fall of Satan from glory.

Job 38:6–7—"On what were its bases sunk, or who laid its cornerstone when the *morning stars* sang together and all the heavenly beings shouted for joy?"

In answering Job out of the whirlwind, the Lord God considers morning stars to be an image of chanting spirits or living beings.

2 Peter 1:19—"So we have the prophetic message more fully confirmed. You will do well to be attentive to this as to a lamp shining in a dark place, until the day dawns and the *morning star* rises in your hearts."

The verse implies that the prophetic word will shine like a guiding lamp, until the light of day. The morning star rising appears to be a light for those coming out of darkness. The illuminating of a dark mind occurs with the light of Christ.

Rev. 2:28—"even as I also received authority from my Father. To the one who conquers I will also give the *morning star.*"

The risen Lord is speaking to the Apostle John. In referring to himself as the *morning star*, he appears to be giving his light to those who overcome.

Rev. 22:16—"It is I, Jesus, who sent my angel to you with this testimony for the churches. I am the root and the descendant of David, the bright *morning star.*"

In one of the final verses of the book of Revelation, we see Jesus referring to himself as the bright morning star.

Glossary of Scientific and Theological Terms

Abiogenesis: The unproven natural process by which life arises from nonliving matter, such as amino acids and simple organic compounds.

Aerospace: A technology and industrial-based business dealing with the design and development of aviation and space products such as aircraft, missiles, and satellites.

Aether Theory: The incorrect belief of a zero-mass medium in outer space through which light and energy travel. The concept was disproven by special relativity.

Albedo: The measurement of the incident light that is reflected back from a celestial surface, such as from the moon or a planet.

Amillennialism: The "no millennium" view affirms that Christ's reign began with his resurrection, continues until now spiritually, and completes at the end of the age. The return or second advent of Jesus Christ will usher in the kingdom of God.

Angular Diameter: The measurement of the size of a celestial body as seen from Earth. The diameter is given in degrees and arc seconds.

Annihilationism: The belief of unrighteous people not experiencing an afterlife. The soul will be completely extinguished after death.

Artificial Satellite: In spaceflight, a manmade object such as spacecraft that orbits a celestial body such as the earth.

Asteroid Belt: The region of space between Mars and Jupiter containing the dwarf planet Ceres and millions of smaller bodies having irregular shapes.

Asthenosphere: The ductile region of the upper mantle. Convective heat transfer from the asthenosphere causes stress in the lithosphere, leading to cracking and displacement.

Astronomy: The science of investigating objects and phenomena beyond the earth. The study determines the location, size, motion, chemical composition, geological features, and atmosphere of celestial bodies.

Aurora: Luminous streams of night light in the north and south poles. Auroras are the result of charged particles from the solar wind precipitating into the atmosphere.

Basalt: A common igneous rock formed from the solidification of magma. Having a gray appearance, it is abundant on the surface of terrestrial planets.

Big Bang: The prevailing cosmological theory explaining the dynamic birth of the universe from a singularity. Evidence comes from an expanding universe and the presence of cosmic microwave background radiation (CMBR).

Black Hole: A black hole is a region of space-time where gravity is so strong that even light cannot escape from it. Some black holes are highly compacted regions of space.

Others are supermassive black holes that locate in the center of galaxies.

Brown Dwarf Star: A substellar object ranging in size between Jupiter and a small star. Brown dwarfs retain low nuclear fusion levels and continue to give off heat.

Cambrian Explosion: The prolific and unparalleled emergence of major classes of species between 540 and 480 million years ago. Before then, most organisms were simple and composed of only a few cells.

Carboniferous Period: The coal-bearing era dating from 360 to 300 million years ago. Dominating the period were amphibians, plant life, and vast swamp lands.

Complementary model: A model seeing scripture and science as working together in a non-intrusive manner. It results in conforming biblical creation to scientific thought.

Conflict model: A model seeing scripture and science as being in direct conflict with one another. The domains are rivals and each one desires to emerge victorious.

Copernican Revolution: The paradigm shift away from the Ptolemaic model of the heavens to Sun-centered cosmology, initiated by Polish mathematician and astronomer Nicolaus Copernicus in 1543. *See* Heliocentrism

Co-presence: A term describing time in eternity, which attaches to ordinary time (t) in the physical universe. Having a past-present-future makeup, co-presence is a substitute term for extra or higher time dimensions.

Core, inner: The spherical center of Earth's inner structure, consisting of an iron-nickel alloy. The solidity or uniformity of the inner core is not known.

Core, outer: The layer of molten metal lying above the inner core and below the mantle. It is composed of a liquid iron-nickel alloy.

Cosmic Microwave Background Radiation (CMBR): Thermal radiation emanating from every direction in the universe. The low-level energy is understood to be remnant radiant heat from the Big Bang expansion.

Cosmic Rays: High energy protons or alpha particles with penetrating power that primarily originate from supernovae in the universe.

Cosmological Constant: The term Einstein uses to describe the opposing force of gravity. The constant increases the expansion rate of the universe and seen in the form of dark energy. *See* Dark Energy

Cosmos: The physical universe seen as a well-ordered and harmonious totality.

Creationism: The belief in the creation of the universe by divine agency. The universe came out of nothing (*ex nihilo*) to form the natural world.

Creation Science: The field providing scientific support to the biblical creation story. The three leading systematic approaches to creationism are Young Earth creationism, Old Earth creationism, and theistic evolution.

Crust: The rigid, outermost layer of Earth. The crust is composed of sedimentary and igneous rock. The expanse covers the continents and the ocean floor.

Dark Energy: A form of energy working to cause the accelerating expanse of the cosmos. Dark energy is not fully understood, but it is estimated to make up 68.3% of the total mass-energy in the universe.

Dark Matter: A form of nonluminous matter, which slows the expansion of the cosmos. Dark matter is not fully understood, but it is estimated to make up 26.8% of the total mass-energy in the universe. *See* Matter, ordinary

Density: A measurement of mass per unit volume.

Dimension: In classical mechanics, space (x, y, z) and time (t) make up the absolute dimensions of the universe. In special relativity, the four dimensions come together as part of the space-time continuum.

Dynamo Theory: The geophysical model explaining how the earth's structure produces a continuous and stable magnetic field through the movement of conductive metal in the outer core. (cf. Magnetosphere)

Eisegesis: Interpreting words and passages in the biblical text by using one's own presuppositions and biases; a.k.a. reading into the text. (cf. Exegesis)

Electromagnetic Spectrum: The range of frequencies covering all electromagnetic radiation. The spectrum's classes of energy include gamma, X-ray, ultraviolet (UV), visible, infrared (IR), microwave, radio/TV, and long waves.

Elementary Particle: An atomic constituent of matter or energy in its simplest form, which cannot be subdivided. Examples include quarks, leptons, bosons, and photons.

End of the Age: The return of Jesus Christ, which begins God's kingdom on Earth. There will be a refreshing of the planet into a sinless environment. The evening sky will include planets, stars, and the multitude of galaxies in the universe.

End of the World: The return of Jesus Christ, which begins God's kingdom on Earth. It requires the eradication of our planet, all celestial bodies, and the universe at large, resulting in a sinless and unimaginable paradise.

Eschatology: Studies concerning the final events of human history. Individual eschatology addresses the destiny of a person, including death, judgment, heaven, and hell.

Eternal Separation: The sentence given to unrepentant people, resulting in unending exile from God. Locations include Hades, hell, and the lake of fire.

Eternity: An everlasting state in the physical universe originating from God's eternal realm. Eternity uses the properties of mass and gravity, while connecting to the world by way of co-presence and extra spatial dimensions.

Ethereal: The realm of nothing from which the universe originates. Nothing now lies beyond the edge of the universe. The ethereal realm has no connection to the universe, lacking in space, time, matter, and energy. *See Ex nihilo* and Nothing

Event Horizon: The outer boundary of a black hole, where gravity becomes overpowering and irreversible. Not even photons of light can escape.

Evolution, natural: The biological theory formulated by Charles Darwin, accepting that all species develop from a common ancestor, undergo random change to advance anatomies, and persevere through natural selection. Colloquial term is "evolution."

Evolution, solar: The formation of the sun from the gravitational collapse of a molecular cloud, which began 4.5 billion years ago. The sun's life cycle continues in the main sequence phase for 1 to 1.5 billion years.

Evolutionary creationism: *See* theistic evolution.

Exegesis: An objective, critical interpretation of the biblical text that draws out and explains the meaning that the author intended for a word or passage. (cf. Eisegesis)

Ex nihilo: The Latin expression *creatio ex nihilo* means "creation out of nothing." The energy for the Big Bang expansion sources from God and comes out of nothing. The nothing now lies beyond the edge of the universe. *See* Ethereal and Nothing

Exoplanet: An exoplanet or extrasolar planet is a planet orbiting a distant star.

Extra dimensions (space): The higher spatial dimensions of eternity. The extra dimensions are not visible but connect to three-dimensional space. In theoretical physics, extra space dimensions exist in the ongoing work of superstring theory.

Extra dimensions (time): *See* Co-presence

Fruitful Integration model: A model showing the Bible and science can be consistent when questioning weak theology and uncertain science. The total vision includes separate metaphysics about space, time, and being. *See* Metaphysics

General Relativity: Einstein's gravitational theory, which fully explains space, time, matter, and energy. General relativity expands upon special relativity by providing a description of gravity as the geometric bending of space-time.

Geochronology: The branch of science that addresses the geological time scale by the dating of rocks, fossils, and sediments.

Geocentricism: The cosmological model developed by Claudius Ptolemaeus, wherein the earth is at the orbital center of all celestial bodies. *See* Ptolemaic System

Geology: The scientific study of the origin, history, structure, and composition of the earth. Disciplines within geology include paleontology, seismology, vulcanology, mineralogy, geochronology, and plate tectonics.

God's Eternal Realm: The domain of God and the spiritual world, which existed before the creation of the universe. Beginning with the Big Bang expansion, the domain enters and becomes part of the physical universe. *See* Eternity

Gradualism: The accumulation of infinitesimally small genetic modifications that are profitable to the evolutionary advancement of a species.

Grand Unified Theory: The GUT is an attempt to bring together the weak, the strong, and the electromagnetic forces. These fundamental forces are part of the Standard Model of particle physics.

Habitable Zone: The orbital region around a star where a planet can have an atmosphere, retain water, and be at temperatures that can support life.

Hades: In the New Testament, a place of temporary confinement for the unrighteous dead under Earth's surface. Lost souls in Hades await final judgment. (cf. Sheol)

Hades, spiritual: The extension of Satan's kingdom beyond the physical confines of the underworld of Hades. The demonic forces of the spiritual domain of Hades influence individuals and infiltrate all nations of the planet.

Hadley Cell: A large-scale atmospheric convection cell. Warm air rises near the equator and travels toward the poles to eventually cool. The cool air then descends and circulates back toward the equator to eventually warm up again.

Heaven: The home of God, the holy angels, and all who have attained salvation. It is a place of unsurpassed beauty, supreme happiness, and ultimate fulfillment.

Heaven, celestial: The present location of heaven within the material universe, where the righteous go after death. The Bible uses the terms "third heaven" or "paradise."

Heaven, on earth: The final relocation of heaven to the paradisical earth. At the end of the age, the return of Jesus Christ will bring a renewing and refreshing to the planet.

Heliocentrism: The cosmological model developed by Nicolaus Copernicus, where the earth and planets of the solar system revolve around the sun. *See* Copernican Revolution

Heliosphere: The spherical expanse of space surrounding the sun that contains the energy from the solar wind. The region extends far beyond the Kuiper Belt.

Hell: A physical location in the universe for eternal separation from God. Deriving from the word *gehenna* in the Gospels, Jesus describes it as a place where the worm never dies and the fire is never quenched. *See* Lake of Fire

Hermeneutics: The study of the principles of interpretation, aiming to analyze truth, value, and meaning. Applied to the Bible, hermeneutics recognizes that both the modern interpreter and the text stand in a given historical context and tradition.

Hierarchy Problem: In quantum physics, the hierarchy problem focuses on the large energy difference between the weak force and gravity. Solutions to the hierarchy problem utilize extra spatial dimensions.

Humanism: A philosophy placing the highest value on human power and endowment. It is skeptical toward religion, while emphasizing reason, scientific inquiry, and mortal fulfillment in the natural world.

Intelligent Design: A scientific belief recognizing that random mutation and natural selection are not adequate to explain the evolutionary process. The origin and development of life requires an intelligent designer.

Interferometry: A family of techniques where the superimposing of electromagnetic waves causes interference, which is used to extract information.

Intermediate State: The condition of a soul after physical death. The soul is a temporary spiritual state, residing in either Hades or the third heaven. All people will ultimately receive a resurrected or immortal spiritual body.

Kuiper Belt: The region of space beyond Neptune, which contain the dwarf planets Pluto, Eris, Makemake, and Haumea, as well as millions of small, icy-rock bodies.

Lake of Fire: A physical place in the universe for eternal separation from God. Sequestering to the lake of fire is the punishment given to the unrighteous at the final judgment in the book of Revelation. *See* Hell

Lava Tube: A natural conduit formed by flowing lava canals. When the outer magna cools and hardens, the inner lava continues to flow, leaving cave-like arteries.

Light Cone: A light cone follows the path that a light source takes traveling through space-time. As part of a Minkowski plot, it originates at a single point and emanates in all directions, allowing forward and backward movement in time.

Lithosphere: The rigid part of the outer earth, consisting of the crust and the underlying upper mantle. The structure divides into tectonic plates. (cf. Plate Tectonics)

Load Cell: A highly sensitive electrical device which measures weight. The transducer converts force into an electrical signal using strain gauges.

LUCA (Last Universal Common Ancestor): The most recent ancestor that unites all of life. Arising three to four billion years ago, it is the single organism to survive from many original organisms, leading to all biological life on the planet.

Macroevolution: A genetic process of major evolutionary transition from one type of organism to another within species. The premise provides support to natural evolution.

Magnetosphere: The magnetic field originating by motion of the liquid outer core. The energy flux extends into outer space and protects Earth's atmosphere by deflecting cosmic rays and particles from the solar wind.

Materialism: The doctrine giving preeminence to matter. Mental thoughts are even attributed to the transfer of matter. Materialism denies the spiritual and the supernatural, looking for physical explanations to all phenomena.

Matter (Ordinary): Any substance with mass, taking up space. Ordinary matter makes up only 4.9% of the universe, but includes all planets, stars, and galaxies.

Mantle: The thick stratum of gummy rock extending from the earth's crust down to the liquid outer core. The two-part mantle divides into the upper and lower sections.

Mass: A fundamental property which measures the quantity of matter in a body. The mass of an object is the same anywhere in the universe.

Mediocrity Principle: A belief suggesting Earth is not a unique or privileged place. The principle asserts that the nurturing environment for life is not special or exceptional in the context of the overall universe.

Metaphysics: The formulation of ideas into strong possibilities or foundational concepts. By relating biblical scriptures and scientific findings, the text uses metaphysics to present new concepts in space, time, and being.

Meteor: An object originating as a meteoroid, comet, or asteroid that passes through the earth's atmosphere. Colloquially called a "shooting star" or a "falling star."

Meteorite: A stone, metal, or stone-metal object that originates in outer space and reaches the surface of the earth.

Microevolution: A genetic process of minor evolutionary transition within species, allowing for environmental adaptation and survival.

Micrometeoroid: A small dust particle traveling at high velocity through outer space.

Millennium: A thousand-year period beginning with the return of Jesus Christ. He will rule in peace and harmony with all the saints on the earth.

Miracle: A real event defying natural laws that is beyond human ability, such as the account of Jesus Christ walking on water or performing a healing. *See* Supernatural

M-theory: A theory attempting to unify five different versions of superstring theory.

Multivalent: In chemistry, the ability of atoms in an element to bond to atoms in another element. In combination, new chemical compounds emerge.

Nadir: The point directly underneath a person on the earth. The direction is 180° opposite of zenith, which is overhead in relation to an observer.

Natural Satellite: A celestial body orbiting another body of typically greater size, such as a star or planet. (e.g., the moon)

Natural Theology: Revelation of the divine attainable through understanding nature and the physical world. In recent decades, natural theology has evolved into a worldview that uses observation to discern the workings of God.

Nebula: A vast cloud of interstellar dust and gas, consisting primarily of hydrogen and helium. It is visible through the telescope as a diffuse patch of light.

Neutron Star: A neutron star is the collapsed core of a massive star. The radical compacting of atomic matter results in a highly dense body of neutrons. *See* Pulsar

Nothing: The absence of matter, energy, space, and time. *See Ex nihilo* and Ethereal

Observable Universe: The spherically-shaped region of the universe containing all matter and energy that can be seen from Earth or space-based telescopes.

Old Earth Creationism (OEC): The creation science accepting divine acts of creation over long periods. God initiates life and then acts at critical stages in order to advance and mature life over hundreds of millions of years. *See* Progressive Creation

Orbital Period: For the planets, the time necessary to complete one revolution around the sun. For the earth, the period is 365.25 days.

Paleontology: The branch of science that examines the fossil record with respect to plants and animals. The field classifies organisms from previous geological periods.

Payload Fairing: The nose cone of a rocket that protects the spacecraft from the launch effects of dynamic air pressure and aerodynamic heating.

Periodic Table of Elements: A table displaying all of the known chemical elements. The elements arrange in order of increasing atomic number.

Phase Diagram: A graph plotting pressure against temperature, which show the phases of a substance. It outlines the solid, liquid, and gas zones.

Photon: A quantum form of electromagnetic radiation found in visible light. Photons have no rest mass and exhibit wave-particle duality.

Physical Cosmology: The scientific study of the origin, formation, evolution, structure, and ultimate fate of the universe.

Physical Universe: The realm consisting of space, time, matter, and energy. The universe contains eternity, a perpetual state interlocking with the material world.

Plate Tectonics: The theory of large and small plates comprising the structure of Earth's crust. Motion of the plates leads to earthquakes, volcanoes, and mountain building.

Positivism, logical: A belief in logic and scientific knowledge as able to solve all human dilemma. Irrelevant are philosophical, spiritual, or metaphysical explanations.

Postmillennialism: The millennium is a "golden age" prior to Christ's return, where the spread of the gospel will Christianize the world. At the end of the age, Jesus Christ will return to usher in the kingdom of God.

Premillennialism: The belief where Jesus Christ returns to the earth in order to remove the church before the tribulation period. He then returns in seven years to usher in the kingdom of God and reigns for one thousand years before the last judgment.

Progressive Creation: In Old Earth creationism, the belief where God creates life in separate stages. The six days of creation represent stages, where the days cover geological eons and eras. (e.g., the Cambrian Explosion).

Pseudoscience: A form of false or counterfeit science, which presents dubious theories and unproven claims. It lacks adherence to the scientific method and is not open to being testable, refutable, or falsifiable.

Ptolemaic System: The second century cosmology model by Claudius Ptolemaeus, wherein the earth is at the orbital center of all celestial bodies. *See* Geocentrism

P-wave: The primary or pressure wave originating at a seismic event, which moves through the earth. The waves travel readily through both solid and liquid mediums.

Pulsar: A neutron star that is highly magnetized and spinning. It releases intense beams of electromagnetic energy from its poles. *See* Neutron Star

Quantum Physics (Mechanics): The branch of physics dealing with forces and the interaction of subatomic particles. Concepts include the quantization of energy, wave-particle duality, and the uncertainty principle.

Radio Telescope: A parabolic dish antenna which can gather radio sources from space. Other uses include tracking and collection of information from satellites.

Radiometric Dating: An accurate and reliable method of dating objects based on the known decay rate of radioactive isotopes. Radiometric dating helps to establish the geological time scale. *See* Geochronology

Rapture: An end-time event when believers who have died will receive their resurrected bodies. Believers who are still alive will rise to meet the Lord in the air.

Red Dwarf Star: A red dwarf is the most common type of star in the Milky Way galaxy. A small and relatively cool star, it has an extremely long lifespan.

Red Shift: The increasing wavelength of light emitted by an object, due to its movement away from the observer. The wave elongation shifts the wave toward the red end of the visible spectrum.

Resurrected Spiritual Body: The permanent state of a person after the final resurrection of all human beings. The immortal spiritual body is imperishable.

Revelation: The self-disclosure and communication of God that conveys knowledge to humans. Special revelation and general revelation serve as the ways through which God communicates his truth.

Revelation, general: The self-disclosure and communication of God using avenues such as the creation, records of history, observation of the natural world, experience, reason, and innate conscience. (cf. Natural Theology)

Revelation, special: The self-disclosure and communication of God to particular people at specific times and places. The Bible, revealing the person of Jesus Christ, provides the primary source for special revelation.

Scientism: The belief in the power of science to answer all questions pertaining to ultimate truth and knowledge.

Being an authoritarian worldview, scientism usurps other viewpoints.

Seismic Tomography: A technique for creating 3-D images of the inner earth using seismic wave propagation.

Seismology: The study of waves generating from seismic events such as earthquakes, volcanic eruptions, and atomic explosions.

Sheol: In the Old Testament, a resting place beneath the surface of the earth where both the righteous and the unrighteous depart after death. (cf. Hades)

Sidereal Day: One complete rotation of a planet about its axis. The rotation orients to a fixed reference frame such as distant stars. (cf. Solar Day)

Singularity Theorem: In general relativity, Penrose–Hawking formulas identifying convergences that lead to a beginning of the universe.

Solar Day: One complete rotation of a planet about its axis. The rotation orients to the sun, rather than to a fixed reference frame such as distant stars. (cf. Sidereal day)

Solar Wind: The continuous stream of high-energy radiation flowing from the sun. The plasma consists of charged particles, such as electrons and protons.

Sovereign model: A model seeing scripture and science as being two separate domains that do not require reconciliation. Ultimate truth cannot be known in this life.

Soul: The soul is the eternal aspect of a person, consisting of one's mind, will, and emotions. At death, the soul departs for either Hades or the third heaven. This text uses the word "soul" to incorporate both "soul and spirit." (cf. Spirit)

Soul Substance: The material substance of a soul. Soul substance has weight, is subject to the laws of gravity, and contains a person's genetic makeup.

Space-time: The merging of three-dimensional space (x, y, z) and the one dimension of time (t) into a single four-dimensional continuum.

Special Relativity: Einstein's theory showing space and time to be a single continuum (space-time). Space and time are not independent, but relative to one another. The theory discloses the equation $E = mc^2$.

Spirit: The conscience of a person, which makes decisions about thoughts and behaviors, discerns right from wrong, and performs ethical judgments. (cf. Soul)

Standard Model: The Standard Model of particle physics classifies known elementary particles and contains three of the four fundamental forces in the universe.

Steady State Theory: The alternate theory to the Big Bang, where the universe has always expanded at a uniform rate with no beginning to time.

String Theory: A theoretical formulation where point-like particles of the Standard Model are replaced by one-dimensional objects called strings.

Superstring Theory: A theory that models the particles and fundamental forces in the Standard Model as vibrations of tiny supersymmetric strings. It requires the use of nine spatial dimensions, plus the time dimension.

Supercritical Fluid: A substance at a pressure and temperature above the critical point of a phase diagram. The medium exhibits the properties of both a gas and a liquid.

Supernatural: An action ascribed to a higher power, such as God. It defies natural laws and is beyond human ability to achieve. *See* Miracle

S-wave: The secondary or shear wave originating at a seismic event, which moves through the earth. The waves travel readily through solid, but not liquid mediums.

Synthetic Aperture Radar (SAR): A remote sensing and mapping technology that uses high-energy radio waves. The outbound and return signals are from an antenna mounted on an airborne platform.

Terminator: The line on a planetary body that divides the sunlit side from the dark side, which is sometimes referred to as the twilight zone.

Theistic Evolution (TE): The creation science accepting natural evolution. Without direct involvement from God, organisms originate from a common ancestor, which evolves via random mutation to advance species. Also known as evolutionary creationism.

Theory of Everything (ToE): A theory reconciling general relativity with quantum physics by bringing gravity together with the weak, strong, and electromagnetic forces.

Tidal Locking: A planetary body with an orbital period matching its rotational period. The moon is tidally locked to the earth, resulting in seeing only one side.

Time: The progression of events from past to present and into the future. Time defines motion in 3-D space. Measurements include hours, minutes, and seconds.

Tribulation: In eschatology, a seven-year period of difficulty where God enacts a series of judgments on the nations of the earth.

Universalism: The restoration of all humanity to a right relationship with God. Spiritual beings undergo a correction, obtaining entry into the kingdom of heaven.

Virga: Precipitation from the clouds that evaporates before reaching the ground.

Volcanism: The activities from volcanoes, geysers, and fumaroles that result in the discharge of molten rock, hot water, steam, and gases onto the surface of a planet.

Vortex: Rapidly rotating liquid or air, which moves around a central axis. In meteorology, the spinning wind of a tornado creates a visible vortex.

Weight: Weight measures the force on an object. On the earth, gravity acts upon the mass of a body, giving rise to the downward force of weight.

Wormhole: A hypothetical tunnel in space-time that connects light-year distances together, allowing for faster-than-light travel through the universe.

X-ray: High energy electromagnetic radiation that is capable of penetrating through materials. Applications include the medical field and airport security scanners.

Young Earth Creationism (YEC): The creation science accepting that the Genesis creation story covers six twenty-four-hour days. It leaves the earth to be less than 10,000 years old. The view contradicts scientific evidence.

Zenith: The point on the celestial sphere, which is directly overhead an observer on the earth. The point is 180° opposite of nadir, which is underfoot.

BIBLIOGRAPHY

Angelo, Joseph A. *Encyclopedia of Space and Astronomy.* New York: Facts on File, Inc., 2006.

Astr 1210 (O'Connell) Study Guide. "Impacts and Bio-Extinctions." http://www.astro.virginia.edu/class/oconnell/astr121/im/asteroid-impact-frequency-NASA.gif.

Astronomy. "A Supermassive Black Hole Spent More Than a Decade Consuming a Star." http://www.astronomy.com/news/2017/02/black-hole-record.

The Astrophysical Journal. "A Revised Exoplanet Yield from the Transiting Exoplanet Survey Satellite." https://iopscience.iop.org/article/10.3847/1538-4365/aae3e9.

Barsukov, V. L., ed. *Venus Geology, Geochemistry and Geophysics: Research Results from the USSR.* Tucson, AZ: University of Arizona Press, 1992.

Bell, Rob. *Love Wins: A Book about Heaven, Hell, and the Fate of Every Person Who Ever Lived.* New York: HarperCollins, 2011.

Bostrom, Nick, and Milan M. Cirkovic, eds. *Global Catastrophic Risks.* New York: Oxford University Press, 2008.

Burgess, Eric. *Venus: An Errant Twin*. New York: Columbia University Press, 1985.

California Institute of Technology (Caltech). "Planets Abound." http://www.caltech.edu/content/planets-abound.

Cao, A., and B. Romanowicz. "Constraints on Shear Wave Attenuation in the Earth's Inner Core from an Observation of PKJKP." *Geophysical Research Letters* 36, no. 9 (May 2009): 5.

CERN Accelerating Science. "The Large Hadron Collider." https://home.cern/science/accelerators/large-hadron-collider.

Chadwick, Henry, trans. *Saint Augustine Confessions*. New York: Oxford University Press, 1998.

CIA World Factbook. "Field Listing – Death Rate." https://www.cia.gov/the-world-factbook/field/death-rate/.

Coogan, Michael D., ed. *The New Oxford Annotated Bible: New Revised Standard Version*. New York: Oxford University Press, 2001.

Crockett, William, ed. *Four Views on Hell*. Grand Rapids, MI: Zondervan, 1992.

Doctrine Commission of the Church of England. *The Mystery of Salvation: The Story of God's Gift*. London: Church House Publishing, 1996.

Draper, Warren F., trans. *The Book of Enoch*. Andover, MA: U.S. Act of Congress, 1882.

EarthSky. *Possible Life Signs in the Clouds of Venus*. https://earthsky.org/space/ phosphine-disequilibrium-venus-atmosphere-pioneer-venus-1978.

Elwell, Walter A., ed. *Baker Encyclopedia of the Bible.* Grand Rapids, MI: Baker Book House, 1988.

Encyclopedia Britannica. *"Primary Wave."* https://www. britannica.com/science/primary-wave.

Estonia News. "ESTCube-1's 651-day Career: 53 Dissertations and a Marriage Proposal." http://news.err.ee/115186/ estcube-1-s-651-day-career-53-dissertations-and-a-marriage-proposal.

European Space Agency. ESA Selects Revolutionary Venus Mission EnVision. https://www.esa.int/Science_Exploration/ Space_Science/ESA_selects_revolutionary_Venus_mission_ EnVision.

Fowler, C.M.R. *The Solid Earth: An Introduction to Global Geophysics,* 2nd ed. Cambridge, UK: Cambridge University Press, 2005.

Gallup News. "In U.S., 42% Believe Creationist View of Human Origins." https://news.gallup.com/poll/170822/ believe-creationist-view-human-origins.aspx.

Gifford Lectures. "The University of Edinburgh, College of Arts, Humanities and Social Sciences." https://www. ed.ac.uk/arts-humanities-soc-sci/news-events/lectures/ gifford-lectures.

Greeley, Ronald. *Lava Tubes in the Solar System.* 6th International Symposium on Vulcanospeleology. Tempe, AZ: Arizona State University Planetary Geology Group, 1992.

Greene, Brian. *The Elegant Universe: Superstrings, Hidden Dimensions, and the Quest for the Ultimate Theory,* 2nd ed. W. W. Norton & Company, 2010. Kindle.

Grinspoon, David H. *Venus Revealed: A New Look Below the Clouds of Our Mysterious Twin Planet.* Reading, MA: Addison-Wesley, 1997.

Hawking, Stephen W. *A Brief History of Time.* New York: Bantam Books, 1998.

Hawking, Stephen W., and George F. R. Ellis. "The Cosmic Black-Body Radiation and the Existence of Singularities in Our Universe." *Astrophysical Journal* 152, (1968): 25–36.

Hawking, Stephen W., and Leonard Mlodinow. *The Grand Design.* New York: Bantam Books, 2010.

Hawking, Stephen, and Roger Penrose. "The Singularities of Gravitational Collapse and Cosmology." *Proceedings of the Royal Society of London*, Series A, 314 (1970): 529-48.

Hodge, Charles. *Systematic Theology, Vol. III.* http://www.ccel.org/ccel/hodge/theology3.

Incorporated Research Institutions for Seismology (IRIS). *Global Seismographic Network.* https://www.iris.edu/hq/programs/gsn.

_____. *Data Services Products: EMC-iasp91 (P & S velocity reference Earth model).* http://ds.iris.edu/ds/products/emc-iasp91/.

International Astronomical Union. "Resolution B5: Definition of a Planet in the Solar System." XXVIth IAU General Assembly (26th). Prague, Czech Republic: IAU, August 24, 2006. 1.

_____. IAU 2006 General Assembly: Result of the IAU Resolution Votes. http://www.iau.org/public_press/news/detail/iau0603/.

Ishida, Masayoshi. "Rebuttal to Claimed Refutations of Duncan MacDougall's Experiment on Human Weight Change at the Moment of Death." *Journal of Scientific Exploration* 24, no. 1 (Spring 2010): 5–39.

Johnson, Phillip E. *Darwin on Trial*. Downers Grove, IL: InterVarsity Press, 2010.

Kastrup, Bernardo. *Why Materialism is Bologna*. Alresford, UK: John Hunt Publishing Ltd., 2014.

Kearny, Cresson H. *Nuclear War Survival Skills*. Cave Junction, OR: Oregon Institute of Science and Medicine, 1987.

Keathley, J. Hampton. "The Pauline Epistles." http://bible.org/seriespage/paulineepistles.

LaHaye, Tim, and Ed Hindson, eds. *The Popular Encyclopedia of Bible Prophecy*. Eugene, OR: Harvest House, 2004.

Lewis, C. S. *The Great Divorce*. New York: MacMillan, 1946.

Libquotes. Francis Bacon Quote. https://libquotes.com/francis-bacon/quote/lbk3m3m.

Luhr, James F. ed. *Smithsonian Institute: Earth*. New York: DK Publ. Inc., 2003.

MacDougall, Duncan. "Hypothesis Concerning Soul Substance Together with Experimental Evidence of the Existence of Such Substance." *American Society for Physical Research*. 1, no. 5 (May 1907): 237–44.

Moore, Patrick. *Venus*. London: Octopus Publishing, 2002.

NASA. "How Do We Know When Voyager Reaches Interstellar Space?" http://www.jpl.nasa.gov/news/news.php?release=2013-278.

———. "Mystery of the Universe's Expansion Rate Widens with New Hubble Data." https://www.nasa.gov/feature/goddard/2019/mystery-of-the-universe-s-expansion-rate-widens-with-new-hubble-data.

———. "NASA Selects 2 Missions to Study 'Lost Habitable' World of Venus." https://www.nasa.gov/press-release/nasa-selects-2-missions-to-study-lost-habitable-world-of-venus.

———. "Spitzer Space Telescope Reveals New Exoplanet Discovery." https://exoplanets.nasa.gov/news/1419/nasa-telescope-reveals-largest-batch-of-earth-size-habitable-zone-planets-around-single-star/.

NASA Science Visualization Studio. "Venus Transit 2012 from Solar Dynamics Observatory." https://svs.gsfc.nasa.gov/3940.

New York Daily News. "President John F. Kennedy Announces He Wants to Put a Man on the Moon." https://www.nydailynews.com/news/national/jfk-announces-1961-put-man-moon-article-1.2648222.

New York Times. "After 350 Years, Vatican Says Galileo Was Right: It Moves." http://www.nytimes.com/1992/10/31/world/after-350-years-vatican-says-galileo-was-right-it-moves.html.

———. "Spacecraft Spots Active Volcanoes on Venus." https://www.nytimes.com/2010/04/10/science/space/10venus.html?searchResultPosition=1.

Oerter, Robert. *The Theory of Almost Everything: The Standard Model, the Unsung Triumph of Modern Physics.* New York: Pearson Educational, Inc., 2006.

Persson, Anders. "Hadley's Principle: Understanding and Misunderstanding the Trade Winds." *History of Meteorology* (Swedish Meteorological Institute, 2006) 3: 17–42.

Peterson, Robert A. *Hell on Trial: The Case for Eternal Punishment.* Phillipsburg, NJ: Presbyterian and Reformed Publishing, 1995.

Phys.org. "Scientists Discover Volcanoes on Venus are Still Active." https://phys.org/news/2020-07-scientists-volcanoes-venus.html.

PNAS.org. "A Globally Fragmented and Mobile Lithosphere on Venus." https://www.pnas.org/content/118/26/e2025919118.

Polkinghorne, John. *Belief in God in an Age of Science.* London: Yale University Press, 2003.

Popper, Karl R. *Conjectures and Refutations: The Growth of Scientific Knowledge,* 2nd ed. London: Butler & Tanner Limited, 1965.

Population Reference Bureau. "How Many People Have Ever Lived on Earth?" http://www.prb.org/Publications/Articles/2002/HowManyPeopleHaveEverLivedonEarth.aspx.

Randall, Lisa. *Knocking on Heaven's Door: How Physics and Scientific Thinking Illuminate the Universe and the Modern World.* New York: HarperCollins Publishers, 2012.

Reasonable Faith. "The Ultimate Question of Origins: God and the Beginning of the Universe." http://www.reasonablefaith.org/the-ultimate-question-of-origins-god-and-the-beginning-of-the-universe.

Reasons to Believe. "Does Macroevolution Fit the Fossil Record?" http://www.reasons.org/explore/topic/evolution.

_____. "The Waters of the Flood." http://www.reasons.org/articles/the-waters-of-the-flood.

Richmond, Michael. *Late Stages of Evolution for Low Mass Stars.* http://spiff.rit.edu/classes/phys230/lectures/planneb/planneb.html

Ross, Hugh. *Beyond the Cosmos: The Transdimensionality of God,* 3rd ed. Covina, CA: RTB Press, 2017. Kindle.

Russell, Robert John. *Cosmology: From Alpha to Omega.* Minneapolis, MN: Fortress Press, 2008.

_____. *Time in Eternity: Pannenberg, Physics and Eschatology in Creative Mutual Interaction.* Notre Dame, IN: University of Notre Dame Press, 2012.

Russell, Robert John, William R. Stoeger, SJ, and George V. Coyre SJ. *Physics, Philosophy and Theology: A Common Quest for Understanding.* Vatican City State: Vatican Observatory Publications, 1988.

Russian Space. "New Promise for the Venera-D Project." http://www.russianspaceweb.com/venera-d-2021.html.

Ryrie, Charles C. *A Survey of Bible Doctrine.* Chicago: Moody Publishers, 1972.

Science Channel. *How the Universe Works.* "Death of the Last Stars." https://www.sciencechannel.com/tv-shows/how-the-universe-works/full-episodes/death-of-the-last-stars.

_____."Planets from Hell." https://www.sciencechannel.com/tv-shows/how-the-universe-works/full-episodes/planets-from-hell.

Science Daily. "A Seismic Mapping Milestone: Team Produces 3-D Map of Earth's Interior." https://www.sciencedaily.com/releases/2017/03/170328135508.htm.

ScienceNews. "The First Picture of a Black Hole Opens a New Era of Astrophysics." https://www.sciencenews.org/article/black-hole-first-picture-event-horizon-telescope.

Scientific American. "Earth-Like Planets May Be Made of Carbon." https://www.scientificamerican.com/article/a-large-lump-of-coal/.

Shearer, Peter M., Catherine A Rycher, and Qinya Liu. "On the Visibility of the Inner-core Shear Wave Phase PKJKP at Long Periods." *Geophysics Journal International* 185, no. 3 (2011): 1379–83.

Sky and Telescope. "Transits of Venus Explained." https://www.skyandtelescope.com/astronomy-news/observing-news/transits-of-venus-explained/.

Song, Xiaodong. "Anisotropy of the Earth's Inner Core." Washington, DC.: American Geophysical Union, August 1997. *Reviews of Geophysics* 35, no. 3 297–313

Space.com. "How a Total Solar Eclipse Helped Prove Einstein Right about Relativity." https://www.space.com/37018-solar-eclipse-proved-einstein-relativity-right.html

———. "How Hot is Mercury?" https://www.space.com/18645-mercury-temperature.html.

Sproul, R.C. *Everyone's a Theologian: An Introduction to Systematic Theology.* Sanford, FL: Reformation Trust Publishing, 2014.

Stein, Seth and Michael Wysession. *An Introduction to Seismology, Earthquakes, and Earth Structure.* Oxford, UK: Blackwell Publishing Ltd., 2003.

Stump, J.B. ed. *Four Views on Creation, Evolution and Intelligent Design.* Grand Rapids, MI: Zondervan, 2017.

Svedhem, Hakan; Dmitry V. Titov; Fredric W. Taylor; and Olivier Witasse. "Venus as a More Earth-like Planet." *Nature* 450, No. 7170 (2007): 629–32.

Taylor, Fredric W. *The Scientific Exploration of Venus.* New York: Cambridge University Press, 2014.

University of Hamburg English Department. "A Virtual Introduction to Science Fiction: Online Toolkit for Teaching SF." http://virtual-sf.com/.

UWNews. "Tidally Locked Exoplanets May Be More Common than Previously Thought." http://www.washington. edu/news/2017/08/14/tidally-locked-exoplanets-may-be-more-common-than-previously-thought/.

Walvoord, John F., and Roy B. Zuck. *The Bible Knowledge Commentary.* Colorado Springs, CO: David C. Cook Publisher, 2002.

Ward, Peter D., and Donald Brownlee. *Rare Earth: Why Complex Life Is Uncommon in the Universe.* New York: Copernicus Books, 2004.

Scripture Index

"f" refers to an entry from a figure.
"t" refers to an entry from a table.
"n" refers to an entry from a footnote.

GENERAL INDEX

"f" refers to an entry from a figure.
"t" refers to an entry from a table.
"n" refers to an entry from a footnote.

Geiger-Müller particle tube 232
general relativity (theory of) 89, 98,
    102–103, 112, 154
general revelation 3, 5–7, 287, 319
The Genesis Flood (Morris) 84
Gentile 48
geocentric model 93, 217
geodesic 98–100
Giant Magellan Telescope 276
Gifford Lectures 6, 327
Glenn, John 23
Global Catastrophic Risks
    (Bostrom) 110–112, 114–
    115, 325
Global Positioning System
    xxvii, 27
Global Seismographic Network
    191, 328
global warming 110–111, 118, 289
God's eternal realm 16, 72, 104–
    108, 142f7, 144, 290, 310
golden age 222, 276, 317
    of exoplanets xxi, xxiv, 22, 276,
        278, 281, 293
    of science fiction 222
gradualism 77–79, 82, 86, 310
The Grand Design (Hawking) 62,
    98–102, 320, 328
Grand Unified Theory xxvii,
    153, 310
graviton 154
gravity 14, 25, 98, 101, 141, 148,
    153–156, 169–171, 264, 273,
    286, 293, 308
    antigravity 112–113
    mass-gravity 148, 155, 157
Great Commission 129
The Great Divorce (Lewis) 32–33,
    222, 329
Great Red Spot 216
great white throne judgment 47,
    49, 51, 140, 267, 290. *See*

also Day of Judgment; final
    judgment
greenhouse effect 10, 110, 232,
    245, 260
G-type main sequence star 117

H
Haarsma, Deborah 74n34
habitable zone 22, 221, 277,
    280, 310
Hades xxiv, 12, 41, 50–52, 138–
    140, 157, 171, 179, 202–207,
    272, 283, 286, 290. *See also*
    Sheol
    confinement of souls in 183
    under the earth 13, 17, 34,
        42–43, 47, 183, 188–190,
        196, 202, 204, 287, 291
    physical location of 16–17
    spiritual domain of 13,
        16–17, 173, 176, 262–263,
        291, 311
    story of Lazarus 252
Hadley cell 238, 311
Hadley, George 238
Ham, Ken 74n34
Hannah (prayer of) 34, 44
Haumea 21, 313
Hawking, Stephen 62, 98–99, 328
Heaven xiii, xv, xxii, 1, 29, 41–44,
    47, 55–57, 71, 91, 103, 119,
    123–127, 130, 138, 157–159,
    189, 273, 295, 305, 331
    celestial xxiii, 138–139, 311
    kingdom of xv, 55, 225, 323
    on Earth 119, 127, 130–132,
        139f6, 210, 214, 266, 273,
        290, 308, 311
    third xv, 43, 48, 125, 139, 149,
        157, 159, 171, 179, 183,
        273, 286, 290, 311
heliosphere 231, 311

Printed in the United States
by Baker & Taylor Publisher Services